Fractal Teletraffic Modeling and Delay Bounds in Computer Communications

T0332914

Fractal Teletraffic Modeling and Delay Bounds in Computer Communications

Ming Li

CRC Press

Taylor & Francis Group

Boca Raton London New York

CRC Press is an imprint of the
Taylor & Francis Group, an **informa** business

First edition published 2022
by CRC Press
6000 Broken Sound Parkway NW, Suite 300, Boca Raton, FL 33487-2742

and by CRC Press
2 Park Square, Milton Park, Abingdon, Oxon, OX14 4RN

CRC Press is an imprint of Taylor & Francis Group, LLC

© 2022 Ming Li

Reasonable efforts have been made to publish reliable data and information, but the author and publisher cannot assume responsibility for the validity of all materials or the consequences of their use. The authors and publishers have attempted to trace the copyright holders of all material reproduced in this publication and apologize to copyright holders if permission to publish in this form has not been obtained. If any copyright material has not been acknowledged please write and let us know so we may rectify in any future reprint.

Except as permitted under U.S. Copyright Law, no part of this book may be reprinted, reproduced, transmitted, or utilized in any form by any electronic, mechanical, or other means, now known or hereafter invented, including photocopying, microfilming, and recording, or in any information storage or retrieval system, without written permission from the publishers.

For permission to photocopy or use material electronically from this work, access www.copyright.com or contact the Copyright Clearance Center, Inc. (CCC), 222 Rosewood Drive, Danvers, MA 01923, 978-750-8400. For works that are not available on CCC please contact mpkbookspermissions@tandf.co.uk

Trademark notice: Product or corporate names may be trademarks or registered trademarks and are used only for identification and explanation without intent to infringe.

ISBN: 978-1-032-21286-9 (hbk)
ISBN: 978-1-032-21526-6 (pbk)
ISBN: 978-1-003-26880-2 (ebk)

DOI: 10.1201/9781003268802

Typeset in Minion
by codeMantra

To Dr. Yonglang Zhang and Joanna Jiayue Li —
for Making It Both Possible and Worthwhile

Contents

Preface

NETWORK TRAFFIC IS A TYPE OF FRACTAL TIME SERIES, ATTRACTING the interest of not only computer scientists but also scientists from various fields, ranging from statistics to engineering. We address our research in fractal traffic modeling and its application to traffic delay bounds.

This monograph consists of 12 chapters. Chapters 1–5 are the fundamental part. The basics of *Time Series* are discussed in Chapter 1. We narrate the basics of the *Fourier Transform* in Chapter 2. Elementary *Applied Functional* in Chapter 3 is explained for our expounding our proof of the existence of the min-plus de-convolution and the representation of the identity in the min-plus algebra system in Chapter 4. It is also used in the optimal approximations in traffic modeling in Hilbert spaces in Chapters 6–8. The *Min-Plus Convolution* is addressed in Chapter 4, which is a promising tool in delay-bound computations. In Chapter 5, we elaborate on the fundamentals of fractional noise and systems.

Chapters 6–9 are for traffic models in time series. In Chapter 6, we treat the traffic modeling using the fractional Gaussian noise. We introduce a novel fractional noise, termed generalized fractional Gaussian noise, and use it in traffic modeling in Chapter 7. We set forth another new fractional noise, called the generalized Cauchy process, and utilize it for traffic modeling in Chapter 8. We introduce a novel traffic bound in Chapter 9 and apply it to traffic delay bounds in Chapter 10. We propose computation formulas of the scale factors of traffic bound in Chapter 11.

The main highlights in this book are as follows:

1. The proof of the existence of the min-plus de-convolution and the representation of the identity in the min-plus convolution algebra system in Chapter 4.

2. Concise description of fractional noise and systems and the representation of fractional order delta function in Chapter 5.

3. Integral representation of fractional Gaussian noise in Chapter 6.

4. Generalized fractional Gaussian noise and its application to traffic modeling in Chapter 7.

5. Generalized Cauchy process and its application to traffic modeling in Chapter 8.

6. A stochastic traffic bound in Chapter 9.

7. A set of expressions of traffic delay bounds in Chapter 10.

8. Computation formulas of the scale factors of traffic bound in Chapter 11.

This monograph may be a reference for computer scientists, researchers, and graduate students.

Ming Li, PhD, Professor

Acknowledgments

THIS WORK WAS SUPPORTED IN PART BY THE NATIONAL NATURAL Science Foundation of China (NSFC) under project grant number 61672238. The views and conclusions contained in this book are those of the author and should not be interpreted as representing the official policies, either expressed or implied, of the Chinese government.

Author

Ming Li PhD, (https://orcid.org/my-orcid?orcid=0000-0002-2725-353X), is a professor at Ocean College, Zhejiang University, as well as at the East China Normal University. He has been an active contributor for many years to the fields of computer communications, applied mathematics and statistics, particularly network traffic modeling, fractal time series, and fractional oscillations. He has authored more than 200 articles and 5 monographs on the subjects. He was identified as the Most Cited Chinese Researcher by Elsevier in 2014–2020. Professor Li was recognized as a top 100,000 scholar in all fields in 2019–2020 and a top 2% scholar in the field of Numerical and Computational Mathematics in 2021 by Prof. John P. A. Ioannidis, Stanford University.

CHAPTER 1

Time Series

We discuss the time series related to traffic modeling in this chapter. It consists of seven parts. In Sections 1.1 and 1.2, we explain the meaning of random processes and ergodicity of a process, respectively. The contents in Sections 1.1 and 1.2 are fundamental for the time series and are worth being paid attention to. We discuss the concepts of three statistical models, namely, probability density function (PDF), autocorrelation function (ACF), and power spectrum density (PSD) function, in Sections 1.3, 1.4, and 1.5, respectively. White noise is described in Section 1.6. Finally, the concepts of long-range dependent processes and $1/f$ noise, which are the basic features of traffic, are given in Section 1.7.

1.1 RANDOM PROCESSES

Let $x(t)$ be a random function. By random, we mean that one does not know what the value of $x(t_1)$ is at t for $t_1 > t$. Due to that, as a variable at t, $x(t)$ is random, where $t \in \mathbf{R}$ (real numbers set). Thus, $t \in \mathbf{R}$ is an attribute of a random variable $x(t)$ that occurs at t.

An environment that $x(t)$ happens is called an experiment. Such an environment may be either natural or artificial. The term "experiment" is neither a teaching experiment in a teaching laboratory nor a science one in a scientific research laboratory. It just implies an abstract environment where $x(t)$ is produced. In other words, a random variable $x(t)$ is a result of that experiment. However, in the field of time series or stochastic processes, one utilizes the term "realization" instead of results to describe

DOI: 10.1201/9781003268802-1

$x(t)$. A realization $x(t)$ of an experiment is also called a sample function or a sample in short.

There are a set of experiments that may produce a set of realizations $x(t)$ s. One says that the nth experiment results in the nth realization or the nth sample function. It is denoted by $x_n(t)$, where $n \in \mathbf{N}$ (the set of natural numbers) and $\mathbf{N}$ is the sample set. Thus, $n \in \mathbf{N}$ is another attribute of a random variable $x_n(t)$. It is clear that, in general,

$$x_m(t) \neq x_n(t), m \neq n. \tag{1.1}$$

Although $x_n(t)$ is random, one is able to obtain its probability for $x_n(t) \leq a$. Denote by $\mathrm{Prob}[x_n(t) \leq a] \in [0, 1]$ the probability of $x_n(t) \leq a$. Then, the number $\mathrm{Prob}[x_n(t) \leq a]$ is the third attribute of a random variable $x_n(t)$. Any $x_n(t)$ corresponds to a probability $\mathrm{Prob}[x_n(t) \leq a]$. Denote by $\mathbf{P}$ the probability set.

Denote by $[\mathbf{N}, \mathbf{R}, \mathbf{P}]$ a probability space. It contains all sample functions $x_n(t)$ ($n = 0, 1, \ldots$). To be precise, $x_n(t) \in [\mathbf{N}, \mathbf{R}, \mathbf{P}]$. The symbol $[\mathbf{N}, \mathbf{R}, \mathbf{P}]$ implies that there are three attributes for a sample function $x_n(t)$. That is, $x_n(t)$ is the nth sample function with the attribute $n \in \mathbf{N}$, and with the other two attributes $\mathrm{Prob}(x_n(t) \leq a)$ and $t \in \mathbf{R}$.

Let $\{x_n(t)\}$ be the set of sample functions. It is called a random process. In other words, a random process designates a set of sample functions $\{x_n(t)\}$. The set $\{x_n(t)\}$ is also called an ensemble of sample functions. All sample functions obey the same probability distribution.

Without confusions occurring, one usually omits the brackets and simply calls $x_n(t)$ a random process. Moreover, by omitting the subscript n, one calls a random process $\{x_n(t)\}$ as a random function and simply denotes it as $x(t)$ (Yaglom [1]).

Since $\{x_n(t)\}$ generally includes infinite sample functions, its mathematical expectation (expectation for short) at time t, using the spatial average (Doob [2], Kolmogorov [3]), is given by

$$\mu_{xx}(t) = \lim_{N \to \infty} \frac{1}{N} \sum_{n=1}^{N} x_n(t). \tag{1.2}$$

Its autocorrelation function (ACF) is given by

$$r_{xx}(t, t+\tau) = \lim_{N \to \infty} \frac{1}{N} \sum_{n=1}^{N} x_n(t) x_n(t+\tau). \tag{1.3}$$

In the theory of stochastic processes, the spatial average plays a role in theory. However, it may be inconvenient in computations in engineering. Practically, infinite sample functions $\{x_n(t)\}$ may not be physically available. For instance, when studying traffic in computer communications, one encounters difficulty in collecting infinite sample functions of traffic during the same period of time. Besides, a practical random function $x(t)$ may not be considered for an infinite length of time, i.e., $t \in \mathbf{R}$, but $t \in [0, T]$, where T is a finite positive number. As a matter of fact, a practical random function or time series is only of single history with finite length (Bendat and Piersol [4]). Consequently, spatial average-based computations are usually inconvenient in practical applications. Fortunately, the ergodicity of stochastic processes provides us with the theory to avoid the mentioned difficulty in computations.

1.2 ERGODICITY

If a process $\{x_n(t)\}$ is stationary and ergodic, the spatial average can be replaced by the time average of any sample function of $\{x_n(t)\}$. Usually, a stationary process $\{x_n(t)\}$ implies that it is ergodic (Priestley [5]). As a matter of fact, when $\{x_n(t)\}$ is stationary, it is challenging to find a process that is non-ergodic. For that reason, in default, we regard a stationary process as an ergodic one.

When $\{x_n(t)\}$ is stationary, one has

$$\mu_{xx}(t) = \lim_{N \to \infty} \frac{1}{N} \sum_{n=1}^{N} x_n(t) = \lim_{T \to \infty} \frac{1}{T} \int_{-\frac{T}{2}}^{\frac{T}{2}} x_n(t)\, dt, \qquad (1.4)$$

where $x_n(t)$ is an arbitrary sample function in the set of $\{x_n(t)\}$. As long as $\{x_n(t)\}$ is stationary, any quantity based on the spatial average is equivalent to the one based on the time average. This much facilitates the application of the theory of stochastic process to practice. We omit the subscript n of $x_n(t)$ and directly consider or write $\{x_n(t)\}$ as a random function $x(t)$ unless otherwise stated in what follows.

1.3 PROBABILITY DENSITY FUNCTION

Let $p(x)$ be a probability density function (PDF) of a random function $x(t)$. PDF $p(x)$ is a type of statistical model of a random function x. It characterizes the occurrence frequency of x with a certain probability p. Denote by $P(X)$ a probability (cumulative) distribution function of $x(t)$. Then,

$$P(X) = P(x \leq X) = \int_{-\infty}^{X} p(x)dx. \qquad (1.5)$$

The general form of the above is

$$P(x) = P(-a < x \leq b) = \int_{-a}^{b} p(x)dx. \qquad (1.6)$$

The above implies

$$p(x) = \frac{dP(x)}{dx}. \qquad (1.7)$$

Both $P(x)$ and $p(x)$ are probability models of $x(t)$. Either contains the probability information of $x(t)$.

The function $P(x)$ has the following properties:

- $P(x < \infty) = 1$.

- $P(-\infty < x) = 1$.

- $P(-a < x < b) = p(\xi)(b-a)$ for $\xi \in (-a, b)$, according to the Lagrange mean value theorem.

The literature of detailed descriptions about PDFs is rich, see e.g., Korn and Korn [6, Chapter 18]. We only mention several that relate to network traffic modeling.

1.3.1 PDF of Brownian Motion

Let $x(t)$ be the Brownian motion (Bm) with zero mean. Its PDF is given by

$$p(x) = \frac{1}{\sqrt{4\pi At}} \exp\left(-\frac{x^2}{4At}\right), \qquad (1.8)$$

where A is a constant.

Since $\mathrm{Var}[x(t)] = 2At$, which implies a time varying variance, the Bm is non-stationary.

Note 1.1. The Bm is Gaussian but non-stationary.

Note 1.2. The PDF of the Bm is exponentially decayed.

1.3.2 Gaussian Distribution

Let $x(t)$ be a random function with mean μ and variance σ^2. If its PDF is given by

$$p(x) = \frac{1}{\sqrt{2\pi}\sigma} e^{-\frac{1}{2}\left(\frac{x-\mu}{\sigma}\right)^2}, \tag{1.9}$$

it is called a Gaussian process. A Gaussian process is specifically termed a normal process. Any other distributions except the normal one are called non-normal distributions. Any other processes except the normal processes are called non-normal processes. Therefore, normal processes play a role in random processes.

The normal probability cumulative function is in the form

$$\Phi(x) = \frac{1}{\sqrt{2\pi}\sigma} \int_{-\infty}^{x} e^{-\frac{1}{2}\left(\frac{x-\mu}{\sigma}\right)^2} dx = \frac{1}{2}\left[1 + \mathrm{erf}\left(\frac{1}{\sqrt{2}}\frac{x-\mu}{\sigma}\right)\right]. \tag{1.10}$$

Let $u = \dfrac{x-\mu}{\sigma}$. It is called the standard normal variable. For u, one has

$$p(u) = \frac{1}{\sqrt{2\pi}\sigma} e^{-\frac{u^2}{2}}. \tag{1.11}$$

The cumulative distribution is given by

$$\Phi(u) = \frac{1}{\sqrt{2\pi}\sigma} \int_{-\infty}^{x} e^{-\frac{u^2}{2}} dx = \frac{1}{2}\left[1 + \mathrm{erf}\left(\frac{u}{\sqrt{2}}\right)\right], \tag{1.12}$$

where $\mathrm{erf}(x)$ is the error function, which is expressed by

$$\mathrm{erf}(u) = -\mathrm{erf}(-u) = \frac{1}{\sqrt{\pi}} \int_{0}^{u} e^{-u^2} du = 2\Phi(u\sqrt{2}) - 1. \tag{1.13}$$

1.3.3 Poisson Distribution

Let x be a discrete random variable. If, for $\xi > 0$ and $x \in \mathbf{N}$, its PDF is in the form

$$p(x) = e^{-\xi} \frac{\xi^x}{x!}, \tag{1.14}$$

$p(x)$ is called the Poisson distribution density function and x is a Poisson random function. For $p(x)$, one has

$$E(x) = \text{Var}(x) = \xi. \tag{1.15}$$

The Poisson distribution plays a key role in the conventional queuing theory in traditional circuit-switched communication networks, such as old telephony networks, see e.g., Gibson [7] and Cooper [8], with the pioneering work by Erlang (Erlang [9], Bojkovic et al. [10]).

In communication networks, one may rewrite the above by

$$p(n \text{ arrivals in time } \tau) = e^{-\lambda|\tau|} \frac{(\lambda|\tau|)^n}{n!}, \tag{1.16}$$

where arrival traffic may be arrival calls, packets, cells, and so on. The parameter λ is the rate of arrivals. Thus,

$$E(n) = \text{Var}(n) = \lambda\tau. \tag{1.17}$$

Note 1.3. The Poisson PDF is exponentially decayed.

1.3.4 Cauchy Distribution

When a PDF of x is in the form

$$p(x) = \frac{1}{\pi\alpha} \frac{1}{1 + \left(\dfrac{x-\xi}{\alpha}\right)^2}, \tag{1.18}$$

where α and ξ are shape and location parameters, respectively, it is called the Cauchy PDF. Since

$$p(x) = \frac{1}{\pi\alpha} \int\limits_{-\infty}^{\infty} \frac{(x-\xi)^n\, dx}{1 + \left(\dfrac{x-\xi}{\alpha}\right)^2} = \infty, \quad (n=1,2), \tag{1.19}$$

the mean and variance of a random function x that follows the Cauchy PDF do not exist.

Note 1.4. If a random function follows the Cauchy PDF, it is a Cauchy process.

Note 1.5. The Cauchy PDF is a power function and hyperbolically decayed.

A remarkable event that happened in the field of computer science is that the scientists found that the traffic on the packet-switched networks, such as the Internet, is non-Poisson (Partridge [11], Willinger and Paxson [12]). According to the theory of fractal time series, therefore, a statistic model of traffic obeys power laws (Li [13]). A traffic time series is of long-range dependence (LRD). The ACF of a time series with LRD is hyperbolically decayed. In this book, we pay attention to the correlation models of traffic.

1.4 CORRELATION FUNCTIONS

We explain four types of correlation functions. They are ACFs, auto-covariance functions, cross-correlation functions, and cross-covariance functions.

1.4.1 Auto-Correlation Functions

Let $x(t_1)$ and $x(t_2)$ be two values of $x(t)$ at t_1 and t_2, respectively. Denote by $r_{xx}(t_1, t_2)$ the ACF of $x(t)$. It is a type of statistical model of a random function x. It is used to measure how a random variable $x(t_1)$ is statistically correlated to another random variable $x(t_2)$. In other words, it characterizes how $x(t)$ at one time t_1 correlates to $x(t)$ at another time t_2. An ACF is defined by

$$r_{xx}(t_1, t_2) = E\left[x(t_1)x(t_2) \right]. \tag{1.20}$$

The expectation is

$$E\left[x(t) \right] = \mu_{xx}(t). \tag{1.21}$$

The above implies that the mean of $x(t)$ is a function of t.

Denote by $\phi_{xx}(t)$ the strength, that is, the average power, of $x(t)$. It is defined by

$$\phi_{xx}(t) = E\left[x^2(t) \right]. \tag{1.22}$$

Since

$$E\left[x^2(t)\right] = r_{xx}(t,t), \tag{1.23}$$

we see that

$$\phi_{xx}(t) = r_{xx}(t,t). \tag{1.24}$$

As the variance of $x(t)$ is given by

$$\mathrm{Var}\left[x(t)\right] = E\left\{x(t) - E\left[x(t)\right]\right\}^2, \tag{1.25}$$

one has

$$\mathrm{Var}\left[x(t)\right] = r_{xx}(t,t) - E\left\{\left[x(t)\right]\right\}^2. \tag{1.26}$$

The above means that Var[$x(t)$] is also a function of t.

One thing important in the above is that a Gaussian process can be uniquely determined by its ACF. In the case of $x(t)$ being stationary, $E[x(t)]$, Var[$x(t)$], and $r_{xx}(t, t)$ are not dependent on time. In that case, letting $t_1 = t$, $t_2 = t_1 + \tau$,

$$r_{xx}(t_1,t_2) = E\left[x(t)x(t+\tau)\right] = r_{xx}(\tau) = \lim_{T \to \infty} \frac{1}{T} \int_{-\frac{T}{2}}^{\frac{T}{2}} x(t)x(t+\tau)dt, \tag{1.27}$$

where τ is the time lag. Besides,

$$E\left[x(t)\right] = \mu_{xx}(t) = \mu_{xx} = \text{constant}, \tag{1.28}$$

$$\phi_{xx}(t) = \phi_{xx} = r_{xx}(0) = \text{constant}, \tag{1.29}$$

$$\mathrm{Var}\left[x(t)\right] = r_{xx}(0) - (\mu_{xx})^2 = \text{constant}. \tag{1.30}$$

There are properties for $r_{xx}(\tau)$. Namely,

$$r_{xx}(0) \geq r_{xx}(\tau), \tag{1.31}$$

$$r_{xx}(\tau) = r_{xx}(-\tau). \tag{1.32}$$

1.4.2 Auto-Covariance Functions

When taking $x(t) - \mu_{xx}$ as a random function, one uses auto-covariance function (ACF again). It is defined by

$$C_{xx}(\tau) = \mathrm{E}\left\{\left[x(t) - \mu_{xx}\right]\left[x(t+\tau) - \mu_{xx}\right]\right\}. \qquad (1.33)$$

From the above, one has

$$\mathrm{Var}\left[x(t)\right] = C_{xx}(0). \qquad (1.34)$$

Similar to $r_{xx}(\tau)$, one has

$$C_{xx}(0) \geq C_{xx}(\tau), \qquad (1.35)$$

$$C_{xx}(\tau) = C_{xx}(-\tau). \qquad (1.36)$$

Denote by $\rho_{xx}(\tau)$ the normalized ACF. By normalization, we mean that $\rho_{xx}(0) = 1$. It is defined by

$$\rho_{xx}(\tau) = \frac{r_{xx}(\tau)}{r_{xx}(0)} = \frac{C_{xx}(\tau)}{C_{xx}(0)}. \qquad (1.37)$$

Consider the ACF of a Poisson random function $x(t)$. A product $x(t)$ $x(t+\tau) = c^2$ if $x(t)$ and $x(t+\tau)$ are of the same sign. Besides, $x(t)x(t+\tau) = -c^2$ when $x(t)$ and $x(t+\tau)$ are of the opposite sign. Thus,

$$r_{xx}(\tau) = \mathrm{E}[x(t)x(t+\tau)] = c^2 \sum_{n=0}^{\infty}(-1)^n P(n) = c^2 e^{-\lambda|\tau|}\sum_{n=1}^{\infty}(-1)^n \frac{\left(\lambda|\tau|\right)^n}{n!} \qquad (1.38)$$

$$= c^2 e^{-2\lambda|\tau|}.$$

Note 1.6. The ACF of the Poisson random function is exponentially decayed.

When taking the function form of a Cauchy PDF as an ACF, one has

$$r_{xx}(\tau) = \frac{1}{1+\tau^2}. \qquad (1.39)$$

Note 1.7. If a random function has an ACF in the above form, it is called a Cauchy class process so as to distinguish it from the one in Note 1.4 (Chiles and Delfiner [14]).

Note 1.8. The ACF of a Cauchy class process is hyperbolically decayed.

The key for the network traffic theory is about a type of ACF that is hyperbolically decayed. We shall mention that later in this book.

1.4.3 Cross-Correlation Functions

Let $x(t)$ and $y(t)$ be two different random functions. Denote by $r_{xy}(\tau)$ the cross-correlation of $x(t)$ and $y(t)$. It is defined by

$$r_{xy}(\tau) = E\left[x(t)y(t+\tau)\right] = \lim_{T \to \infty} \frac{1}{T} \int_{-\frac{T}{2}}^{\frac{T}{2}} x(t)y(t+\tau)dt. \tag{1.40}$$

The cross-correlation $r_{xy}(\tau)$ exhibits how a random function $x(t)$ at t correlates to the other random function $y(t)$ at $t+\tau$. It has properties different from those of ACF. Generally, $r_{xy}(0)$ may not be the maximum of $r_{xy}(\tau)$. It may be positive or negative. When $r_{xy}(\tau) > 0$, we say that $x(t)$ and $y(t+\tau)$ have a positive correlation, implying that they have the same statistical persistence. On the other hand, if $r_{xy}(\tau) < 0$, $x(t)$ and $y(t+\tau)$ have a negative correlation, meaning they have the statistical anti-persistence.

In general, $r_{xy}(\tau) \neq r_{yx}(\tau)$. However,

$$r_{xy}(\tau) = r_{yx}(-\tau). \tag{1.41}$$

In fact,

$$E\left[y(t)x(t+\tau)\right] = r_{yx}(\tau) = \lim_{T \to \infty} \frac{1}{T} \int_{-\frac{T}{2}}^{\frac{T}{2}} y(t)x(t+\tau)dt$$

$$= \lim_{T \to \infty} \frac{1}{T} \int_{-\frac{T}{2}}^{\frac{T}{2}} y(t)x(t+\tau)d(t+\tau) \overset{\text{letting } t+\tau=u}{=} \lim_{T \to \infty} \frac{1}{T} \int_{-\frac{T}{2}+\tau}^{\frac{T}{2}+\tau} y(u-\tau)x(u)du \tag{1.42}$$

$$= r_{xy}(-\tau).$$

The cross-correlation function $r_{xy}(\tau)$ has the bound expressed by the cross-correlation inequality in the form

$$|r_{xy}(\tau)|^2 \le r_{xx}(0)\, r_{yy}(0). \tag{1.43}$$

As a matter of fact, since the Cauchy–Schwartz inequality is given by

$$\left[\int_{-\infty}^{\infty} x(t)y(t)dt\right]^2 \le \int_{-\infty}^{\infty} x^2(t)dt \int_{-\infty}^{\infty} y^2(t)dt, \tag{1.44}$$

we have

$$|r_{xy}(\tau)|^2 = \left[\lim_{T\to\infty}\frac{1}{T}\int_{-\frac{T}{2}}^{\frac{T}{2}} x(t)y(t+\tau)dt\right]^2 \le \lim_{T\to\infty}\frac{1}{T}\int_{-\frac{T}{2}}^{\frac{T}{2}} x^2(t)dt \lim_{T\to\infty}\frac{1}{T}\int_{-\frac{T}{2}}^{\frac{T}{2}} y^2(t+\tau)dt$$

$$= r_{xx}(0)r_{yy}(0). \tag{1.45}$$

Another cross-correlation function inequality is expressed by

$$|r_{xy}(\tau)| \le \frac{1}{2}\left[r_{xx}(0)+r_{yy}(0)\right]. \tag{1.46}$$

As a matter of fact, for $a>0$ and $b>0$, one has $\sqrt{ab} \le \dfrac{a+b}{2}$. Because $r_{xx}(0)\ge 0$ and $r_{yy}(0)\ge 0$, we have $|r_{xy}(\tau)| \le \dfrac{r_{xx}(0)+r_{yy}(0)}{2}$.

1.4.4 Cross-Covariance Functions

When considering the cross-correlation between two random functions $[x(t)-\mu_{xx}]$ and $[y(t)-\mu_{yy}]$, we have the cross-covariance function, denoted by $C_{xy}(\tau)$, in the form

$$C_{xy}(\tau)= E\left\{\left[x(t)-\mu_{xx}\right]\left[y(t+\tau)-\mu_{yy}\right]\right\}= r_{xy}(\tau)-\mu_{xx}\mu_{yy}. \tag{1.47}$$

Similar to $r_{xy}(\tau)$, one has

$$C_{xy}(\tau)= C_{yx}(-\tau), \tag{1.48}$$

$$|C_{xy}(\tau)|^2 \le C_{xx}(0)C_{yy}(0), \tag{1.49}$$

$$|C_{xy}(\tau)| \le \frac{C_{xx}(0)+C_{yy}(0)}{2}. \tag{1.50}$$

When $x=y$, $C_{xy}(\tau)$ reduces to $C_{xx}(\tau)=r_{xx}(\tau)-\mu_{xx}\,\mu_{xx}$. Due to $0\le|r_{xy}(\tau)|^2\le r_{xx}(0)$ $r_{yy}(0)$, one has

$$0 \le \frac{r_{xy}(\tau)}{\sqrt{r_{xx}(0)r_{yy}(0)}} \le 1. \tag{1.51}$$

Denote by $\rho_{xy}(\tau)$ the normalized cross-correlation function. Then,

$$\rho_{xy}(\tau) = \frac{r_{xy}(\tau)}{\sqrt{r_{xx}(0)r_{yy}(0)}}. \tag{1.52}$$

Note 1.9. The normalized cross-correlation function is a quantity to measure the similarity between $x(t)$ and $y(t)$ (Li [15]).

1.5 POWER SPECTRA

We discuss two types of power spectra. One is the power auto-spectrum density function (power spectrum density, PSD for short). The other is the power cross-spectrum density function.

1.5.1 Power Auto-Spectrum Density Functions

Denote by $X(\omega)$ the Fourier transform of a random function $x(t)$. Then, $X(\omega)$ and $x(t)$ have the same statistical properties. The difference between the two is that $x(t)$ is in the time domain while $X(\omega)$ is in the frequency domain. A considerably important result in time series is that $|X(\omega)|^2$ is a deterministic function, called the PSD function.

Denote the PSD of x by $S_{xx}(\omega)$. Then, $S_{xx}(\omega)=|X(\omega)|^2$. It is a statistical model of $x(t)$ in the frequency domain. According to the Wiener–Khinchin relation (Khinchin [16], Wiener [17]), for $i=\sqrt{-1}$,

$$S_{xx}(\omega) = \int_{-\infty}^{\infty} r_{xx}(t)e^{-i\omega t}\,dt. \tag{1.53}$$

For a Poisson random function, its PSD is given by

$$S_{\text{Poisson}}(\omega) = \int_{-\infty}^{\infty} r_{xx}(t)e^{-i\omega t}\, dt = \int_{-\infty}^{\infty} c^2 e^{-2\lambda|t|}e^{-i\omega t}\, dt = c^2\frac{4\lambda}{4\lambda^2+\omega^2}. \quad (1.54)$$

For a Cauchy class random function, its PSD is expressed by

$$S_{\text{Cauchy class}}(\omega) = \int_{-\infty}^{\infty} r_{xx}(t)e^{-i\omega t}\, dt = \int_{-\infty}^{\infty} \frac{1}{1+t^2} e^{-i\omega t}\, dt = \sqrt{\frac{2|\omega|}{\pi}} K_{0.5}(|\omega|), \quad (1.55)$$

where $K_\nu(z)$ is the modified Bessel function of the second kind (Lim and Li [18, p. 2942]).

Let x be a fractional Gaussian noise (fGn). Its PSD is given by (Li and Lim [19])

$$S_{\text{fGn}}(\omega) = \sigma^2 \sin(H\pi)\Gamma(2H+1)|\omega|^{1-2H}, \quad (1.56)$$

where σ^2 is the strength of fGn and $0 < H < 1$ is the Hurst parameter. When $0.5 < H < 1$, we have $S_{\text{fGn}}(0) = \infty$, which implies $1/f$ noise.

1.5.2 Power Cross-Spectrum Density Functions

Let $S_{xy}(\omega)$ be the power cross-spectrum density (cross PSD for short) of $x(t)$ and $y(t)$. Following the Wiener–Khinchin relation (Khinchin [16], Wiener [17]),

$$S_{xy}(\omega) = \int_{-\infty}^{\infty} r_{xy}(t)e^{-i\omega t}\, dt. \quad (1.57)$$

Generally, $S_{xy}(\omega)$ is not an even function in terms of ω. It is usually a complex function. However,

$$S_{xy}(\omega) = S_{yx}(-\omega). \quad (1.58)$$

In fact,

$$S_{xy}(\omega) = \int_{-\infty}^{\infty} r_{xy}(t)e^{-i\omega t}\, dt = \int_{-\infty}^{\infty} r_{yx}(-t)e^{-i\omega t}\, dt = S_{yx}(-\omega). \quad (1.59)$$

1.6 WHITE NOISE

Denote by $w(t)$ the white noise. By white noise, we mean that the PSD of $w(t)$ is a constant. Let $S_{ww}(\omega)$ be the PSD of $w(t)$. Then,

$$S_{ww}(\omega) = \sigma^2, \tag{1.60}$$

where σ^2 is the strength of $w(t)$. Let $r_{ww}(\tau)$ be the ACF of $w(t)$. The meaning of white noise also says that $w(t)$ is a random function that is uncorrelated at any two different time points. Thus, one has

$$r_{ww}(\tau) = \sigma^2 \delta(\tau), \tag{1.61}$$

where $\delta(\tau)$ is the delta function. The normalized white noise implies that $S_{ww}(\omega) = 1$ and accordingly $r_{ww}(\tau) = \delta(\tau)$.

Let $\phi(\omega)$ be a random function. Denote by $W(\omega)$ the Fourier transform of $w(t)$. Then, when

$$W(\omega) = \exp[i\phi(\omega)], \tag{1.62}$$

we have the normalized white noise given by

$$w(t) = \mathrm{F}^{-1}\{\exp[i\phi(\omega)]\}, \tag{1.63}$$

because

$$|W(\omega)|^2 = 1. \tag{1.64}$$

1.7 RANDOM FUNCTIONS OF INTEREST IN TRAFFIC THEORY

Let $x(t)$ be a traffic time series. In the theory of traffic models, we are interested in a type of random functions and their ACFs are slowly decayed such that

$$\int_{-\infty}^{\infty} r_{xx}(\tau)d\tau = \infty. \tag{1.65}$$

A random process with the above property is called the LRD process or long memory process (Beran [20]).

When $S_{xx}(0)=0$, one writes $S_{xx}(\omega) \sim 1/\omega$ for $\omega \to 0$. In that case, we say that $x(t)$ is an $1/f$ noise (Mandelbrot [21]). Note that $S_{xx}(\omega) = \int_{-\infty}^{\infty} r_{xx}(t)e^{-i\omega t} dt$. If $x(t)$ is of LRD, one has

$$S_{xx}(0) = \infty. \qquad (1.66)$$

Thus, an LRD process is a $1/f$ noise [22]. Traffic modeling is interested in LRD processes.

REFERENCES

1. A. M. Yaglom, *An Introduction to the Theory of Stationary Random Functions*, Prentice-Hall, London, 1962.
2. J. L. Doob, *Stochastic Processes*, John Wiley & Sons, New York, 1953.
3. A. N. Kolmogorov, *Foundations of the Theory of Probability*, 2nd Ed., Chelsea Publishing Company, New York, 1956.
4. J. S. Bendat and A. G. Piersol, *Random Data: Analysis and Measurement Procedure*, 4th Ed., John Wiley & Sons, New York, 2010.
5. M. B. Priestley, *Spectral Analysis and Time Series*, Academic Press, London/ New York, 1981.
6. G. A. Korn and T. M. Korn, *Mathematical Handbook for Scientists and Engineers*, McGraw-Hill, New York, 1961.
7. J. D. Gibson, editor-in-chief, *The Communications Handbook*, IEEE Press, New York, 1997.
8. R. B. Cooper, *Introduction to Queueing Theory*, 2nd Ed., Elsevier, New York/ Oxford, 1981.
9. A. K. Erlang, Telefon-Ventetider. Et Stykke Sandsynlighedsregning. *Matematisk Tidsskrift* B, 1920, 25–42.
10. Z. Bojkovic, M. Bakmaz, and B. Bakmaz, Originator of teletraffic theory. *Proc. IEEE*, 98(1) 2010, 123–127.
11. C. Partridge, The end of simple traffic models (editor's notes), *IEEE Net.*, 7 1993, 3.
12. W. Willinger and V. Paxson, Where mathematics meets the Internet, *Not. AMS*, 45(8) 1998, 961–970.
13. M. Li, Fractal time series—a tutorial review, *Math. Prob. Eng.*, 2010 2010, Article ID 157264, 26 p. Doi:10.1155/2010/157264.
14. J.-P. Chiles and P. Delfiner, *Geostatistics, Modeling Spatial Uncertainty*, Wiley, New York, 1999.
15. M. Li, An iteration method to adjusting random loading for a laboratory fatigue test, *Int. J. Fatigue*, 27(7) 2005, 783–789.

16. A.J. Khinchin, *Mathematical Foundation of Statistical Mechanics*, Dover Publications, Inc., New York, 1949.
17. N. Wiener, *Extrapolation, Interpolation, and Smoothing of Stationary Time Series*, The Technology Press of the MIT and John Wiley & Sons, New York, 1964.
18. S. C. Lim and M. Li, A generalized Cauchy process and its application to relaxation phenomena, *J. Phys. A: Math. Gen.*, 39(12) 2006, 2935–2951.
19. M. Li and S. C. Lim, A rigorous derivation of power spectrum of fractional Gaussian noise, *Fluct. Noise Lett.*, 6(4) 2006, C33–C36.
20. J. Beran, *Statistics for Long-Memory Processes*, Chapman & Hall, New York, 1994.
21. B. B. Mandelbrot, *Multifractals and 1/f Noise*, Springer, New York/Berlin, 1998.
22. M. Li and W. Zhao, On 1/f noise, *Math. Prob. Eng.*, 2012 23 Oct. 2012, Article ID 673648, 22 p.

CHAPTER 2

Fourier Transform

The Fourier transform plays a crucial role in time series (S. Makridakis, A survey of time series, *Int. Stat. Rev./Revue Internationale de Statistique*, 44(1) 1976, 29–70.). In this chapter, we discuss four main parts regarding the Fourier transform: (1) the Fourier transform for ordinary functions, (2) delta function and nascent delta functions, (3) the Fourier transform in generalized functions, and (4) convolutions. These are needed in traffic modeling and delay-bound computations. When dealing with the issue of the existence of the inverse min-plus convolution and the identity in the min-plus convolution system in Chapter 4, we need the delta function series. Consequently, the delta function and its nascent ones are essential. Since traffic is of long-range dependence, its spectrum power density function has to be dealt with in the domain of generalized functions. Hence, the Fourier transform in generalized functions is desired. Because the min-plus convolution plays a role in dealing with traffic delay bounds, its analogy, namely the conventional convolution, is stressed.

2.1 BASIC IN FOURIER TRANSFORM

Let $f(t)$ be a function for $t \in (-\infty, \infty)$. Denote by $F(\omega)$ its Fourier transform. It is given by

$$F(\omega) = \int_{-\infty}^{\infty} f(t)e^{-i\omega t} \, dt, \qquad (2.1)$$

DOI: 10.1201/9781003268802-2   17 where $\omega = 2\pi f$ is the angular frequency and f is the frequency. One usually uses F as the operator of the Fourier transform. Then, $F(\omega) = F[f(t)]$. It is a function in the frequency domain for $\omega \in (-\infty, \infty)$. It reveals frequency components of $f(t)$. The function $F(\omega)$ is called the frequency spectrum function (spectrum for short) of $f(t)$.

For $F(\omega)$, it corresponds to a time function $f(t)$ expressed by

$$f(t) = \frac{1}{2\pi} \int_{-\infty}^{\infty} F(\omega) e^{i\omega t} \, d\omega. \tag{2.2}$$

The above is the inverse Fourier transform of $F(\omega)$. Denote by F^{-1} the operator of the inverse Fourier transform. Then, $f(t) = F^{-1}[F(\omega)]$. Two functions, $f(t)$ and $F(\omega)$, may be expressed by

$$f(t) \leftrightarrow F(\omega). \tag{2.3}$$

In some literature, the Fourier transform of $f(t)$ is in the form

$$F(\omega) = \int_{-\infty}^{\infty} f(t) e^{i\omega t} \, dt.$$

The inverse operation of the above is given by

$$f(t) = \frac{1}{2\pi} \int_{-\infty}^{\infty} F(\omega) e^{-i\omega t} \, d\omega,$$

see e.g., Gelfand and Vilenkin [1]. We use (2.1) and (2.2) for the Fourier transform and its inverse.

For two functions $f_1(t)$ and $f_2(t)$, one says that $[f_1(t) - f_2(t)]$ is a null function if

$$\int_{-\infty}^{\infty} \left[f_1(t) - f_2(t) \right] e^{-i\omega t} \, dt = 0. \tag{2.4}$$

Suppose $f_1(t) \leftrightarrow F_1(\omega)$ and $f_2(t) \leftrightarrow F_2(\omega)$. If $[f_1(t) - f_2(t)]$ is a null function, we say that $F_1(\omega) = F_2(\omega)$ even if $f_1(t) \neq f_2(t)$. On the other hand, when $[f_1(t) - f_2(t)]$ is a null function, we say that $f_1(t) = f_2(t)$ in the sense of $F_1(\omega) = F_2(\omega)$.

Example 2.1 (Null function)

Consider the signum function in two different forms:

$$\text{sgn}_1(t)=\begin{cases} 1, t>0 \\ -1, t\le 0 \end{cases}, \quad \text{sgn}_2(t)=\begin{cases} 1, t\ge 0 \\ -1, t<0 \end{cases}. \tag{2.5}$$

Then, $\text{sgn}_2(t)-\text{sgn}_1(t)$ is a null function.

Proof. Since

$$\text{sgn}_2(t)-\text{sgn}_1(t)=\begin{cases} 1 & t=0 \\ 0 & \text{elsewhere} \end{cases}, \tag{2.6}$$

we have

$$\int_{-\infty}^{\infty} [\text{sgn}_2(t)-\text{sgn}_1(t)]e^{-i\omega t}\, dt=0. \tag{2.7}$$

Thus, $\text{sgn}_2(t)-\text{sgn}_1(t)$ is a null function. Accordingly, $\text{F}[\text{sgn}_1(t)]=\text{F}[\text{sgn}_2(t)]$.

The Fourier transform is a one-to-one mapping. For $f_1(t) \leftrightarrow F_1(\omega)$ and $f_2(t) \leftrightarrow F_2(\omega)$, $F_1(\omega)=F_2(\omega)$ if $[f_1(t)-f_2(t)]$ is a null function. Therefore, from a view of the Fourier transform, $\text{sgn}_1(t)=\text{sgn}_2(t)$ in the sense of $\text{F}[\text{sgn}_1(t)]=\text{F}[\text{sgn}_2(t)]$.

Mathematically, the position of $f(t)$ is the same as that of $F[f(t)]$. Both $f(t)$ and $F(\omega)$ contain the same information. For instance, if $f(t)$ is white noise, $F[f(t)]$ is white noise too (Robinson [2]). The difference between the two is that $f(t)$ is in the time domain while $F[f(t)]$ is in the frequency domain.

Function $F(\omega)$ is complex, in general. Expressing it by

$$F(\omega)= \int_{-\infty}^{\infty} f(t)e^{-i\omega t}\, dt = \int_{-\infty}^{\infty} f(t)(\cos\omega t - i\sin\omega t)\, dt \tag{2.8}$$

yields

$$F(\omega)= \text{Re}[F(\omega)]+i\,\text{Im}[F(\omega)]= A(\omega)+iB(\omega), \tag{2.9}$$

where

$$A(\omega) = \int_{-\infty}^{\infty} f(t)\cos\omega t \, dt, \tag{2.10}$$

$$B(\omega) = -\int_{-\infty}^{\infty} f(t)\sin\omega t \, dt. \tag{2.11}$$

In polar coordinates, $F(\omega)$ is expressed by

$$F(\omega) = |F(\omega)| e^{i\varphi(\omega)}, \tag{2.12}$$

where $|F(\omega)| = \sqrt{A^2(\omega) + B^2(\omega)}$ and $\varphi(\omega) = \arctan\dfrac{B(\omega)}{A(\omega)}$.

Example 2.2

Consider the Fourier transform of a single-side exponentially decayed function in the form

$$f(t) = Ee^{-at}u(t), \quad a > 0, \tag{2.13}$$

where $u(t)$ is the unit step function and E is the magnitude. Its Fourier transform is given by

$$F(\omega) = \int_{-\infty}^{\infty} Ee^{-at}u(t)e^{-i\omega t} \, dt = \int_{0}^{\infty} Ee^{-at}e^{-i\omega t} \, dt = \frac{E}{a + i\omega}. \tag{2.14}$$

The amplitude-frequency spectrum of $f(t)$ is given by

$$|F(\omega)| = \frac{E}{\sqrt{a^2 + \omega^2}}. \tag{2.15}$$

Its phase is given by

$$\varphi(\omega) = -\arctan\frac{a}{\omega}. \tag{2.16}$$

Example 2.3

Consider the Fourier transform of a two-side exponentially decayed function in the form

$$f(t) = Ee^{-|a|t}, \quad a > 0. \tag{2.17}$$

Its Fourier transform is given by

$$F(\omega) = \int_{-\infty}^{\infty} Ee^{-a|t|}e^{-i\omega t}\, dt = \frac{2aE}{a^2 + \omega^2}. \tag{2.18}$$

Note that the phase spectrum of $f(t)$ is zero.

Example 2.4

Study the Fourier transform of the single rectangular pulse function given by

$$f(t) = \begin{cases} E, & -\dfrac{\tau}{2} < t < \dfrac{\tau}{2} \\ 0, & \text{elsewhere} \end{cases} \tag{2.19}$$

Its Fourier transform is given by

$$F(\omega) = \int_{-\infty}^{\infty} f(t)e^{-i\omega t}\, dt = 2E\int_{0}^{\frac{\tau}{2}} \cos\omega t\, dt = E\tau \text{Sa}\left(\frac{\omega\tau}{2}\right). \tag{2.20}$$

2.2 DELTA FUNCTION

Suppose that ϕ is a function that is continuous and rapidly decays on (a, b) and its derivatives of all orders exist. Then, it is called a test function on (a, b), where a may be minus infinity and b may be infinity. The set of all test functions is denoted by **D**. Now, we say that whether a function $f(t)$ can be defined or not does not rely on whether the value of $f(t)$ is finite or not. Instead, it simply depends on whether the operation $\langle f(t), \phi(t) \rangle$ is convergent or not. A commonly used operation is integral. That is,

$\langle f(t), \phi(t) \rangle = \int_a^b f(t)\phi(t)\,dt.$ Therefore, if that integral is convergent, we say that $f(t)$ is defined as a function. When a function is defined in that way, it is called a generalized function (Gelfand and Vilenkin [1]). A generalized function $f(t)$ is also called a Schwartz distribution.

Several properties of generalized functions are listed below.

Lemma 2.1

Any generalized function is infinitely differentiable [1].
Proof is omitted.

Lemma 2.2

There exists the Fourier transform of any generalized function [1].
Proof is omitted.

Lemma 2.3

The limit of the sequence of a generalized function is unique with a possible difference in a null function [1].
Proof is omitted.

Lemma 2.4

The product of generalized functions is undefined [1].
Proof is omitted.

Lemma 2.5

Limit operation and integral one are interchangeable for any generalized function [1].
Proof is omitted.

Lemma 2.6

If, for any $\phi \in \mathbf{D}$, there exists

$$\lim_{\nu \to \infty} \int_{-\infty}^{\infty} f_\nu(t)\phi(t)\,dt = \int_{-\infty}^{\infty} f(t)\phi(t)\,dt, \qquad (2.21)$$

for $f_1, f_2, \ldots, f_\nu, \ldots$, which is a sequence of a generalized function, the sequence $\{f_\nu\}$ is convergent to f [1].

Proof is omitted.

Lemma 2.7

The derivative of a generalized function f is another generalized function given by

$$\int_{-\infty}^{\infty} \frac{df(t)}{dt}\phi(t)\,dt = -\int_{-\infty}^{\infty} f(t)\frac{d\phi(t)}{dt}\,dt. \qquad (2.22)$$

Because of infinitely differentiable, one has

$$\int_{-\infty}^{\infty} f^{(n)}(t)\phi(t)\,dt = (-1)^n \int_{-\infty}^{\infty} f(t)\phi^{(n)}(t)\,dt. \qquad (2.23)$$

Proof is omitted.

Lemma 2.8

The Fourier kernel $e^{-i\omega t}$ is a test function.
Proof is omitted.

Example 2.5

Denote by $\delta(t)$ the delta function. For all $\phi \in \mathbf{D}$, it is defined by

$$\int_{-\infty}^{\infty} \delta(t)\phi(t)\,dt = \phi(0). \qquad (2.24)$$

Proof is omitted.

Example 2.6

For all $\phi \in$ **D**, following Lemma 2.7, its derivative of order n is defined by

$$\int_{-\infty}^{\infty} \delta^{(n)}(t)\phi(t)\,dt = (-1)^{(n)} \int_{-\infty}^{\infty} \delta(t)\phi^{(n)}(t)\,dt = (-1)^{(n)}\phi^{(n)}(0). \qquad (2.25)$$

Proof is omitted.

There is a relationship between $\delta(t)$ and $u(t)$ in the form (Xia and Yan [3])

$$\delta(t) = \frac{du(t)}{dt}. \qquad (2.26)$$

The integral relationship between $\delta(t)$ and $u(t)$ is expressed by

$$\int_{-\infty}^{t} \delta(t)\,dt = u(t). \qquad (2.27)$$

From the definition of $u(t)$ and according to the above, we see that $\delta(t)$ has the property given by

$$\delta(t) = 0 \quad (t \neq 0). \qquad (2.28)$$

Example 2.7

$\delta(t)$ is an even function.

   Proof. According to (2.24), we have

$$\int_{-\infty}^{\infty} \delta(-t)\phi(t)\,dt \overset{t=-u}{=} -\int_{\infty}^{-\infty} \delta(u)\phi(-u)\,du = \int_{-\infty}^{\infty} \delta(u)\phi(-u)\,du = \phi(0). \qquad (2.29)$$

Thus,

$$\delta(t) = \delta(-t). \qquad (2.30)$$

The proof completes.

Example 2.8

$\delta'(t)$ is an odd function.

Proof. Based on (2.25), we have

$$\int\limits_{-\infty}^{\infty} \delta'(t)\phi(t)\,dt = -\int\limits_{-\infty}^{\infty} \delta(t)\phi'(t)\,dt = -\phi'(0). \qquad (2.31)$$

On the other hand,

$$\int\limits_{-\infty}^{\infty} \delta'(-t)\phi(t)\,dt \overset{t=-u}{=} -\int\limits_{\infty}^{-\infty} \delta(u)\phi'(-u)\,du = \int\limits_{-\infty}^{\infty} \delta(u)\phi'(-u)\,du = \phi'(0). \quad (2.32)$$

Therefore, we have

$$\delta'(-t) = -\delta'(t). \qquad (2.33)$$

This finishes the proof.

Example 2.9

$$t\delta(t) = 0.$$

Proof. Based on (2.24), we have

$$\int\limits_{-\infty}^{\infty} t\delta(t)\phi(t)\,dt = \int\limits_{-\infty}^{\infty} \delta(t)[t\phi(t)]\,dt = [t\phi(t)]_{t=0} = 0. \qquad (2.34)$$

This completes the proof.

I emphasize that $\delta(t)$ at $t=0$ is undefined. From the point of view of generalized functions, we do not care whether $\delta(0)$ is defined or not. Due to (2.26), $\delta(0)$ is never a number. As a matter of fact, $\delta(0)$ just taken ∞ as a limit.

Example 2.10

The Fourier transform of $\delta(t)$ is given by

$$\int_{-\infty}^{\infty} \delta(t)e^{-i\omega t}\, dt = e^{-i\omega t}\Big|_{t=0} = 1. \tag{2.35}$$

The above exhibits a particular property of $\delta(t)$. To be precise, its spectrum is constant over $\omega \in (-\infty, \infty)$.

The above-mentioned $\delta(t)$ is often called the Dirac-delta function, see e.g., Robinson [2], so as to memorialize the famous physicist P.A.M. Dirac [4]. However, mathematicians, such as Fourier, Cauchy, Poisson, et al., had introduced the function $\delta(t)$ to study the issues of divergent series and integrals before the age of Dirac (see Laugwitz [5], Hoskins [6], and Lützen [7]). Thus, this book uses the term delta function without the prefix Dirac.

Note that the function $\delta(t)$ has to be defined in the domain of generalized functions. In the domain of ordinary functions, it cannot be defined. In fact, if defining $\delta(t)$ by

$$\delta(t) = \begin{cases} \infty, & t = 0, \\ 0, \text{elsewhere}, \end{cases} \tag{2.36}$$

we encounter a contradiction. For instance, when $A > 1$, we have

$$A\delta(t) = \begin{cases} \infty, & t = 0, \\ 0, \text{elsewhere}. \end{cases} \tag{2.37}$$

Thus, we have the contradiction expressed by

$$A\delta(t) = \delta(t), \quad A > 1. \tag{2.38}$$

The above implies

$$(A-1)\delta(t) = 0. \tag{2.39}$$

Since $A > 1$, the above means, for all t,

$$\delta(t) = 0. \tag{2.40}$$

That is another contradiction.

In order to avoid the symbol ∞ in the expression of $\delta(t)$, one uses the expression in the form

$$\begin{cases} \delta(t) = 0, \quad t = 0, \\ \int\limits_{-\infty}^{\infty} \delta(t)\,dt = 1, \end{cases} \tag{2.41}$$

see e.g., Dirac [4, p. 58]. Since

$$\begin{cases} \delta(t) = 0, \quad t \neq 0 \\ \int\limits_{-\infty}^{\infty} \delta(t)\,dt = 1 \end{cases} = \begin{cases} \delta(-t) = 0, \quad t \neq 0 \\ \int\limits_{-\infty}^{\infty} \delta(-t)\,dt = 1 \end{cases}, \tag{2.42}$$

we immediately, for $A > 0$, have

$$\int\limits_{-\infty}^{\infty} A\delta'(t)\,dt = 0. \tag{2.43}$$

The above implies that

$$\begin{cases} A\delta'(t) = 0, \quad t = 0, \\ \int\limits_{-\infty}^{\infty} A\delta'(t)\,dt = 0. \end{cases} \tag{2.44}$$

Thus,

$$\begin{cases} \delta(t) + A\delta'(t) = 0, \quad t = 0, \\ \int\limits_{-\infty}^{\infty} [\delta(t) + A\delta'(t)]\,dt = 1. \end{cases} \tag{2.45}$$

The above exhibits the contradiction given by

$$\delta(t) + A\delta'(t) = \delta(t). \tag{2.46}$$

It is not difficult to show more contradictions regarding $\delta(t)$ if it is defined in the domain of ordinary functions.

Proposition 2.1

Using $\delta(t)$, we have

$$\int_{-\infty}^{\infty} \cos \omega t \, d\omega = 2\pi\delta(t), \qquad (2.47)$$

and

$$\int_{-\infty}^{\infty} \sin \omega t \, d\omega = 0. \qquad (2.48)$$

Proof. Doing the inverse Fourier transform of 1 yields

$$\frac{1}{2\pi} \int_{-\infty}^{\infty} e^{-i\omega t} \, d\omega = \delta(t). \qquad (2.49)$$

From the above, we have

$$\int_{-\infty}^{\infty} \cos \omega t \, d\omega - i \int_{-\infty}^{\infty} \sin \omega t \, d\omega = 2\pi\delta(t). \qquad (2.50)$$

Because $\delta(t)$ is real, we have (2.47) and (2.48).

From Proposition 2.1, we have the following corollary.

Corollary 2.1

Let $\delta(\omega)$ be the delta function in the frequency domain. Then,

$$\int_{-\infty}^{\infty} \cos \omega t \, dt = 2\pi\delta(\omega), \qquad (2.51)$$

and

$$\int_{-\infty}^{\infty} \sin \omega t \, dt = 0. \tag{2.52}$$

Proof. Replacing t by ω and changing ω with t in (2.47) and (2.48) produce (2.51) and (2.52).

2.3 NASCENT DELTA FUNCTIONS

Let $f_v(t)$ be a function with a parameter v. Then, for $a \neq 0$ and $b \neq 0$, when the following limit holds

$$\lim_{v \to 0^+} \int_a^b f_v(t) \, dt = \begin{cases} 1, & a < 0 < b \\ 0, & a < b < 0 \text{ and } 0 < a < b \end{cases} \tag{2.53}$$

and it is a continuous function, we say that $f_v(t)$ is a nascent delta/impulse function. An alternative definition of a nascent delta function can be expressed as follows.

Let $f_v(t)$ be a function with a parameter v. It is a nascent delta function if it is a continuous function in the form

$$\lim_{v \to 0} \int_{-\infty}^{t} f_v(t) \, dt = u(t) = \begin{cases} 1, & t \geq 0 \\ 0, & t < 0 \end{cases}. \tag{2.54}$$

Example 2.11

Consider a rectangular function in the form

$$f_v(t) = \text{rect}(t) = \begin{cases} \dfrac{1}{v}, & -\dfrac{v}{2} < t < \dfrac{v}{2}, \quad v > 0. \\ 0, \text{otherwise} \end{cases} \tag{2.55}$$

Because

$$\lim_{v \to 0} \int_{-\infty}^{t} \text{rect}(t) \, dt = u(t) = \begin{cases} 1, & t > 0 \\ 0, & t < 0 \end{cases}, \tag{2.56}$$

rect(t) is a nascent delta function. It can be expressed by

$$\delta(t) = \lim_{v \to 0} \text{rect}(t). \qquad (2.57)$$

Since the limit $v \to 0$ cannot be realized by any practical machine, we can only set a small value for the pulse width $v = \varepsilon$. So long as v is much smaller than the transient response time of a system, ε can be considered infinitesimal in engineering. Accordingly, rect(t) may be taken as a practical delta function without the need of $v \to 0$.

Example 2.12

Consider a function that takes the form of the Cauchy probability density. It is given by

$$f_v(t) = \text{Cauchy}(t) = \frac{1}{\pi} \frac{v}{t^2 + v^2}. \qquad (2.58)$$

Then, $f_v(t)$ is a nascent delta function.
   Proof. Since

$$\int_a^b \text{Cauchy}(t)dt = \frac{1}{\pi}\left(\text{arctg}\frac{b}{v} - \text{arctg}\frac{a}{v}\right) = \begin{cases} 1, a < 0 < b, \\ 0, \text{elsewhere}, \end{cases} \qquad (2.59)$$

we have

$$\delta(t) = \frac{1}{\pi} \lim_{v \to 0^+} \frac{v}{t^2 + v^2}. \qquad (2.60)$$

Thus, Cauchy(t) is a nascent delta function.
   Keep in mind that $\delta(t)$ is an abstract symbol of the delta function. Practical methods for its realizations in engineering are simply nascent ones.

2.4 BASIC PROPERTIES OF FOURIER TRANSFORM

We brief some properties of $F(\omega)$. Interesting readers may refer to Papoulis [9] or Priestley [10] for details. Note that Fourier transform is a kind of linear operation. It satisfies the superposition. That is, if

$$f_n(t) \leftrightarrow F_n(\omega), \sum_{n=0}^{\infty} a_n f_n(t) \leftrightarrow \sum_{n=0}^{\infty} a_n F_n(\omega).$$

Property 2.1

$A(\omega)$ is an even function while $B(\omega)$ is odd.

Proof. According to (2.10), we have $A(\omega)=A(-\omega)$. On the other hand, in (2.11), one has $B(-\omega)=-B(\omega)$. The proof finishes.

Property 2.2

$A^2(\omega)$ and $B^2(\omega)$ are even functions.

Proof. Since $A(\omega)$ is even, $A^2(\omega)$ is even. In addition, $B^2(\omega)$ is even because $B(\omega)$ is odd.

Property 2.3

$|F(\omega)|$ is an even function while $\varphi(\omega)$ is odd.

Proof. According to (2.12), we see that $|F(\omega)|$ is even while $\varphi(\omega)$ is odd. The proof completes.

Property 2.4

If $f(t)$ is an even function, $F(\omega)=A(\omega)$ is even. If $f(t)$ is an odd function, $F(\omega)=iB(\omega)$ is odd.

Proof. If $f(t)$ is even, $f(t)\sin\omega t$ is odd in terms of t. Thus, $B(\omega)=0$ and $F(\omega)=A(\omega)$ when $f(t)$ is even. On the other hand, if $f(t)$ is odd, $f(t)\cos\omega t$ is odd in terms of t. Thus, $A(\omega)=0$ and $F(\omega)=iB(\omega)$ when $f(t)$ is odd when $f(t)$ is odd.

Property 2.5 (Symmetry)

If $f(t)\leftrightarrow F(\omega), F(t)\leftrightarrow 2\pi f(-\omega)$.

Proof. In $F(\omega)=\displaystyle\int_{-\infty}^{\infty} f(t)e^{-i\omega t}\,dt$, changing variable t with ω produces

$$F(t)=\int_{-\infty}^{\infty} f(\omega)e^{-i\omega t}\,d\omega = \frac{1}{2\pi}\int_{-\infty}^{\infty} 2\pi f(-\omega)e^{i(-\omega)t}d(-\omega). \qquad (2.61)$$

Thus, $F(t)\leftrightarrow 2\pi f(-\omega)$. The proof completes.

Property 2.5 is particularly useful for dealing with divergent integrals.

Example 2.13

Denote by rect(t) the single rectangular pulse in the form

$$\text{rect}(t) = \begin{cases} E, -\dfrac{\tau}{2} < t < \dfrac{\tau}{2} \\ 0 \end{cases}. \tag{2.62}$$

Its Fourier transform is $E\tau\text{Sa}(\omega\tau/2)$
  Proof. Note that

$$\text{F}[\text{rect}(t)] = \int\limits_{-\frac{\tau}{2}}^{\frac{\tau}{2}} Ee^{-i\omega t}\, dt = E\tau\text{Sa}\left(\frac{\omega\tau}{2}\right). \tag{2.63}$$

Using Property 2.5, one has

$$E\tau\text{Sa}\left(\frac{t\tau}{2}\right) \leftrightarrow 2\pi\text{rect}(\omega). \tag{2.64}$$

Example 2.14

The Fourier transform of $\cos\omega_0 t$ is given by

$$\cos\omega_0 t \leftrightarrow \pi\left[\delta(\omega+\omega_0)+\delta(\omega-\omega_0)\right]. \tag{2.65}$$

Proof. Due to $\delta(t) \leftrightarrow 1$, one has $1 \leftrightarrow 2\pi\delta(\omega)$ based on symmetry. Thus,

$$\cos\omega_0 t \leftrightarrow \int\limits_{-\infty}^{\infty} \frac{e^{i\omega_0 t}+e^{-i\omega_0 t}}{2}e^{-i\omega t}\, dt = \int\limits_{-\infty}^{\infty} \frac{e^{i(\omega_0-\omega)t}+e^{-i(\omega_0+\omega)t}}{2}\, dt$$

$$= \pi\left[\delta(\omega+\omega_0)+\delta(\omega-\omega_0)\right]. \tag{2.66}$$

This finishes the proof.

Example 2.15

The Fourier transform of $\sin \omega_0 t$ is expressed by

$$\sin \omega_0 t \leftrightarrow i\pi\left[\delta(\omega+\omega_0)-\delta(\omega-\omega_0)\right]. \qquad (2.67)$$

Proof. Due to

$$\sin \omega_0 t \leftrightarrow \int_{-\infty}^{\infty} \frac{e^{i\omega_0 t}-e^{-i\omega_0 t}}{2i}e^{-i\omega t}\,dt = \int_{-\infty}^{\infty} \frac{e^{i(\omega_0-\omega)t}-e^{-i(\omega_0+\omega)t}}{2i}dt, \qquad (2.68)$$

one has (2.67).

Property 2.6 (Time Shifting)

If $f(t)\leftrightarrow F(\omega), f(t-t_0)\leftrightarrow F(\omega)e^{-i\omega t_0}$.
   Proof. In fact,

$$f(t-t_0)\leftrightarrow \int_{-\infty}^{\infty} f(t-t_0)e^{-i\omega t}\,dt = \int_{-\infty}^{\infty} f(t-t_0)e^{-i\omega(t-t_0)}e^{-i\omega t_0}d(t-t_0)$$

$$= e^{-i\omega t_0}\int_{-\infty}^{\infty} f(u)e^{-i\omega u}\,du = F(\omega)e^{-i\omega t_0}. \qquad (2.69)$$

The proof completes.

Example 2.16

If $f(t)\leftrightarrow F(\omega), f(t-t_0)+f(t+t_0)\leftrightarrow 2F(\omega)\cos\omega t_0$.
Proof. Since $f(t-t_0)\leftrightarrow F(\omega)e^{-i\omega t_0}$ and $f(t+t_0)\leftrightarrow F(\omega)e^{i\omega t_0}$, we have

$$f(t-t_0)+f(t+t_0)\leftrightarrow F(\omega)e^{-i\omega t_0}+F(\omega)e^{i\omega t_0} = 2F(\omega)\cos\omega t_0. \qquad (2.70)$$

The proof finishes.

Property 2.7 (Frequency Shifting)

If $f(t) \leftrightarrow F(\omega)$, $f(t)e^{i\omega_0 t} \leftrightarrow F(\omega - \omega_0)$.
    Proof. Due to

$$f(t)e^{i\omega_0 t} \leftrightarrow \int_{-\infty}^{\infty} f(t)e^{i\omega_0 t}e^{-i\omega t}\,dt = \int_{-\infty}^{\infty} f(t)e^{-i(\omega - \omega_0)t}\,dt = F(\omega - \omega_0), \quad (2.71)$$

the property holds.

Example 2.17

If $f(t) = e^{-at}$,

$$F[f(t)] = 2\pi\delta(\omega - ia). \quad (2.72)$$

Proof. Since

$$1 \leftrightarrow 2\pi\delta(\omega), \quad (2.73)$$

in addition,

$$e^{-at} = e^{i(iat)}, \quad (2.74)$$

using the property of frequency scaling, we have (2.72).

Example 2.18

If $f(t) \leftrightarrow F(\omega)$,

$$f(t)\cos\omega_0 t \leftrightarrow \frac{1}{2}[F(\omega - \omega_0) + F(\omega + \omega_0)]. \quad (2.75)$$

Proof. Since $f(t)\cos\omega_0 t = 0.5\{[f(t)\exp(i\omega_0 t)] + [f(t)\exp(-i\omega_0 t)]\}$, with the property of frequency scaling, we have (2.75).
Equation (2.75) represents the modulation theorem in electronics engineering (Zheng et al. [8]).

Example 2.19

Let $f(t)$ be a periodic signal with period T_0. Then,

$$F[f(t)] = a_0\pi\delta(\omega) + \sum_{n=1}^{\infty}\left\{\begin{array}{l}a_n\pi[\delta(\omega+n\omega_0)+\delta(\omega-n\omega_0)]\\ +ib_n\pi[\delta(\omega+n\omega_0)-\delta(\omega-n\omega_0)]\end{array}\right\}, \qquad (2.76)$$

where $\omega_0 = \dfrac{2\pi}{T_0}$, a_0, a_n, and b_n are Fourier coefficients.

Proof. Extending $f(t)$ into its Fourier series yields

$$f(t) = \frac{a_0}{2} + \sum_{n=1}^{\infty}(a_n\cos n\omega_0 t + b_n\sin n\omega_0 t). \qquad (2.77)$$

According to Examples 2.14 and 2.15, we have

$$\begin{aligned}\cos n\omega_0 t &\leftrightarrow \pi[\delta(\omega+n\omega_0)+\delta(\omega-n\omega_0)],\\ \sin n\omega_0 t &\leftrightarrow i\pi[\delta(\omega+n\omega_0)-\delta(\omega-n\omega_0)].\end{aligned} \qquad (2.78)$$

In addition, $\dfrac{a_0}{2} \leftrightarrow a_0\pi\delta(\omega)$. Thus, with the superposition, we have

$$f(t) \leftrightarrow F\left(\frac{a_0}{2}\right) + F\left(\sum_{n=1}^{\infty}(a_n\cos n\omega_0 t + b_n\sin n\omega_0 t)\right)$$

$$= a_0\pi\delta(\omega) + \sum_{n=1}^{\infty}[a_n F(\cos n\omega_0 t) + b_n F(\sin n\omega_0 t)]$$

$$= a_0\pi\delta(\omega) + \sum_{n=1}^{\infty}\left\{\begin{array}{l}a_n\pi[\delta(\omega+n\omega_0)+\delta(\omega-n\omega_0)]\\ +ib_n\pi[\delta(\omega+n\omega_0)-\delta(\omega-n\omega_0)]\end{array}\right\} \qquad (2.79)$$

The proof completes.

Property 2.8 (Differential)

If $f(t) \leftrightarrow F(\omega)$, $f^{(n)}(t) \leftrightarrow (i\omega)^n F(\omega)$.

Proof. According to Lemma 2.7, we have

$$f^{(n)}(t) \leftrightarrow \int_{-\infty}^{\infty} f^{(n)}(t)e^{-i\omega t}\,dt = (-1)^n \int_{-\infty}^{\infty} f(t)\left(e^{-i\omega t}\right)^{(n)}\,dt$$

$$= (-1)^{2n}(i\omega)^n \int_{-\infty}^{\infty} f(t)e^{-i\omega t}\,dt = (i\omega)^n F(\omega). \qquad (2.80)$$

This completes the proof.

Example 2.20

Let $\delta(t)$ be the impulse function. Then,

$$\delta^{(n)}(t) \leftrightarrow (i\omega)^n. \qquad (2.81)$$

Proof. Letting $f(t) = \delta(t)$ in Property 2.8 yields (2.81).

Example 2.21

Let $\delta(\omega)$ be the delta function in the frequency domain. Then,

$$t^n \leftrightarrow 2\pi(-i)^n \delta^{(n)}(-\omega). \qquad (2.82)$$

Proof. According to the property of symmetry, using (2.81), one has $(it)^n \leftrightarrow 2\pi\delta^{(n)}(-\omega)$. Moving i^n from the left to the right yields (2.82). This finishes the proof.

Example 2.22

Let $\delta(\omega)$ be the delta function in the frequency domain. Then,

$$e^t \leftrightarrow \int_{-\infty}^{\infty} e^t e^{-i\omega t}\,dt = \int_{-\infty}^{\infty} \left(\sum_{n=0}^{\infty} \frac{t^n}{n!}\right) e^{-i\omega t}\,dt = 2\pi \sum_{n=0}^{\infty} \frac{(-i)^n \delta^{(n)}(-\omega)}{n!}. \qquad (2.83)$$

Proof. According to Example 2.21 and the superposition property of the Fourier transform, when expanding exp(t) using its Taylor expansion produces the above.

Example 2.23

There exists the equality in the form

$$\sum_{n=0}^{\infty} \frac{(-i)^n \delta^{(n)}(-\omega)}{n!} = \delta(\omega + i). \tag{2.84}$$

Proof. Let $a = -1$ in (2.72). We have

$$e^t \leftrightarrow 2\pi\delta(\omega + i). \tag{2.85}$$

Consider (2.83), we have (2.84).

Example 2.24

There is the equality in the form

$$\sum_{n=0}^{\infty} \frac{(-i)^n \delta^{(n)}(t)}{n!} = \delta(i - t). \tag{2.86}$$

Proof. Replacing ω with $-t$ yields the above, according to (2.84).
An alternative of the above is given by

$$\sum_{n=0}^{\infty} \frac{\delta^{(n)}(t)}{n!} = i^n \delta(i - t). \tag{2.87}$$

Example 2.25

The signum function is in the form

$$\text{sgn}(t) = \begin{cases} 1, & t \geq 0 \\ -1, & t < 0 \end{cases}. \tag{2.88}$$

Its Fourier transform is given by

$$\text{sgn}(t) \leftrightarrow \frac{2}{i\omega}. \tag{2.89}$$

Proof. The function sgn(t) is odd. Thus, $\dfrac{d\,\mathrm{sgn}(t)}{dt}$ is even. In fact,

$$\frac{d\,\mathrm{sgn}(t)}{dt} = 2\delta(t) \leftrightarrow 2.$$

According to the differential property, we have

$$\frac{d\,\mathrm{sgn}(t)}{dt} \leftrightarrow i\omega F[\mathrm{sgn}(t)] = 2. \tag{2.90}$$

Thus, $F[\mathrm{sgn}(t)] = \dfrac{2}{i\omega}$.

Example 2.26

The Fourier transform of the unit step function $u(t)$ is in the form

$$u(t) \leftrightarrow \pi\delta(\omega) + \frac{1}{i\omega}. \tag{2.91}$$

Proof. Because $u(t) = \dfrac{1}{2} + \dfrac{1}{2}\mathrm{sgn}(t)$, by superposition, we have

$$u(t) \leftrightarrow F\left(\frac{1}{2}\right) + F\left(\frac{1}{2}\mathrm{sgn}(t)\right) = \pi\delta(\omega) + \frac{1}{i\omega}. \tag{2.92}$$

This completes the proof.

Mathematically, because of

$$u(t) \leftrightarrow \int_0^\infty u(t)e^{-i\omega t}\,dt = \int_0^\infty (\cos\omega t - i\sin\omega t)\,dt = \pi\delta(\omega) + \frac{1}{i\omega},$$

we have

$$\int_0^\infty \cos\omega t\,dt = \pi\delta(\omega), \tag{2.93}$$

and

$$\int_0^\infty \sin \omega t \, dt = \frac{1}{\omega}. \tag{2.94}$$

Property 2.9 (Integral)

If $f(t) \leftrightarrow F(\omega)$,

$$\int_{-\infty}^t f(t) \, dt \leftrightarrow \pi \delta(\omega) F(0) + \frac{F(\omega)}{i\omega}. \tag{2.95}$$

Proof. Since

$$\int_{-\infty}^t f(t) \, dt = \left(\int_{-\infty}^t f(t) \, dt \right) * \delta(t), \tag{2.96}$$

with Lemma 2.10, one has

$$\int_{-\infty}^t f(t) \, dt = f(t) * \int_{-\infty}^t \delta(t) \, dt = f(t) * u(t). \tag{2.97}$$

According to Lemma 2.11, we have

$$\int_{-\infty}^t f(t) \, dt = f(t) * u(t) \leftrightarrow \left[\pi \delta(\omega) + \frac{1}{i\omega} \right] F(\omega) = \pi \delta(\omega) F(0) + \frac{F(\omega)}{i\omega}. \tag{2.98}$$

The proof completes.

Under the condition of $F(0) = 0$, one has

$$\int_{-\infty}^t f(t) \, dt \leftrightarrow \frac{F(\omega)}{i\omega}. \tag{2.99}$$

Property 2.10 (Scaling)

If $f(t) \leftrightarrow F(\omega)$,

$$f(at) \leftrightarrow \frac{1}{|a|} F\left(\frac{\omega}{a}\right). \tag{2.100}$$

Proof. As a matter of fact,

$$\int_{-\infty}^{\infty} f(at)e^{-i\omega t}\, dt = \frac{1}{a} \int_{-\infty}^{\infty} f(at)e^{-i\frac{\omega}{a}at}\, dat. \tag{2.101}$$

If $a > 0$, $\dfrac{1}{a} \displaystyle\int_{-\infty}^{\infty} f(at)e^{-i\frac{\omega}{a}at}\, dat = \dfrac{1}{a} F\left(\dfrac{\omega}{a}\right)$. When $a < 0$,

$$\frac{1}{a} \int_{-\infty}^{\infty} f(at)e^{-i\frac{\omega}{a}at}\, dat = \frac{1}{a} \int_{\infty}^{-\infty} f(u)e^{-i\frac{\omega}{a}u}\, du$$

$$= -\frac{1}{a} \int_{-\infty}^{\infty} f(u)e^{-i\frac{\omega}{a}u}\, du = \frac{1}{|a|} \int_{-\infty}^{\infty} f(u)e^{-i\frac{\omega}{a}u}\, du. \tag{2.102}$$

The proof completes.

Example 2.27

If $f(t) \leftrightarrow F(\omega)$,

$$f(-t) \leftrightarrow F(-\omega). \tag{2.103}$$

Proof. Using $a = -1$ in (2.100) yields the above.

Lemma 2.9 (Parseval's Rule)

If $f(t) \leftrightarrow F(\omega)$,

$$\int_{-\infty}^{\infty} |f(t)|^2 \, dt = \int_{-\infty}^{\infty} |F(\omega)|^2 \, d\omega. \tag{2.104}$$

Proof. Let $f(t)$ be a current that passes through a resistor with $1\ \Omega$. Then, $|f(t)|^2$ is the power. Accordingly, $\int_{-\infty}^{\infty} |f(t)|^2 \, dt$ is the energy the resistor consumes over the time interval $(-\infty, \infty)$. Since the Fourier transform is a one-to-one mapping in mathematics, $\int_{-\infty}^{\infty} |f(t)|^2 \, dt$ must equal to the energy represented in the frequency domain, that is, $\int_{-\infty}^{\infty} |F(\omega)|^2 \, d\omega$. According to the energy conservation law, (2.104) holds. The proof completes.[1]

Example 2.28

Prove the integral below

$$\int_{-\infty}^{\infty} \left(\mathrm{Sa}\,\frac{\omega}{2} \right)^2 \, d\omega = 1. \tag{2.105}$$

Proof. Let $f(t)$ be a rectangular pulse rect(t) with the width $\tau = 1$ and the magnitude $E = 1$. Then,

$$\int_{-\infty}^{\infty} |f(t)|^2 \, dt = 1. \tag{2.106}$$

Since $f(t) \leftrightarrow \mathrm{Sa}\,\dfrac{\omega}{2}$, according to the Parsavel's rule, we have (2.105).

Example 2.29

Prove the integral below

---

[1] I purposely prove the well-known Parsaval's rule based on the energy conservation law.

$$\int\limits_{-\infty}^{\infty}\left(\text{Sa}\frac{\omega\tau}{2}\right)^2 d\omega = \frac{1}{\tau}. \qquad (2.107)$$

Proof. Let $f(t)$ be a rectangular pulse rect(t) with the width τ and the magnitude $E = 1$. Then,

$$\int\limits_{-\infty}^{\infty}\left|f(t)\right|^2 dt = \tau. \qquad (2.108)$$

As

$$f(t) \leftrightarrow \tau\text{Sa}\frac{\omega\tau}{2}, \qquad (2.109)$$

based on the Parsavel's rule, we have

$$\int\limits_{-\infty}^{\infty}\left(\tau\text{Sa}\frac{\omega\tau}{2}\right)^2 d\omega = \tau. \qquad (2.110)$$

Thus, (2.107) holds.

2.5 CONVOLUTION

For two functions $f_1(t), f_2(t)$, $-\infty < t < \infty$, the convolution of $f_1(t)$ and $f_2(t)$ is a specific product defined by

$$f_1(t) * f_2(t) = \int\limits_{-\infty}^{\infty} f_1(u)f_2(t-u)\,du. \qquad (2.111)$$

In algebra, convolution follows the laws of commutative, associative, and distributive, respectively. The commutative implies that

$$f_1(t) * f_2(t) = f_2(t) * f_1(t) = \int\limits_{-\infty}^{\infty} f_2(u)f_1(t-u)\,du. \qquad (2.112)$$

In fact,

$$f_1(t) * f_2(t) = -\int_{-\infty}^{\infty} f_1(\tau) f_2(t-\tau) d(t-\tau) \overset{u=t-\tau}{=} -\int_{\infty}^{-\infty} f_1(u-t) f_2(u) du$$

(2.113)

$$= \int_{-\infty}^{\infty} f_1(t-u) f_2(u) du = f_2(t) * f_1(t).$$

The associative means

$$f_1(t) * \left[f_2(t) * f_3(t) \right] = \left[f_1(t) * f_2(t) \right] * f_3(t).$$ (2.114)

As a matter of fact, the right side of the above is

$$f_1(t) * \left[f_2(t) * f_3(t) \right] = \int_{-\infty}^{\infty} \left[\int_{-\infty}^{\infty} f_1(\lambda) f_2(\tau-\lambda) d\lambda \right] f_3(t-\tau) d\tau$$

$$= \int_{-\infty}^{\infty} f_1(\lambda) \left[\int_{-\infty}^{\infty} f_2(\tau-\lambda) f_3(t-\tau) d\tau \right] d\lambda$$ (2.115)

$$= \int_{-\infty}^{\infty} f_1(\lambda) \left[\int_{-\infty}^{\infty} f_2(\tau) f_3(t-\tau-\lambda) d\tau \right] d\lambda$$

$$= f_1(t) * [f_2(t) * f_3(t)].$$

The distributive says

$$f_1(t) * \left[f_2(t) + f_3(t) \right] = \left[f_1(t) * f_2(t) \right] + \left[f_1(t) * f_3(t) \right].$$ (2.116)

Note that

$$f_1(t) * \left[f_2(t) + f_3(t) \right] = \int_{-\infty}^{\infty} f_1(\tau) \left[f_2(t-\tau) + f_3(t-\tau) \right] d\tau$$

$$= \int_{-\infty}^{\infty} f_1(\tau) f_2(t-\tau) d\tau + \int_{-\infty}^{\infty} f_1(\tau) f_3(t-\tau) d\tau$$ (2.117)

$$= f_1(t) * f_2(t) + f_1(t) * f_3(t).$$

Lemma 2.10 (Differential of Convolution)

Let $g(t) = f_1(t) * f_2(t)$. If $n = l + m (l, m \geq 0)$, we have

$$g^{(n)}(t) = f_1^{(n)}(t) * f_2(t) = f_1(t) * f_2^{(n)}(t) = f_1^{(l)}(t) * f_2^{(m)}(t). \quad (2.118)$$

Proof. In fact,

$$g^{(n)}(t) = \frac{d^n \left[f_1(t) * f_2(t) \right]}{dt^n} = \frac{d^n}{dt^n} \int_{-\infty}^{\infty} f_1(t - \tau) f_2(\tau) d\tau$$

$$= \frac{d^l}{dt^l} \frac{d^m}{dt^m} \int_{-\infty}^{\infty} f_1(t - \tau) f_2(\tau) d\tau = \frac{d^l}{dt^l} \int_{-\infty}^{\infty} \frac{d^m}{dt^m} f_1(t - \tau) f_2(\tau) d\tau$$

$$= \frac{d^l}{dt^l} \left[\frac{d^m}{dt^m} f_1(t) * f_2(t) \right] = \frac{d^l}{dt^l} \int_{-\infty}^{\infty} \frac{d^m}{d\tau^m} f_1(\tau) f_2(t - \tau) d\tau$$

$$= \int_{-\infty}^{\infty} \frac{d^m}{d\tau^m} f_1(\tau) \frac{d^l}{dt^l} f_2(t - \tau) d\tau = \frac{d^m}{dt^m} f_1(t) * \frac{d^l}{dt^l} f_2(t). \quad (2.119)$$

This finishes the proof.

Example 2.30

Prove

$$g^{(n)}(t) = \delta^{(n)}(t) * g(t). \quad (2.120)$$

Proof. Since

$$g(t) = \delta(t) * g(t), \quad (2.121)$$

we have

$$g^{(n)}(t) = \left[\delta(t) * g(t) \right]^{(n)} = \delta^{(n)}(t) * g(t). \quad (2.122)$$

The proof is finished.

Lemma 2.11 (Convolution Rule in the Time Domain)

If $f_1(t) \leftrightarrow F_1(\omega)$ and $f_2(t) \leftrightarrow F_2(\omega)$, one has

$$f_1(t) * f_2(t) \leftrightarrow F_1(\omega)F_2(\omega). \tag{2.123}$$

Proof. Because

$$f_1(t) * f_2(t) \leftrightarrow \int_{-\infty}^{\infty} \left[\int_{-\infty}^{\infty} f_1(t-\tau)f_2(\tau)d\tau \right] e^{-i\omega t} dt$$

$$= \int_{-\infty}^{\infty} f_2(\tau)d\tau \int_{-\infty}^{\infty} f_1(t-\tau)e^{-i\omega t} dt = \int_{-\infty}^{\infty} f_2(\tau)e^{-i\omega \tau} d\tau F_1(\omega)$$

$$= F_1(\omega)F_2(\omega), \tag{2.124}$$

(2.123) holds.

Example 2.31

Consider the proof for the equation below.

$$\delta(t) * f(t) = f(t). \tag{2.125}$$

Proof. Let $f(t) \leftrightarrow F(\omega)$. According to Lemma 2.11 and due to $\delta(t) \leftrightarrow 1$, we have

$$\delta(t) * f(t) \leftrightarrow F(\omega). \tag{2.126}$$

Thus, (2.125) is valid.

Note that $\delta(t) = \dfrac{du(t)}{dt}$. Thus,

$$\delta(t) * f(t) = \frac{du(t)}{dt} * f(t) = u(t) * \frac{df(t)}{dt} \leftrightarrow \left[\pi\delta(\omega) + \frac{1}{i\omega} \right] F(\omega)$$

$$= \pi\delta(\omega)F(0) + \frac{F(\omega)}{i\omega}. \tag{2.127}$$

The above is the integral property of the Fourier transform.

On the other hand,

$$\delta'(t) * f(t) = \delta(t) * f'(t) \leftrightarrow i\omega F(\omega). \qquad (2.128)$$

The above is the differential property of the Fourier transform. In fact, since

$$\delta^{(n)}(t) \leftrightarrow (i\omega)^n,$$

one has

$$\delta^{(n)}(t) * f(t) \leftrightarrow (i\omega)^n F(\omega). \qquad (2.129)$$

The above again gives the differential property of the Fourier transform.

Example 2.32

Prove the following

$$\delta(t - t_0) * f(t) = f(t - t_0). \qquad (2.130)$$

Proof. Let $f(t) \leftrightarrow F(\omega)$. According to Lemma 2.11 and due to $\delta(t - t_0) \leftrightarrow e^{-i\omega t_0}$, we obtain

$$\delta(t - t_0) * f(t) \leftrightarrow F(\omega)e^{-i\omega t_0}. \qquad (2.131)$$

Since

$$F(\omega)e^{-i\omega t_0} \leftrightarrow f(t - t_0), \qquad (2.132)$$

(2.130) holds.

From the above, we have

$$\delta(t + t_0) * f(t) \leftrightarrow F(\omega)e^{i\omega t_0}. \qquad (2.133)$$

Thus, considering the convolution given by

$$[\delta(t - t_0) + \delta(t + t_0)] * f(t), \qquad (2.134)$$

we have

$$\left[\delta(t-t_0)+\delta(t+t_0)\right]*f(t) \leftrightarrow F(\omega)e^{-i\omega t_0} + F(\omega)e^{i\omega t_0}$$

$$= F(\omega)\left(e^{-i\omega t_0} + e^{i\omega t_0}\right) = 2F(\omega)\cos\omega t_0. \qquad (2.135)$$

The above is the modulation rule represented by convolution.

Lemma 2.12 (Convolution Rule in the Frequency Domain)

Let $f_1(t) \leftrightarrow F_1(\omega)$ and $f_2(t) \leftrightarrow F_2(\omega)$. Then,

$$f_1(t)f_2(t) \leftrightarrow \frac{1}{2\pi}F_1(\omega)*F_2(\omega). \qquad (2.136)$$

Proof is omitted.

As mentioned previously, the product of generalized functions is not defined. To describe that, we let $f(t) = \delta(t)$. Thus, following Lemma 2.12, we have

$$2\pi\delta(t)\delta(t) \leftrightarrow \{\mathrm{F}[\delta(t)]*\mathrm{F}[\delta(t)]\} = 1*1. \qquad (2.137)$$

Since the right side of the above is undefined, $\delta(t)\delta(t)$ is undefined. In general, the product of generalized functions is not defined (refer to Li [11–13] for the products of generalized functions).

REFERENCES

1. I. M. Gelfand and K. Vilenkin, *Generalized Functions*, Vol. 1, Academic Press, New York, 1964.
2. E. A. Robinson, A historical perspective of spectrum estimation, *Proc. IEEE*, 70(9) 1982, 885–907.
3. D. X. Xia and S. Z. Yan, *Real Functions and Foundation of Applied Functional Analysis*, Shanghai Science and Technology Publishing House, Shanghai, 1982. In Chinese.
4. P. A. M. Dirac, *Quantum Mechanics*; 4th Ed., Oxford University Press, Oxford, 1958.
5. D. Laugwitz, Early delta functions and the use of infinitesimals in research, *Revue d'histoire des sciences*, 45(1) 1992, Etudes sur Cauchy (1789–1857), 115–128.
6. R. F. Hoskins, *Delta Functions: An Introduction to Generalized Functions*, Woodhead Publishing Limited, Oxford, 2009.

7. J. Lützen, *The Prehistory of the Theory of Distributions, Studies in the History of Mathematics and Physical Sciences*, vol. 7, Springer, New York-Berlin 1982, pp. 112–115.

8. J. L. Zheng, Q. Y. Ying, and W. L. Yang, *Signals and Systems*, 2nd Ed., Vol. 1, Higher Education Press, Beijing, 2000. In Chinese.

9. A. Papoulis, *The Fourier Integral and Its Applications*, McGraw-Hill Inc., New York, 1962.

10. M. B. Priestley, *Spectral Analysis and Time Series*, Vol. 1, Academic Press, New York, 1981.

11. C. K. Li, The powers of the Dirac delta function by Caputo fractional derivatives, *J. Fract. Calculus Appl.*, 7(1) 2016, 12–23.

12. C. K. Li, The product and fractional derivative of analytic functionals, *Int. J. Math. Analy.*, 11(20) 2017, 955–972.

13. Y. Q. Li, The products of generalized functions x_+^λ and x_-^μ *Scientia Sinica*, *Spec. Issue Math (I)*, 1979, 103–123. In Chinese.

CHAPTER 3

Applied Functional

There are two tough or open problems in the aspect of the min-plus convolution system, which is a key tool for computing traffic delay bounds. One is whether the inverse min-plus convolution exists. An alternative problem of that is whether the identity exists in the min-plus convolution system. The other is how to represent the identity if it exists. In order to solve the problems, we need the inverse operator theorem of Banach, which is essential in functional analysis. In the aspect of traffic modeling, we may use the optimal approximation in Hilbert spaces for evaluating the degree of modeling accuracy. For those reasons and for the sake of completeness, we discuss the basics of applied function in this chapter, which may suffice for the related contents in applied functional used in this monograph.

3.1 LINEAR SPACES

3.1.1 Notion of Linear Spaces

Definition 3.1 (Linear Spaces)

Denote by E a non-empty set. It is called a linear space if the following three axioms hold.

I. (Addition) $\forall x, y \in E, \exists z \in E$ such that

$$z = x + y, \tag{3.1}$$

where $+$ stands for an operation.

II. (Scale multiplication) $\forall x \in$ **E** and $\forall \lambda \in$ **R**, where **R** is the set of real numbers, $\exists z \in$ **E** so that

$$z = \lambda x. \tag{3.2}$$

III. $\forall x, y, z \in$ E, $\forall \lambda, \mu \in$ R, the following operations are satisfied.

$$1. \ (\text{Alternative}) x + y = y + x \tag{3.3}$$

$$2. \ (\text{Associative}) x + (y + z) = (x + y) + z; \lambda(\mu x) = (\lambda \mu) x \tag{3.4}$$

3. There exists unique null element;

$$4. \ (\text{Distributive}) \lambda(x + y) = \lambda x + \lambda y; \ (\lambda + \mu) x = \lambda x + \mu x. \tag{3.5}$$

In the definition of linear spaces, + is usually termed addition. However, it may or may not be ordinary addition.

3.1.2 Isomorphism of Linear Spaces

Definition 3.2 (Isomorphism)

For two linear spaces **X** and **Y**, if the mapping φ: **X** $\rightarrow$ **Y** is one-to-one and linear, that is,

$$1. \ \varphi(x) = y. \tag{3.6}$$

$$2. \ \varphi(x + y) = \varphi(x) + \varphi(y), \text{ and } \varphi(\lambda x) = \lambda \varphi(x), \tag{3.7}$$

X and **Y** are isomorphic and φ is called isomorphism mapping.

Note 3.1. If two linear spaces **X** and **Y** are isomorphism, they are equivalent in algebra.

Example 3.1

The Fourier transform is an isomorphism mapping. So is the Laplace transform.

3.1.3 Subspaces and Affine Manifold

Definition 3.3 (Subspaces)

Let **L** be a subspace of linear space **E**. If **L** is a linear space, we say that **L** is a subspace of **E**.

Definition 3.4 (Affine Manifold)

Let **L** be a proper subspace of **E**. Then, for $x \in$ **E**, the following set is called an affine manifold of **L** in **E**.

$$\mathbf{A} = \{x + l; l \in \mathbf{L}\}. \tag{3.8}$$

Note 3.2. Affine manifold is also termed linear variety, linear affine, or affine subspace, see e.g., Abels [1] and Xia and Yan [2]. As a matter of fact, an element in the affine manifold $\{x + l; l \in$ **L**$\}$ is the element $l \in$ **L** plus a constant x. Thus, the affine manifold is the translation of **L** in **E**.

Remark 3.1

L may in general not be isomorphic to its affine manifold.

Proof. For $x_1, x_2 \in$ **E**, we have $x_1 + l$ and $x_2 + l$ in **A**. On the other hand, for $x_1 + x_2 \in$ **E**, we have $x_1 + x_2 + l$ in **A**. Thus, in general, **A** may not be a linear subspace of **E**. Consequently, there is no issue of isomorphism in an affine manifold.

3.1.4 Convex Sets

Definition 3.5

Let **E** be a linear space. Then, a set **M** in **E**, i.e., **M** $\subset$ **E**, is said to be convex if for $\forall \lambda, \mu \in [0, 1]$, with the restriction $\lambda + \mu = 1$, there exists $\lambda x + \lambda y \in$ **M**.

Proposition 3.1

Let **E** be a linear space. Then, the necessary and sufficient condition of **V** $\subset$ **E** to be an affine manifold of **E** is that **V** is convex in **E**.

Proof. Let **V** be an affine manifold of **E**. That is, **V** $= x_0 +$ **L** for $x_0 \in$ **E**, where **L** is a proper subspace of **E**. We shall address the necessity and sufficiency, respectively.

Suppose $x \in$ **V**, $x = x_0 + \tilde{x}$ for $\tilde{x} \in$ **L**. Also, we assume $y \in$ **V**, $y = y_0 + \tilde{y}$ for $\tilde{y} \in$ **L**. Thus,

$$\lambda x + \lambda y = (\lambda + \mu)x_0 + \lambda \tilde{x} + \mu \tilde{y} = x_0 + \lambda \tilde{x} + \mu \tilde{y} \in \mathbf{L}. \tag{3.9}$$

Since **L** is a linear space, we have $\lambda \tilde{x} + \mu \tilde{y} \in$ **L**. Therefore, $\lambda x + \mu y \in$ **V**. This implies the necessity.

Suppose there is a subset $\mathbf{V} \subset \mathbf{E}$. We select $x_0 \in \mathbf{V}$ and define $\mathbf{L} = \{x - x_0 | x \in \mathbf{V}\}$. Therefore, we only need to prove that $\mathbf{L}$ is a linear subspace.

Let $\tilde{x}, \tilde{y} \in \mathbf{V}$. Let $x = \tilde{x} - x_0$ and $y = \tilde{y} - y_0$. Suppose $\lambda + \mu = 1$ for $\forall \lambda, \mu \in [0, 1]$. Because

$$2\lambda\tilde{x} + (1 - 2\lambda)x_0 = 2\lambda(x + x_0) + (1 - 2\lambda)x_0 = 2\lambda x + x_0 \in \mathbf{V}, \quad (3.10)$$

$$2\mu\tilde{y} + (1 - 2\mu)y_0 = 2\mu y + y_0, \quad (3.11)$$

we have

$$0.5\left[2\lambda\tilde{x} + (1 - 2\lambda)x_0\right] + 0.5\left[2\mu\tilde{y} + (1 - 2\mu)y_0\right]$$

$$= \lambda(\tilde{x} - x_0) + \mu(\tilde{y} - y_0) + x_0 \in \mathbf{V}. \quad (3.12)$$

Thus,

$$\lambda x + \mu y + x_0 \in \mathbf{V}. \quad (3.13)$$

Consequently,

$$\lambda x + \mu y \in \mathbf{L}. \quad (3.14)$$

The above implies $\mathbf{V} = x_0 + \mathbf{L}$. This completes the proof.

3.2 METRIC SPACES

As known, the concept of limit is a key in mathematics analysis. The linear spaces discussed previously do not relate to this concept. In metric spaces, however, we can consider the limit.

The limit $x_n \to x_0$ implies that $\forall \varepsilon > 0$, $\exists N(\varepsilon)$ such that $|x_n - x_0| < \varepsilon$ for $n > N(\varepsilon)$. Thus, one may use the concept of the metric between x_n and x_0, which is denoted by $d(x_n, x_0)$, to represent $|x_n - x_0|$. That is, $|x_n - x_0| = d(x_n, x_0)$.

3.2.1 Concept of Metric Spaces

Definition 3.6 (Metric and Metric Space)

Denote by $\mathbf{X}$ a non-empty set. If $\forall x, y \in \mathbf{X}$, there is a real number denoted by $d(x, y)$ such that the following three axioms hold. Then, $d(x, y)$ is called the metric or distance between x and y. $\mathbf{X}$ is called the metric space.

I. (Nonnegative): $d(x,y) \geq 0$ and $d(x,y) = 0$ if and only if $x = y$. (3.15)

II. (Symmetry): $d(x,y) = d(y,x)$. (3.16)

III. (The triangle inequality): $d(x,y) \leq d(x,z) + d(y,z)$ for $z \in \mathbf{X}$. (3.17)

Note 3.3. A metric space consists of two. One is the set $\mathbf{X}$ and the other is the metric $d(x, y)$ that is equipped with $\mathbf{X}$. It may be written by $(\mathbf{X}, d(x, y))$.

Example 3.2

The set of real numbers $\mathbf{R}$ is a metric space.

Example 3.3

Denote by $\mathbf{R}_n$ the n-dimensional vector space. For any $x \in \mathbf{R}_n$ and $y \in \mathbf{R}_n$, denote $x = [\xi_i]$ and $y = [\eta_i]$ for $i = 1, \ldots, n$. Then, $(\mathbf{R}_n, d_1(x, y))$, $(\mathbf{R}_n, d_p(x, y))$ $(p > 1)$, and $(\mathbf{R}_n, d_\infty(x, y))$ are metric spaces, where

$$d_1(x,y) = \Sigma |\xi_i - \eta_i|, i = 1, \ldots, n,$$ (3.18)

$$d_p(x,y) = \Sigma |\xi_i - \eta_i|^p, i = 1, \ldots, n, p > 1,$$ (3.19)

$$d_\infty(x,y) = \max |\xi_i - \eta_i|, 1 \leq i \leq n.$$ (3.20)

Example 3.4

Denote by $C[a, b]$ the set of continuous functions. For any $x(t), y(t) \in C[a, b]$, define

$$d(x,y) = \max |x(t) - y(t)|, t \in [a,b].$$ (3.21)

Then, $(C[a, b], d(x, y))$ is a metric space.

Proof. The above metric is non-negative and symmetrical. Moreover,

$$|x(t) - y(t)| \leq |x(t) - z(t)| + |z(t) - y(t)| \leq \max |x(t) - z(t)|$$

$$+ \max |z(t) - y(t)| = d(x,z) + d(z,y).$$ (3.22)

Thus,

$$d(x,y) \leq d(x,z) + d(z,y). \tag{3.23}$$

3.2.2 Limit in Metric Spaces

Definition 3.7 (Limit)

Denote by **X** a non-empty set. Denote by $\{x_n\}$ a sequence in a metric space $(\mathbf{X}, d)$. If there is $x \in \mathbf{X}$ such that $\lim d(x_n, x) = 0$ for $n \to \infty$, we say that $\{x_n\}$ is convergent and x is its limit denoted by $x_n \to x$.

Remark 3.2

The limit is unique if it exists.

Proof. In fact, if x and y were the limits of x, one has, by the triangle inequality,

$$0 \leq d(x,y) \leq d(x,x_n) + d(x_n,y). \tag{3.24}$$

In the case of $n \to \infty$, we have $d(x, x_n) = 0$ and $d(x_n, y) = 0$. Therefore, $x = y$.

3.2.3 Balls Viewed from Metric Spaces

Definition 3.8 (Balls)

Denote by **X** a non-empty set. For $r > 0$, the set given by

$$S(x_0, r) = \{x \in \mathbf{X}, d(x_0, x) < r\} \tag{3.25}$$

is called a ball in the metric space $(\mathbf{X}, d)$, where x_0 is the center of the ball and r is its radius. When $r = \varepsilon$, where ε is a small positive number, $S(x_0, r)$ is a ball-type neighborhood of x_0. If the ball is defined by

$$S(x_0, r) = \{x \in \mathbf{X}, d(x_0, x) \leq r\}, \tag{3.26}$$

it is a closed ball.

Definition 3.9 (Inner Point)

Let **M** be a subset of the metric space $(\mathbf{X}, d)$. If, for $x \in \mathbf{M}$, there exists a neighborhood described by the ball $S(x_0, r)$ that satisfies $S(x_0, r) \subset \mathbf{M}$, we say that x is an inner point in **M**.

Definition 3.10 (Open Set)

In Definition 3.9, if all elements of **M** are inner points in **M**, we say that **M** is an open set.

Example 3.5

The ball defined by (3.25) is an open ball. It is an open set.

Example 3.6

Let $a, b \in \mathbf{R}$. Then, (a, b) is an open set.

Definition 3.11 (Cluster Point)

Let $x \in \mathbf{X}$ and $\mathbf{M} \subset (\mathbf{X}, d)$. If there exists a point that is different from $x_0 \in S(x_0, r)$ for any $r > 0$, then x_0 is said to be a cluster point (or limit point) of **M**.

Note 3.4. The necessary and sufficient condition for x_0 to be a cluster point of **M** is that there is a sequence $\{x_n\}$ $(n = 1, \ldots, \infty)$ in **M**, which differs from x_0, such that $x_n \to x_0$.

A cluster point of **M** may not necessarily belong to **M**. For instance, for the set $\mathbf{M} = \{1, 1/2, 1/3, \ldots\} \in \mathbf{R}$, $0 \in \mathbf{R}$ is a cluster point of **M** but $0 \notin \mathbf{M}$.

Note 3.5. An equivalent definition of cluster point can be described as follows. Denote by ϕ the empty set. Then, x_0 is a cluster point of **M** if

$$\forall \varepsilon > 0 \big(S(x_0, \varepsilon) \cap (\mathbf{M} - \{x_0\}) \neq \phi \big). \tag{3.27}$$

Definition 3.12 (Derived Set) (Xia and Yan [2])

Denote by $\mathbf{M}'$ the set that contains all cluster points of $\mathbf{M} \subset (\mathbf{X}, d)$. Then, $\mathbf{M}'$ is called the derived set of **M**.

Definition 3.13

Let $\mathbf{M}^0 = \mathbf{M}' \cup \mathbf{M}$. Then, $\mathbf{M}^0$ is called the closure of **M**.

Note 3.6. The set $\mathbf{M}'$ of $\mathbf{M}$ is closed.

Note 3.7. The closure of $\mathbf{M}$ is a closed set but not vice versa.

3.2.4 Postscript

By introducing the concept of metric, we have viewed the important concepts, such as limit, convergence, inner point, cluster point, open sets, closed sets, derived sets, and closure, from the point of view of abstract analysis, although they appear similar in structure to those in mathematics analysis. More discussions about the contents in metric spaces refer to Deza and Deza [3].

According to the theory of metric spaces, any set can be constructed as a metric space as long as it is equipped with a metric. A metric space may or may not be linear since it does not relate to the property of linearity of a space.

3.3 LINEAR NORMED SPACES

We are familiar with the absolute value denoted by $|x|$ for $x \in \mathbf{R}$ and the module denoted by $|z|$ for a complex number $z \in C$, where C is the set of complex numbers. Both have the sense of "length". In normed spaces, the notion of length is generalized to characterize the length of an element that may not be a number. That is called the norm of an element in a normed space as described below.

3.3.1 Notion of Norm and Normed Spaces

Definition 3.14 (Norm)

Denote by $\mathbf{E}$ a linear space. $\forall x \in \mathbf{E}$, if there is a real number denoted by $\|x\|$ that corresponds to x and $\|x\|$ satisfies the following three axioms, $\|x\|$ is termed the norm of x and $\mathbf{E}$ is called linear normed space with the norm $\|x\|$.

i. (Nonnegative): $\|x\| \geq 0$ and $\|x\| = 0$ if and only if x

$= \theta$, where θ is the null element in $\mathbf{E}$. (3.28)

ii. (Scale multiplication): $\|\lambda x\| = |\lambda| \|x\|, \lambda \in \mathbf{R}$. (3.29)

iii. $\left(\text{The triangle inequality}\right)$: $\|x+y\| \le \|x\| + \|y\|, x, y \in E$. (3.30)

Note 3.8. Three axioms for defining a norm are similar to those for defining an absolute value. However, $x \in E$ may not be a number in general but $\|x\| \in R$. Thus, the notion of norm implies an abstract length of an element. In the case of $E = R$, $|x|$ becomes a special case of $\|x\|$.

Note 3.9. If there is a real number that corresponds to an element x in a linear space E and that number satisfies the above three axioms, one can construct a normed space.

Note 3.10. The metric $d(x, y)$ can be defined by a norm. That is,

$$d(x,y)=\|x-y\|.$$ (3.31)

Proof. Obviously, $\|x - y\|$ is non-negative. Besides, since

$$\|x-y\|=\|(-1)(y-x)\|=|-1|\|y-x\|=\|y-x\|,$$ (3.32)

$\|x - y\|$ satisfies the symmetry of a metric. Finally, as

$$d(x,y)=\|x-y\|=\|(x-z)+(z-y)\|\le\|(x-z)\|+\|z-y\|$$
$$=d(x,z)+d(z,y),$$ (3.33)

(3.31) satisfies the triangle inequality. This completes the proof.

3.3.2 Norms

As discussed above, we see that a linear normed space is a linear space equipped with a norm. Therefore, a linear space equipped with different kinds of norms produces different kinds of normed spaces. We talk about some commonly used norms with examples.

Example 3.7

Denote by R_n the n-dimensional vector space. For any $x \in R_n$, denote $x = [\xi_i]$ for $i = 1, \dots, n$. Then, $\|x\|_2$, $\|x\|_p$, and $\|x\|_\infty$ described below are norms,

$$\|x\|_2 = \left(\Sigma |\xi_i|^2 \right)^{1/2}, i = 1, \dots, n, \tag{3.34}$$

$$\|x\|_p = \left(\Sigma |\xi_i|^p \right)^{1/p}, i = 1, \dots, n, \tag{3.35}$$

$$\|x\|_\infty = \max |\xi_i|, \ 1 \le i \le n. \tag{3.36}$$

Proof. It is obvious that $\|x\|_2 \ge 0$, $\|x\|_p \ge 0$, and $\|x\|_\infty \ge 0$. In addition, it is easily seen that $\|x\|_2 = 0$, $\|x\|_p = 0$, and $\|x\|_\infty = 0$ if and only if $x = \theta$. Besides, for $\lambda \in \mathbf{R}$, $\|\lambda x\|_2 = |\lambda| \|x\|_2$, $\|\lambda x\|_p = |\lambda| \|x\|_p$, and $\|\lambda x\|_\infty = |\lambda| \|x\|_\infty$. Moreover, $\|x + y\|_2 \le \|x\|_2 + \|y\|_2$, $\|x + y\|_p \le \|x\|_p + \|y\|_p$, and $\|x + y\|_\infty \le \|x\|_\infty + \|y\|_\infty$, according to the Minkowski inequality. Thus, $\|x\|_2$, $\|x\|_p$, and $\|x\|_\infty$ are norms.

Note 3.11. $\mathbf{R}_n$ equipped with $\|x\|_2$ is denoted by l_n^2. If $\mathbf{R}_n$ is equipped with $\|x\|_p$, it is denoted by l_n^p. Use l_n^∞ for $\mathbf{R}_n$ equipped with $\|x\|_\infty$.

Note 3.12. $\|x\|_2$ is also called the Euclidian norm. Consequently, l_n^2 is a Euclidian space.

Example 3.8

Denote by $C[a, b]$ the set of continuous functions. For any $x(t) \in C[a, b]$, define

$$\|x(t)\| = \max |x(t)|, t \in [a, b]. \tag{3.37}$$

Then, $C[a, b]$ is a linear normed space equipped with the norm expressed by (3.37).

Example 3.9

For any $x(t) \in C[a, b]$, define

$$\|x(t)\|_p = \left(\int_a^b |x(t)|^p \, dt \right)^{\frac{1}{p}}. \tag{3.38}$$

Then, $C[a, b]$ is a linear normed space specifically denoted by $L_p[a, b]$ or $L^p[a, b]$.

Note 3.13. In the case of $p = 2$ in (3.38), we have the following $\|x\|_2$. The space $C[a, b]$ with $\|x\|_2$ is often denoted by $L_2[a, b]$ or $L^2[a,b]$, see e.g., Leigh [4].

$$\|x(t)\|_2 = \sqrt{\int_a^b |x(t)|^2 \, dt}. \qquad (3.39)$$

In $L^2[a,b]$, a and b are allowed to be $-\infty$ and ∞, respectively. In this case, it is written by $L^2(-\infty,\infty)$.

3.3.3 Equivalence of Norms

Given a linear space **E**, one may use different kinds of norms to construct different kinds of normed spaces as can be seen from the previous discussions. On the one hand, this characteristic of normed spaces provides us with a flexible tool for various issues in engineering. For instance, one may select the control principle of H_2 type, which is based on L^2 or l^2 norm, or H_∞, which is based on L^∞ or l^∞, according to specific issues encountered in control engineering, see e.g., Leigh [4], Thompson [5], Williams [6], and Li et al. [7]. On the other hand, one may select a kind of norm according to his preference among the norms that are equivalent in mathematics without affecting the performances of control systems or algorithms (Li [8]). Therefore, the equivalence of norms as well as normed spaces is meaningful in either mathematics or engineering.

Definition 3.15 (Equivalence of Norms)

Denote by $\|\cdot\|_{(1)}$ and $\|\cdot\|_{(2)}$ two different norms in a linear space **E**, respectively. If there exist constants $\alpha > 0$ and $\beta > 0$ such that the following holds for any $x \in$ **E**,

$$\alpha \|\cdot\|_{(1)} \le \|\cdot\|_{(2)} \le \beta \|\cdot\|_{(1)}, \qquad (3.40)$$

we say that $\|\cdot\|_{(1)}$ and $\|\cdot\|_{(2)}$ are equivalent. Equivalent norms $\|\cdot\|_{(1)}$ and $\|\cdot\|_{(2)}$ are denoted by

$$\|\cdot\|_{(1)} \sim \|\cdot\|_{(2)}. \qquad (3.41)$$

As a matter of fact, by $\|\cdot\|_{(1)} \sim \|\cdot\|_{(2)}$, we mean that

$$\exists \alpha > 0, \beta > 0, \ \forall x \in \mathbf{E}\left(\alpha\|x\|_{(1)} \le \|x\|_{(2)} \le \beta\|x\|_{(1)}\right). \tag{3.42}$$

Alternatively, (3.40) implies the following

$$\|x_n - x_0\|_{(1)} \to 0 \Leftrightarrow \|x_n - x_0\|_{(2)} \to 0. \tag{3.43}$$

In other words, the norm equivalence implies the equivalence of convergence.

Proposition 3.2 (Norm Equivalence)

Any norm is equivalent in finite dimensional spaces (Jarvinen [9]).

Proof. Let $\mathbf{E}$ be an n-dimensional linear normed space. Denote by $\{e_i\}_{i=1}^{n}$ a base of $\mathbf{E}$. For $x \in \mathbf{E}$, denote $x = [\xi_i] = \sum_{i=1}^{n} \xi_i e_i$. Then, one has

$$\|x\| = \left\|\sum_{i=1}^{n} \xi_i e_i\right\| \le \sum_{i=1}^{n} |\xi_i| \|e_i\| \le \sqrt{\sum_{i=1}^{n} \|e_i\|^2} \sqrt{\sum_{i=1}^{n} |\xi_i|^2} = \beta\|x\|_2,$$

where $\beta = \sqrt{\sum_{i=1}^{n} \|e_i\|^2} > 0$.

For any $y = \dfrac{x}{\|x\|_2} \in \mathbf{E}$. Denote $y = \sum_{i=1}^{n} \eta_i e_i$. Then, we have $\left\|\dfrac{x}{\|x\|_2}\right\| \ge \alpha$. Therefore,

$$\alpha\|x\|_2 \le \|x\| \le \beta\|x\|_2.$$

The above is valid for $x = \theta$. Thus, any norm $\|x\|$ in an n-dimensional space $\mathbf{E}$ is equivalent to $\|x\|_2$. Consequently, any norm is equivalent in finite dimensional spaces.

The above proposition is useful in engineering. In fact, because issues in practice are often considered in spaces of finite dimensions, one may select a norm according to his or her preference, see e.g., Li [10,11].

3.3.4 Equivalence of Linear Normed Spaces

Definition 3.16 (Equivalence of Linear Normed Spaces)

Denote two different linear normed spaces, respectively, by **X** and **Y**. The norms in **X** and **Y** are denoted by $\|x\|_X$ and $\|y\|_Y$, respectively. If there exists an isomorphic mapping $\varphi: \mathbf{X} \to \mathbf{Y}$ such that $\varphi(x) = y, \forall x \in \mathbf{X}, \forall y \in \mathbf{Y}$, and

$$\|y\|_Y = \|\varphi(x)\|_Y = \|x\|_X, \tag{3.44}$$

we say that **X** and **Y** are isometrically isomorphic.

Note 3.14. If **X** and **Y** are isomorphic, their algebra structures are equivalent. If **X** and **Y** are isometrically isomorphic, their mathematics structures are equivalent or identical.

3.4 BANACH SPACES

The famous theorem of Banach regarding the existence of inverse operator is a key point we shall use to deal with the identity in min-plus algebra. Thus, we need the brief of Banach spaces.

3.4.1 Concept of Banach Spaces

Definition 3.17 (Cauchy Sequence)

Denote by **X** a linear normed space. Denote an infinite sequence by $\{x_n\}$ $\in$ **X** for $n = 1, \ldots$. If, for natural number N and m, the following holds

$$\forall \varepsilon > 0 \left(\exists N (n > N \Rightarrow \|x_{n+m} - x\| < \varepsilon) \right), \tag{3.45}$$

we say that $\{x_n\}$ is a Cauchy sequence, which is also called a basic sequence.

Definition 3.18 (Banach Space)

Denote by **X** a linear normed space. If, for $n = 1, \ldots$, any Cauchy sequence $\{x_n\} \in \mathbf{X}$ converges to $x \in \mathbf{X}$, **X** is called a complete linear normed space. A complete linear normed space is specifically termed Banach space.

Note 3.15. A consequence of a Banach space **X** is that any Cauchy sequence in **X** is convergent.

Note 3.16. In mathematics analysis, Cauchy sequences are in $\mathbf{R}_n$. In fact, since $\mathbf{R}_n$ is complete, Cauchy sequences in mathematics analysis are convergent (Rudin [12], Aliprantis and Burkinsaw [13]).

Any convergent sequence in a linear normed space **E** is a Cauchy sequence in **E** but not vice versa. This property of Cauchy sequences differs from that in mathematics analysis, where a Cauchy sequence is always convergent, since **E** may not be complete, Liu [14].

3.4.2 Completeness

As can be seen from the discussions above, completeness is a crucial property of Banach spaces. Commonly used complete spaces are $\mathbf{R}_n$, $C^k[a, b]$, where k is a natural number, l_n^2, $L^p[a,b]$ for $p \geq 1$ (Xia and Yan [2]).

Proposition 3.3

Any finite dimensional linear normed spaces are complete and accordingly Banach (Jarvinen [9]).

Proof. According to Proposition 3.2, any norm is equivalent in finite dimensional spaces. Thus, any finite dimensional linear normed spaces are complete. Therefore, any finite dimensional linear normed spaces are Banach ones.

A natural consequence of Proposition 3.3 is given below.

Corollary 3.1

A finite dimensional subspace of any linear normed space is closed.

Proof. Let **E** be an n-dimensional subspace of a linear normed space **X**. Denote by $\{e_i\}_{i=1}^n$ a base of **E**. For $x, y \in \mathbf{E}$, denote $x = [\xi_i] = \sum_{i=1}^n \xi_i e_i$ and $y = [\eta_i] = \sum_{i=1}^n \eta_i e_i$. Then, we have

$$\big\| \|x\| - \|y\| \big\| \leq \|x - y\| \leq \beta \sqrt{\sum_{i=1}^n |\xi_i - \eta_i|^2},$$

where $\beta = \sqrt{\sum_{i=1}^{n} \|e_i\|^2} > 0$. The above implies that $\|x\|$ can be taken as a n-dimensional function in terms of ξ_i for $i = 1, \ldots, n$. In the bounded closed set $S = \left\{ x \in \mathbf{E}; \|x\|_2 = 1 \right\} = \left\{ x \in \mathbf{E}; \sum_{i=1}^{n} |\xi_i|^2 = 1 \right\}$, it reaches its infimum $\alpha = \inf_{x \in S} \|x\|$. Since S does not include null element, $\alpha > 0$. In addition, S is an n-dimensional closed unit ball, $\mathbf{E}$ is closed (Liu [14, pp. 18–19]).

3.4.3 Series in Banach Spaces
Definition 3.19 (Series)

Denote by $\mathbf{X}$ a linear normed space. Denote a sequence in $\mathbf{X}$ by $\{x_n\}$ for $n = 1, \ldots$ If $s_n = \sum_{k=1}^{n} x_k$ converges to $s \in \mathbf{X}$, we say that the series is convergent and $s = \sum_{n=1}^{\infty} x_n$.

Definition 3.20

Denote by $\mathbf{X}$ a linear normed space. Denote a sequence in $\mathbf{X}$ by $\{x_n\}$ for $n = 1, \ldots$ If the numeric series $\sum_{n=1}^{\infty} \|x_n\|$ is convergent, the series $\sum_{n=1}^{\infty} x_n$ is absolutely convergent.

Proposition 3.4

The necessary and sufficient condition for $\sum_{n=1}^{\infty} x_n$ in a Banach space to be convergent is as follows. If $\forall \varepsilon > 0$, there exists a natural number N such that when $n > N, m > N$, $\left\| \sum_{k=n}^{n+m} x_k \right\| < \varepsilon$.

Proof is omitted.

A consequence of Proposition 3.4 is the following corollary.

Corollary 3.2

$\sum_{n=1}^{\infty} x_n$ is convergent if it is absolutely convergent in a Banach space.

Proof. According to the Cauchy convergence criterion, for $n, m > N \in$ **N**, one has

$$\left\| s_{n+m} - s_n \right\| = \left\| \sum_{k=n+1}^{n+m} x_k \right\| \le \sum_{k=n+1}^{n+m} \left\| x_k \right\| \to 0 \text{ when } n \to \infty.$$

Since $\Sigma \| x_k \|$ converges, (s_n) is a Cauchy sequence in a Banach space. Thus, $\sum_{n=1}^{\infty} x_n$ converges to a member of the space (Griffel [15, p. 218]).

Note 3.17. In general, an element x in a Banach space **X** may not be a number though its norm $\|x\|$ is a number. Thus, series in Banach spaces are useful for non-numeric series, such as matrix series, see e.g., Dorf and Bishop [16], Ling [17], Grote and Antonsson [18], and Gabel and Roberts [19].

3.4.4 Separable Banach Spaces and Completion of Spaces

The density of a linear normed space is an important property used in separable Banach spaces.

Definition 3.21

Let **M** be a subset of a linear normed space **X**. If $\forall x \in$ **X** and $\forall \varepsilon > 0$, there exists $m \in$ **M** such that

$$\|x - m\| < \varepsilon, \tag{3.46}$$

we say that **M** is dense in **X**.

Definition 3.22

If there are countable and dense subsets in a linear normed space **X**, **X** is said to be separable.

Example 3.10

R_n is separable.

Proof. Denote by Q_n the space of n-dimensional rational numbers. Since Q_n is countable and $Q_n \subset R_n$, R_n is separable.

Example 3.11

$C[a, b]$ is separable.

Proof. Denote by $P[a, b]$ the space of polynomials with real coefficients. Let $P_0[a, b]$ be the space of polynomials with rational coefficients. Then, $P_0[a, b] \subset P[a, b] \subset C[a, b]$. Denote by $P_0^n[a,b]$ the space of polynomials with rational coefficients of order n. Then, $P_0^n[a,b]$ and Q_{n+1} are one-to-one correspondence. Thus, $P_0^n[a,b]$ is dense and $C[a, b]$ is separable.

Example 3.12

$L^\infty[a,b]$ is non-separable.

Proof. The norm of $x \in L^\infty[a,b]$ is given by $\|x\|_\infty = \text{ess} \sup_{a \le t \le b} |x(t)|$, where ess sup means essential supremum. Since $[0, 1]$ is non-countable, $L^\infty[a,b]$ is non-separable.

Proposition 3.5

Let X be a Banach space. If the base of X is countable, X is separable.

Proof. Let $\{e_i\}_{i=1}^n$ be a countable base of a Banach space X. Denote by M the set of all linear combinations of $\sum_{i=1}^n \xi_i e_i$, where ξ_I is a rational number and $n \in N$. Then, M is a dense subset of X. Hence, X is separable.

A space that is not complete may be completed in a way.

Proposition 3.6

Any linear normed space X can be isometrically embedded in a Banach space $\hat{X}$, and that normed space is isomorphic with a dense subspace of $\hat{X}$.

Proof is omitted.

3.5 HILBERT SPACES

Banach spaces are a class of linear normed spaces that are complete. A specific class of Banach spaces, called Hilbert spaces, plays a role in functional analysis as well as in engineering.

In geometry, the norm $\|x\|$ in a Banach space $\mathbf{X}$ represents the length of $x \in \mathbf{X}$. It does not give the information of the location of x in $\mathbf{X}$. Suppose two vectors $\vec{a}$ and $\vec{b}$ in a Euclidian space $\mathbf{E}$. Then, the dot product is given by

$$\vec{a} \cdot \vec{b} = |\vec{a}| \cdot |\vec{b}| \cos(\vec{a}, \vec{b}), \tag{3.47}$$

$$\vec{a} \cdot \vec{a} = |\vec{a}|^2. \tag{3.48}$$

The dot product expressed by (3.48) provides the information of the length of a vector while (3.47) exhibits the included angle between $\vec{a}$ and $\vec{b}$. Hence, (3.47) gives the information of the location of $\vec{a}$ and $\vec{b}$. The dot product in elementary geometry may be substantially extended to its abstract form called inner product, which is a skillful work in Hilbert spaces.

3.5.1 Inner Product Spaces

3.5.1.1 Concept of Inner Product Spaces

Definition 3.23 (Inner Product)

Denote by $\mathbf{E}$ a real linear space. If $\forall x \in \mathbf{E}$, $\forall y \in \mathbf{E}$, $\forall z \in \mathbf{E}$, there exists a real number denoted by (x, y) that satisfies the following four axioms, (x, y) is called an inner product. $\mathbf{E}$ is called inner product space.

I. $(x,x) \geq 0$. $(x,x) = 0$ if $x = \theta$ (null element in $\mathbf{E}$). (3.49)

II. $(\text{Symmetry})(x,y) = (y,x)$. (3.50)

III. $\lambda(x,y) = (\lambda x, y) = (x, \lambda y)$ $(\lambda \in \mathbf{R})$. (3.51)

IV. $(x+z, y) = (x, y) + (z, y)$. (3.52)

Note 3.18 (Pre-Hilbert space). An inner product space is called pre-Hilbert space. This is because that the inner product space is the first condition of a space to be Hilbert.

An inner product (x, y) contains the information of the location of x and y in an inner product space. The length of x in an inner product space can be expressed by (x, x).

Note 3.19. By using the inner product, $\|x\|$ is expressed by

$$\|x\| = \sqrt{(x,x)}. \tag{3.53}$$

Proof: First, (3.53) implies that $\|x\| \geq 0$. $\|x\| = 0$ if and only if $x = \theta$. Thus, (3.53) satisfies the first axiom of the definition of a norm. Second,

$$\|\lambda x\| = \sqrt{(\lambda x, \lambda x)} = \sqrt{\lambda(x, \lambda x)} = \sqrt{\lambda^2 (x,x)} = |\lambda| \cdot \|x\|. \tag{3.54}$$

Therefore, (3.53) satisfies the second axiom in the definition of a norm. Finally, according to the Cauchy–Schwarz inequality, one has

$$\left\|(x,y)\right\| \leq \sqrt{(x,x)}\sqrt{(y,y)} = \|x\| \cdot \|y\|. \tag{3.55}$$

Thus, (3.53) holds.

Example 3.13

Let $x(t)$, $y(t) \in L^2[a,b]$. Then, the inner product of $x(t)$ and $y(t)$ can be defined by

$$(x, y) = \int_a^b x(t)y(t)dt. \tag{3.56}$$

If $w(t) \in L^2[a,b]$ and $w(t) > 0$, (x, y) can be defined by

$$(x, y) = \int_a^b x(t)y(t)w(t)dt, \tag{3.57}$$

where $w(t)$ is a weighing function.

Example 3.14

In the discrete case, if $x, y \in l_\infty^2$, where $x = [x_1, x_2, \ldots]$, $y = [y_1, y_2, \ldots]$, (x, y) can be defined by

$$(x, y) = \sum_{i=1}^{\infty} x_i y_i. \tag{3.58}$$

Similar to $w(t) \in L^2[a,b]$, we use $w > 0$ and $w \in l_\infty^2$, where $w = [w_1, w_2, \ldots]$ is a weighing sequence. In this case, (x, y) can be given by

$$\left(x, y\right) = \sum_{i=1}^{\infty} x_i y_i w_i. \tag{3.59}$$

3.5.1.2 Orthogonality

One of the important properties of inner product spaces is orthogonality.

Definition 3.24 (Orthogonality)

Let **E** be an inner product space. If, for $x, y \in$ **E**,

$$\left(x, y\right) = 0, \tag{3.60}$$

we say that x and y are orthogonal. The symbol $x \perp y$ is used for $(x, y) = 0$.

3.5.1.3 Continuity

Proposition 3.7

Let **E** be an inner product space. Let $\{x_n\}$, $\{y_n\}$, $x, y \in$ **E**. If, in the norm sense, $x_n \to x$ and $y_n \to y$ for $n \to \infty$, then

$$\left(x_n, y_n\right) \to \left(x, y\right) \text{ for } n \to \infty. \tag{3.61}$$

Proof. Using inequality (3.55), one has

$$\left\|\left(x_n, y_n\right) - \left(x, y\right)\right\| \leq \left|\left(x_n - x, y_n\right) - \left(x, y_n - y\right)\right| \leq \|y_n\| \|x_n - x\|$$
$$+ \|x\| \|y_n - y\| \to 0 \text{ for } n \to \infty.$$

The proof is finished.

Note 3.20. The above proposition implies the following operations regarding limit.

$$\lim_{n \to \infty} (x_n, y_n) = \left(\lim_{n \to \infty} x_n, \lim_{n \to \infty} y_n \right), \tag{3.62}$$

$$\lim_{n \to \infty} (x_n, y) = \left(\lim_{n \to \infty} x_n, y \right), \tag{3.63}$$

$$\lim_{n \to \infty} (x, y_n) = \left(x, \lim_{n \to \infty} y_n \right). \tag{3.64}$$

3.5.2 Hilbert Spaces

Definition 3.25 (Hilbert Space)

Let **E** be an inner product space. Then, **E** is a Hilbert space if it is complete.

Note 3.21. Let **H** be a Hilbert space. Then, it is a Banach space.

Proof. **H** is a complete normed space with the norm defined by the inner product. Hence, it is a Banach space.

Note 3.22. Let **H** be a finite dimensional space. Then, it is of Hilbert.

Proof. When **H** is a finite dimensional space, it is a complete inner product space with the inner product defined by a norm. Hence, it is of Hilbert.

Let **X** be a metric space. Let $\mathbf{B} \subseteq \mathbf{X}$. Denote by $d(x, \mathbf{B})$ the distance from x to the set **B**. That is,

$$d(x, \mathbf{B}) = \inf d(x, y) \text{ for } y \in \mathbf{B}. \tag{3.65}$$

If there is y such that the above holds, $y \in \mathbf{B}$ is called the optimal approximation of $x \in \mathbf{X}$.

Theorem 3.1 (Optimal Approximation in Hilbert Spaces)

Let **B** be the convex subspace of a Hilbert space **H**. Let $x \in \mathbf{H}$ but $x \notin \mathbf{B}$, there exists unique $y \in \mathbf{B}$ such that

$$\|x - y\| = \inf \|x - z\| \text{ for } z \in \mathbf{B}. \tag{3.66}$$

Proof. Let $d = d(x, \mathbf{B}) = \inf d(x, y)$ for $y \in \mathbf{B}$. For any natural number $n \in \mathbf{N}$, there exists $y_n \in \mathbf{B}$ such that

$$d \le \|x - y_n\| \le d + 1/n. \tag{3.67}$$

For $(x - y_n)$ and $(x - y_m)$, using the parallelogram law yields

$$2\|x - y_n\|^2 + 2\|x - y_m\|^2 = \|2x - y_n - y_m\|^2 + \|y_n - y_m\|^2. \tag{3.68}$$

Since $\mathbf{B}$ is convex, $\dfrac{y_n + y_m}{2} \in \mathbf{B}$. Therefore,

$$\|2x - y_n - y_m\|^2 = 4\left\|x - \frac{y_n + y_m}{2}\right\|^2 \ge 4d^2. \tag{3.69}$$

According to (3.67) and (3.68),

$$
\begin{aligned}
\|y_n - y_m\|^2 &= 2\|x - y_n\|^2 + 2\|x - y_m\|^2 - \|2x - y_n - y_m\|^2 \\
&\le 2\left(d + \frac{1}{n}\right)^2 + 2\left(d + \frac{1}{m}\right)^2 - 4d^2 \\
&= \frac{4d}{n} + \frac{4d}{m} + \frac{2}{n^2} + \frac{2}{m^2}.
\end{aligned}
\tag{3.70}
$$

The above implies that $\{y_n\}$ is a basic sequence. Thus, due to $\mathbf{B}$ being closed, there exists $y \in \mathbf{B}$ such that $y_n \to y$. Considering (3.67) for $n \to \infty$, we have

$$\|x - y\| = d. \tag{3.71}$$

Suppose that there is another element $z \in \mathbf{B}$ such that $\|x - z\| = d$. In this case, we have

$$4d^2 = 2\|x - y\|^2 + 2\|x - z\|^2 = \|y - z\|^2 + 4\left\|x - \frac{y + z}{2}\right\|^2 \ge \|y - z\|^2 + 4d^2. \tag{3.72}$$

The above means that $\|y - z\| \le 0$, which implies $z = y$. Therefore, the optimal approximation element $y \in \mathbf{B}$ for $\|x - y\| = d$ is unique.

A consequence of the above is as follows. Let **L** be a closed subspace of a Hilbert space **H**. Let $x \in$ **H** but $x \notin$ **L**, there exists unique $l \in$ **L** such that

$$\|x - l\| = d(x, \mathbf{L}).\tag{3.73}$$

3.6 BOUNDED LINEAR OPERATORS

Definition 3.26 (Linear Operators)

Let **X** and **Y** be linear normed spaces. If an operator $T: \mathbf{X} \to \mathbf{Y}$ is linear, then $T(ax + by) = aT(x) + bT(y) \ \forall \ a, b \in \mathbf{R}$ and $\forall x, y \in \mathbf{X}$.

Definition 3.27

Let $T: \mathbf{X} \to \mathbf{Y}$ be an operator, where **X** and **Y** are normed spaces. The operator is said to be bounded if there exists a number $m > 0$ such that

$$\|Tx\|_{\mathbf{y}} \le m\|x\|_{\mathbf{X}}.\tag{3.74}$$

Proposition 3.8 (Continuity of Linear Operators)

Let $T: \mathbf{X} \to \mathbf{Y}$ be an operator. If T is bounded, T is continuous.

Proof. If T is bounded, one has $\|Tx\|_{\mathbf{y}} \le m\|x\|_{\mathbf{X}}$. Thus, for $x_n, x_0 \in D(T)$,

$$\|Tx_n - Tx_0\|_{\mathbf{y}} \left\|T(x_n - x_0)\right\|_{\mathbf{y}} \le m\|x_n - x_0\|_{\mathbf{X}}.$$

Therefore, T is continuous.

Proposition 3.9 (Boundedness of Linear Operators)

Let $T: \mathbf{X} \to \mathbf{Y}$ be an operator. If T is continuous, T is bounded.

Proof. Assume that T is continuous but unbounded. Then, for $n \in \mathbf{N}$, there exists a non-null element $x_n \in D(T)$ such that $\|Tx_n\|_{\mathbf{y}} > n\|x_n\|_{\mathbf{X}}$. Let $y_n = \dfrac{x_n}{n\|x_n\|}$. Then, $\|y_n\| = \dfrac{1}{n} \to 0$ if $n \to \infty$. That implies that $y_n \to \theta$ for $n \to \infty$. Since T is continuous, we have $Ty_n \to \theta$. However, because

$$\|Ty_n\| = \frac{\|Tx_n\|}{n\|x_n\|} > 1.$$

The above contradiction says that T must be bounded.

Definition 3.28 (Norm of Linear Operators)

Let $T: \mathbf{X} \to \mathbf{Y}$ be a bounded linear operator, where $\mathbf{X}$ and $\mathbf{Y}$ are normed spaces. The norm of T is defined by

$$\|T\| = \sup_{\|x\|=1} \frac{\|T(x)\|}{\|x\|} = \sup_{\|x\|\neq\theta} \frac{\|T(x)\|}{\|x\|} = \sup_{\|x\|\leq 1} \frac{\|T(x)\|}{\|x\|}. \tag{3.75}$$

Proposition 3.10 (Existence of Inverse Operators)

Let $T: \mathbf{X} \to \mathbf{Y}$ be a linear operator. Denote by T^{-1} the inverse of T. Then, T^{-1} exists and it is bounded if and only if there exists $m > 0$ such that

$$\|Tx\|_y \geq m\|x\|_{\mathbf{X}}, \tag{3.76}$$

where x belongs to the domain of T, which is included by $\mathbf{X}$.

Proof. Let $N(T) = \{\theta\}$, where θ is the null element. Then, that T^{-1} exists and it is bounded $\Leftrightarrow \exists m > 0 \left(\forall x \in D(T) \left(\|Tx\|_y \geq m\|x\|_{\mathbf{X}} \right) \right) \Leftrightarrow \exists m > 0$ $\left(\forall x \in D(T) \left(\forall y \in R(T) \left(\|y\|_y \geq m\|T^{-1}y\|_{\mathbf{X}} \right) \right) \right)$. Therefore, $\forall y \in D(T^{-1})$, $\|T^{-1}y\|_{\mathbf{X}} \leq m^{-1}\|y\|_y$. Thus, if T^{-1} exists and it is bounded, we have $Tx = \theta$ for $x \in N(T) \Rightarrow \|x\|_{\mathbf{X}} = 0 \Rightarrow x = \theta \Rightarrow N(T) = \{\theta\}$.

Theorem 3.2 (The Inverse Operator Theorem of Banach)

Let $T: \mathbf{X} \to \mathbf{Y}$ be a linear one-to-one operator. Let $\mathbf{X}$ and $\mathbf{Y}$ be Banach spaces. If T^{-1} exists, T^{-1} is a bounded linear operator. The proof refers to Istratescu [20] or Ye [21, pp. 107–110].

Theorem 3.3

Let $T: \mathbf{X} \to \mathbf{X}$ be a linear one-to-one operator. Let $\mathbf{X}$ be a Banach space. Then, $L(\mathbf{X}, \mathbf{X})$ is a Banach space [20,21].

REFERENCES

1. H. Abels, Properly discontinuous groups of affine transformations: A survey. *Geometriae Dedicata*, 87(1–3) 2001, 309–333.
2. D.-X. Xia and S.-Z. Yan, *Introduction to Real Analysis and Functional Analysis*, Press of Shanghai Science and Technology, Shanghai, 1987. In Chinese.
3. M. M. Deza and E. Deza, *Encyclopedia of Distances*, Heidelberg/New York, Springer, 2009.
4. J. R. Leigh, *Functional Analysis and Linear Control Theory*, Academic Press, London/New York, 1980.
5. S. Thompson, Robust control—an introduction. *Measure Control*, 26 1993, 235–241.
6. S. J. Williams, H_∞ for the layman. *Measure Control*, 24 1991, 18–21.
7. M. Li, B.-H. Xu, and Y.-S. Wu, An H_2-optimal control of random loading for a laboratory fatigue test. *J. Test. Eval.*, 26(6) 1998, 619–625.
8. M. Li, An iteration method to adjusting random loading for a laboratory fatigue test, *Int. J. Fatigue*, 27(7) 2006, 783–789.
9. R. D. Jarvinen, *Finite and Infinite Dimensional Linear Spaces*, Marcel Dekker, Inc., New York/Basel, 1981.
10. M. Li, Modeling autocorrelation functions of long-range dependent teletraffic series based on optimal approximation in Hilbert space-a further study, *Appl. Math. Model.*, 31(3) 2007, 625–631.
11. M. Li, Generalized fractional Gaussian noise and its application to traffic modeling, *Physica A*, 579 2021, 1236137 (22 p).
12. W. Rudin, *Real and Complex Analysis*, 2nd Ed., McGraw-Hill, New York, 1974.
13. C. D. Aliprantis and O. Burkinsaw, *Principles of Real Analysis*, 3rd Ed., Elsevier, Singapore, 2008.
14. Z.-K. Liu, *Applied Functional Analysis*, National Defense Industry Press, Beijing, 1985. In Chinese.
15. D. H. Griffel, *Applied Functional Analysis*, John Wiley & Sons, New York, 1981.
16. R. C. Dorf and R. H. Bishop, Modern Control Systems, 9th Ed., Prentice Hall, London, 2002.
17. F. F. Ling, Editor-in-chief, *Vibration Dynamics and Control*, Springer, New York, 2008.
18. I. K.-H. Grote and G. Antonsson, Eds., *Springer Handbook of Mechanical Engineering*, Springer, New York, 2009.
19. R. A. Gabel and R. A. Roberts, *Signals and Linear Systems*, John Wiley & Sons, New York, 1973.
20. VI. Istratescu, *Introduction to Linear Operator Theory*, Marcel Dekker, New York/Basel, 1981.
21. H. A. Ye, *Functional Analysis*, Anhui Education Press, Hefei, 1984.

CHAPTER 4

Min-Plus Convolution

Due to the importance of the min-plus convolution in traffic delay-bound computations, we brief the main results of the conventional convolution in Section 4.1. Theoretically speaking, the conventional convolution may not be a necessary topic to mention. However, it is helpful in the education of min-plus convolution since the conventional one is well known in many fields of sciences and engineering. The min-plus convolution is explained in Section 4.2, which is followed by the description of the conventional identity in Section 4.3. The contributions in this chapter are in four aspects. We propose the problem statements with respect to the identity in the min-plus convolution system in Section 4.4, bring forward the existence of the min-plus de-convolution in Section 4.5, address the condition of the existence of the min-plus de-convolution in Section 4.6, and present the representation of the identity in the min-plus convolution in Section 4.7. An application area of the min-plus convolution is the computations of traffic delay bounds to be addressed in Chapter 10.

4.1 CONVENTIONAL CONVOLUTION

We mentioned the conventional convolution in Chapter 2 from a view of signals and systems. We now mention it again in this chapter for the purpose of taking it as an analogy of the min-plus convolution so as to facilitate the discussions, in particular, for the purpose of bringing forward

DOI: 10.1201/9781003268802-4

the existence of the min-plus de-convolution and the representation of the identity in the min-plus convolution system.

A function $f(t) \in L^p(a,b)$ implies $\int_a^b |f(u)|^p \, du < \infty$. When a is allowed to be $-\infty$ and b is allowed to be ∞, we mean

$$\int_{-\infty}^{\infty} |f(u)|^p \, du = \lim_{b \to \infty} \int_{-b}^{b} |f(u)|^p \, du. \tag{4.1}$$

Suppose that there exist two functions $f(t), g(t) \in L(-\infty, \infty)$. Then, one says that $f(t)$ convolutes $g(t)$ if

$$f_1(t) * f_2(t) = \int_{-\infty}^{\infty} f_1(u) f_2(t-u) du, \tag{4.2}$$

where * implies the operation of convolution. We call it the conventional convolution so as to distinguish it from the min-plus convolution in min-plus algebra we are discussing in this book.

Lemma 4.1

In the algebra system $(L; *)$, the conventional convolution is commutative.

Proof. For $f_1(t), f_2(t) \in L$, when replacing $\tau = t - u$ on the right side of the following,

$$f_1(t) * f_2(t) = \int_{-\infty}^{\infty} f_1(u) f_2(t-u) du = -\int_{-\infty}^{\infty} f_1(u) f_2(t-u) d(t-u),$$

one has

$$-\int_{-\infty}^{\infty} f_1(u) f_2(t-u) d(t-u) = \int_{-\infty}^{\infty} f_1(t-u) f_2(\tau) d\tau.$$

Thus, $f_1(t) * f_2(t) = f_2(t) * f_1(t)$. The proof completes.

Lemma 4.2 (Closure of *)

If $f_1(t), f_2(t) \in L, f_1(t) * f_2(t) \in L$.

Lemma 4.3

In the algebra system $(L; +, *)$, where $+$ implies the ordinary addition,$*$ with respect to $+$ is distributive.

Proof. For $f_1(t), f_2(t) \in L$, one has

$$y(t) * [f_1(t) + f_2(t)] = \int_{-\infty}^{\infty} y(u)[f_1(t-u) + f_2(t-u)] du$$

$$= y(t) * f_1(t) + y(t) * f_2(t).$$

The proof finishes.

Lemma 4.4

For $a \in \mathbf{R}, [af_1(t)] * f_2(t) = f_1(t) * [af_2(t)] = a[f_1(t) * f_2(t)]$.

Lemma 4.5

For $f_1(t), f_2(t), f_3(t) \in L$, $*$ is associative.
Proof. Because

$$[f_1(t) * f_2(t)] * f_3(t) = \int_{-\infty}^{\infty} \left[\int_{-\infty}^{\infty} f_1(\lambda) f_2(\tau - \lambda) d\lambda \right] f_3(t - \tau) d\tau$$

$$= \int_{-\infty}^{\infty} f_1(\lambda) \left[\int_{-\infty}^{\infty} f_2(\tau - \lambda) f_3(t - \tau) d\tau \right] d\lambda$$

$$= \int_{-\infty}^{\infty} f_1(\lambda) \left[\int_{-\infty}^{\infty} f_2(\tau) f_3(t - \tau - \lambda) d\tau \right] d\lambda$$

$$= f_1(t) * [f_2(t) * f_3(t)],$$

Lemma 4.5 holds.

Theorem 4.1

The identity in $(L; *)$ is the delta function $\delta(t)$ defined by

$$f(t) = \int_{-\infty}^{\infty} f(u)\delta(t-u)\,du, \qquad (4.3)$$

where $f(t) \in L(-\infty, \infty)$ is continuous at t.

Proof. In the domain of generalized functions, we have

$$\int_{-\infty}^{\infty} \delta(u)\,du = \int_{-\infty}^{\infty} |\delta(u)|\,du < \infty. \qquad (4.4)$$

Therefore, $\delta(t) \in L(-\infty, \infty)$. In addition,

$$f(t)*\delta(t) = \delta(t)*f(t) \text{ for any } f(t) \in L(-\infty, \infty). \qquad (4.5)$$

Assume there is another element $e(t) \in L(-\infty, \infty)$ such that

$$f(t)*e(t) = e(t)*f(t) = f(t). \qquad (4.6)$$

Then,

$$f(t)*\delta(t) - f(t)*e(t) = f(t)*\big(\delta(t) - e(t)\big) = f(t) - f(t) = 0. \quad (4.7)$$

The above implies that $\delta(t) - e(t) = 0$. Consequently, the identity $\delta(t)$ is unique.

Since $\delta(t)$ is a generalized function (Lighthill [1]), it is the identity in $(L; *)$ in the domain of generalized functions.

According to the theory of algebra, the inverse of the conventional convolution discussed by, for instance, Mikusinski [2], Bracewell [3], Gold and Rader [4], Gabel and Roberts [5], Press et al. [6], McGillem and Cooper [7] exists because the necessary and sufficient condition that the inverse of an operation exists is that there exists identity in that system (see e.g., Korn and Korn [8], Zhang [9], Riley et al. [10], Bronshtein et al. [11], and Stillwell [12]) but it is in the domain of generalized functions. As a matter of fact, the convolution operation is in that domain (Smith [13]).

Theorem 4.2

The convolution system $(L; *)$ is a group.

Proof. First, the operation $*$ is closed in L. Second, $*$ is associative. Finally, there exists the left identity denoted by $\delta(t)$ and the right one again denoted by $\delta(t)$ in $(L; *)$ such that they are identical.

Thus, $(L; *)$ is a group.

Lemma 4.6 (Derivative)

For $x(t), y(t) \in L$,

$$\frac{d^n[x(t)*y(t)]}{dt^n} = x^{(n)}(t)*y(t) = x(t)*y(t)^{(n)} = x^{(m)}(t)*y(t)^{(l)}, \quad (4.8)$$

where $l + m = n$, and l, m, n are positive integers.

Proof. Note that

$$\frac{d^n[x(t)*y(t)]}{dt^n} = \frac{d^n}{dt^n}\int_{-\infty}^{\infty} x(t-\tau)y(\tau)d\tau = \frac{d^l}{dt^l}\frac{d^m}{dt^m}\int_{-\infty}^{\infty} x(t-\tau)y(\tau)d\tau$$

$$= \frac{d^l}{dt^l}\int_{-\infty}^{\infty}\frac{d^m x(t-\tau)}{dt^m}y(\tau)d\tau = \frac{d^l[x^{(m)}(t)*y(t)]}{dt^l}$$

$$= \frac{d^l}{dt^l}\int_{-\infty}^{\infty} x^{(m)}(\tau)y(t-\tau)d\tau = \int_{-\infty}^{\infty} x^{(m)}(\tau)\frac{d^l y(t-\tau)}{dt^l}d\tau$$

$$= x^{(m)}(t)*y^{(l)}(t). \quad (4.9)$$

The proof completes.

Example 4.1

Using $f(t) = \dfrac{t^n}{n!}$, we may express 0 with

$$0 = \delta^{(n+1)}(t) * \frac{t^n}{n!}. \tag{4.10}$$

Proof. According to Lemma 4.6, we have

$$\delta^{(n+1)}(t) * f(t) = \delta(t) * f^{(n+1)}(t). \tag{4.11}$$

Because $f^{(n+1)}(t) = 0$, Example 4.1 holds.

Example 4.2

With $f(t) = \dfrac{t^n}{n!}$, constant 1 may be expressed by

$$1 = \delta^{(n)}(t) * \frac{t^n}{n!}. \tag{4.12}$$

Proof. Following Lemma 4.6, the right side of the above may be rewritten by

$$\delta^{(n)}(t) * \frac{t^n}{n!} = \delta(t) * \frac{d^n}{dt^n} \frac{t^n}{n!}. \tag{4.13}$$

As $\dfrac{d^n}{dt^n} \dfrac{t^n}{n!} = 1$, we see that Proposition 4.2 holds.

Lemma 4.7 (Integral)

For $x(t), y(t) \in L$,

$$\left[x(t) * y(t) \right]^{(-n)} = x^{(-n)}(t) * y(t) = x(t) * y(t)^{(-n)} = x^{(-m)}(t) * y(t)^{(-l)}, \tag{4.14}$$

where $l + m = n$, and l, m, n are positive integers.

The proof is similar to that of Lemma 4.6. It is omitted.

Example 4.3

The integral of $f(t)$ may be expressed by

$$\int_{-\infty}^{t} f(t)dt = \delta^{(-1)}(t) * f(t). \tag{4.15}$$

Proof. Note that

$$\delta^{(-1)}(t) = \int_{-\infty}^{t} \delta(t)dt. \tag{4.16}$$

Thus, according to Lemma 4.7, (4.15) holds.

Example 4.4

The function $f(t) = \dfrac{t^n}{n!}u(t)$ may be expressed by

$$\frac{t^n}{n!}u(t) = \delta^{(-n)}(t). \tag{4.17}$$

Proof. Since

$$\delta^{(-1)}(t) = \int_{-\infty}^{t} \delta(t) = u(t), \tag{4.18}$$

$$\delta^{(-2)}(t) = \int_{-\infty}^{t} u(t)dt = tu(t). \tag{4.19}$$

By induction, we see that (4.17) holds.

Proposition 4.1

Constant 1 may be in the form

$$1 = \delta^{(-1)}(t) + \delta^{(-1)}(-t). \tag{4.20}$$

Proof. Because

$$\delta^{(-1)}(t) = u(t), \tag{4.21}$$

$$\delta^{(-1)}(-t) = u(-t), \tag{4.22}$$

we have

$$\delta^{(-1)}(t) + \delta^{(-1)}(-t) = u(t) + u(-t) = 1. \tag{4.23}$$

The proof finishes.

4.2 MIN-PLUS CONVOLUTION

Considering the property of wide sense increasing of accumulated traffic, we denote by S the set that contains all functions that are greater than or equal to zero and that are wide sense increasing. In addition, we assume here and below that functions belonging to S are causal. By causal, we mean $X(t) = 0$ for $t < 0$.

Definition 4.1

Let $X_1(t)$, $X_2(t) \in S$. Then, the following operation is called the min-plus convolution

$$X_1(t) \otimes X_2(t) = \inf_{0 \le u \le t} \{X_1(t-u) + X_2(u)\}, \tag{4.24}$$

where $\otimes$ represents the operation of the min-plus convolution.

Example 4.5

Let $X(t) = t^2$ for $t > 0$ and 0 elsewhere. Then, $X(t) \otimes X(t) = t^2/2$ for $t > 0$ and 0 otherwise.

Lemma 4.8 (Closure of $\otimes$)

Let $X_1(t)$, $X_2(t) \in S$. Then, $X_1(t) \otimes X_2(t) \in S$.

Proof: Because $X_1(t)$ and $X_2(t)$ are wide sense increasing, then, for $0 \le t_1 < t_2$ and $\forall u \in \mathbf{R}$, one has

$$X_1(t_1 - u) + X_2(u) \le X_1(t_2 - u) + X_2(u).$$

Since $X_1(t)$ and $X_2(t)$ are causal, the above implies

$$\inf_{0 \le u \le t_1} \{X_1(t_1 - u) + X_2(u)\} = X_1(t_1) \otimes X_2(t_1)$$

$$\le \inf_{0 \le u \le t_2} \{X_1(t_2 - u) + X_2(u)\} = X_1(t_2) \otimes X_2(t_2).$$

Therefore, the function $X_1(t) \otimes X_2(t)$ is wide sense increasing. Thus, this lemma holds.

Lemma 4.9

The operation $\otimes$ is commutative. That is,

$$X_1(t) \otimes X_2(t) = X_2(t) \otimes X_1(t) \text{ for } X_1(t), X_2(t) \in \mathbf{S} \qquad (4.25)$$

Proof: In $X_1(t) \otimes X_2(t) = \inf_{0 \le u \le t} \{X_1(t - u) + X_2(u)\}$, we replace $(t - u)$ by v. Since

$$0 \le u \Rightarrow v < t; u < t \Rightarrow 0 \le v,$$

we have $0 \le u < t \Rightarrow 0 \le v < t$. On the other side,

$$X_1(t - u) + X_2(u) = X_1(v) + X_2(t - v).$$

Therefore,

$$\inf_{0 \le u \le t} \{X_1(t - u) + X_2(u)\} = \inf_{0 \le u \le t} \{X_1(v) + X_2(t - v)\}.$$

This completes the proof.

Lemma 4.10

The operation $\otimes$ is associative. That is, for $X_1(t)$, $X_2(t)$, $X_3(t) \in \boldsymbol{S}$,

$$\left[X_1(t) \otimes X_2(t)\right] \otimes X_3(t) = X_1(t) \otimes \left[X_2(t) \otimes X_3(t)\right]. \qquad (4.26)$$

Proof: $\left[X_1(t) \otimes X_2(t)\right] \otimes X_3(t) = \inf_{0 \leq u \leq t} \left\{ \inf_{0 \leq v \leq t-u} \left\{ X_1(t-u-v) + X_2(v) \right\} + X_3(u) \right\}$

$$= \inf_{0 \leq u \leq t} \left\{ \inf_{u \leq u' \leq t} \left\{ X_1(t-u') + X_2(u'-u) \right\} + X_3(u) \right\}.$$

$$= \inf_{0 \leq u' \leq t} \left\{ \inf_{0 \leq u \leq u'} \left\{ X_1(t-u') + X_2(u'-u) \right\} + X_3(u) \right\}$$

$$= \inf_{0 \leq u' \leq t} \left\{ X_1(t-u') + \inf_{0 \leq u \leq u'} \left\{ X_2(u'-u) + X_3(u) \right\} \right\}$$

$$= \inf_{0 \leq u' \leq t} \left\{ X_1(t-u') + \left[X_2(u') \otimes X_3(u') \right] \right.$$

$$= X_1(t) \otimes \left[X_2(t) \otimes X_3(t) \right].$$

Define another operation that is denoted by $\wedge$ such that

$$X_1(t) \wedge X_2(t) = \inf\left[X_1(t), X_2(t)\right] \text{ for } X_1(t), X_2(t) \in \boldsymbol{S}. \qquad (4.27)$$

Then, we have an algebra system denoted by $(\boldsymbol{S}, \wedge, \otimes)$ that follows the distributive law.

Lemma 4.11

The operation $\otimes$ with respect to $\wedge$ is distributive. That is, for $X_1(t)$, $X_2(t)$, $X_3(t) \in \boldsymbol{S}$,

$$\left[X_1(t) \wedge X_2(t)\right] \otimes X_3(t) = \left[X_1(t) \otimes X_3(t)\right] \wedge \left[X_2(t) \otimes X_3(t)\right]. \qquad (4.28)$$

Proof is omitted.

The following rule is useful.

Lemma 4.12

Suppose $K \in \mathbf{R}$. Then, for $X_1(t), X_2(t) \in \mathbf{S}$, we have

$$[X_1(t)+K] \otimes X_2(t) = X_1(t) \otimes X_2(t) + K. \qquad (4.29)$$

Proof: Note that $[X_1(t)+K] \otimes X_2(t) = \inf_{0 \le u \le t} \{X_1(t-u)+X_2(u)+K\}$. Thus,

$$\inf_{0 \le u \le t} \{X_1(t-u)+X_2(u)+K\} = \inf_{0 \le u \le t} \{X_1(t-u)+X_2(u)\} + K$$

$$= X_1(t) \otimes X_2(t) + K.$$

4.3 IDENTITY IN THE MIN-PLUS CONVOLUTION

Denote by $I_1(t)$ the conventional identity in min-plus algebra. It is defined by

$$I_1(t) = \begin{cases} \infty, & t > 0 \\ 0, & t < 0 \end{cases}, \qquad (4.30)$$

see Chang [14], Boudec [15], Bouillard et al. [16], Jiang [17], Burchard et al. [18], Golestani [19], Starobinski et al. [20], Pyun et al. [21], Fidler [22], and Mao and Panwar [23].

It seems obvious when one takes $I_1(t)$ as the identity in min-plus algebra since the following appears sound

$$X(t) \otimes I_1(t) = I_1(t) \otimes X(t) = X(t) \text{ for } X(t) \in \mathbf{S}. \qquad (4.31)$$

However, we shall soon point to the problems or the contradictions when taking $I_1(t)$ as the identity.

4.4 PROBLEM STATEMENTS

Denote by $u(t)$ the unit step function. Then,

$$u(t) = \begin{cases} 1, & t > 0 \\ 0, & t < 0 \end{cases}. \qquad (4.32)$$

For $K \in \mathbf{R}$, we have

$$Ku(t) = \begin{cases} K, t > 0 \\ 0, t < 0 \end{cases}.$$ (4.33)

If using (4.30), we have

$$I_1(t) + Ku(t) = \begin{cases} \infty + K, \ t > 0 \\ 0, \ t < 0 \end{cases} \quad \text{(Contradiction 1)}.$$

$$= \begin{cases} \infty, \ t > 0 \\ 0, \ t < 0 \end{cases} = I_1(t)$$ (4.34)

We call (4.34) contradiction 1 regarding the conventional identity defined by (4.30).

In addition to the above contradiction, we now state another problem regarding (4.30). As a matter of fact, if we let $X_1(t) = I_1(t)$ and $K = Ku(t)$ in Lemma 4.11, then, on the left side of (4.29), we have

$$[I_1(t) + Ku(t)] \otimes X_2(t) = I_1(t) \otimes X_2(t) = X_2(t).$$ (4.35)

On the right side of (4.29), we have

$$[I_1(t) + Ku(t)] \otimes X_2(t) = I_1(t) \otimes X_2(t) + Ku(t) = X_2(t) + Ku(t).$$ (4.36)

Comparing the right sides of (4.35) with that of (4.36) yields another contradiction expressed by

$$X_2(t) = X_2(t) + Ku(t) \ \text{(Contradiction 2)}.$$ (4.37)

The above discussions imply that the conventional representation of the identity defined by (4.30) in min-plus algebra may be improper as can be seen from (4.34) and (4.37). Consequently, the identity in min-plus algebra needs to be studied.

In fact, for $X(t) \in \mathbf{S}$, there is

$$I_1(t) + X(t) = I_1(t).$$ (4.38)

Thus, $I_1(t)$ is not unique. Consequently, it is not an identity from the point of view of algebra.

4.5 EXISTENCE OF MIN-PLUS DE-CONVOLUTION

Due to the importance of generalized functions, we brief them again.

4.5.1 Preliminaries

Definition 4.2

Let supp(f) be the support of a function $f: \mathbf{R} \to \mathbf{C}$. It implies $\{t: f(t) \neq 0\}$. The function is said to have a bounded support if there exists $a, b \in \mathbf{R}$ such that supp(f) $\subset [a, b]$.

Definition 4.3

A function $f: \mathbf{R} \to \mathbf{C}$ is said to have n time-continuous derivatives if its first n derivatives exist and are continuous. If its derivatives of all orders exist and are continuous, f is said to be infinitely differentiable. In this case, f is said to be a smooth.

Definition 4.4

A test function is a smooth $\mathbf{R} \to \mathbf{C}$ with supp(f) $\subset [a, b]$. The set of all test functions is denoted by $\mathbf{D}$.

Definition 4.5

A linear functional f on $\mathbf{D}$ is a map $f: \mathbf{D} \to \mathbf{C}$ such that, for $a, b \in \mathbf{C}$ and ϕ, $\psi \in \mathbf{D}$, $f(a\phi + b\psi) = af(\phi) + bf(\psi)$.

Definition 4.6

Denote by (ϕ_n) a sequence of test functions and Φ another test function. We say that $\phi_n \to \Phi$ if the following two properties hold.

1. There is an interval $[a, b]$ that contains supp(Φ) and supp(ϕ_n) for all n.
2. $\lim_{n \to \infty} \phi_n^{(k)}(t) \to \Phi^{(k)}(t)$ uniformly for $t \in [a, b]$.

Definition 4.7

A functional f on D is continuous if it maps every convergent sequence in D into a convergent sequence in C. A continuous linear functional f on D is termed a generalized function. It is often called a Schwartz distribution.

Definition 4.8

A function f: $R \to C$ is locally integrable if $\int_a^b f(t)dt < \infty$ for all a, b.

Lemma 4.13

Any continuous, including piecewise continuous, function is locally integrable.

Lemma 4.14 (Regular)

Any locally integrable function f is a generalized function. In this case, f is called regular.

Lemma 4.15

Any generalized function has derivatives of all orders.

Lemma 4.16

There exists the Fourier transform of any generalized function.

Definition 4.9 (Rapid Decay Function)

A function of rapid decay is a smooth function ϕ: $R \to C$ such that $t^n\phi^{(r)}(t) \to 0$ as $t \to \pm\infty$ for all $n, r \geq 0$, where C is the space of complex numbers. The set of all functions of rapid decay is denoted by S.

Lemma 4.17

Every function belonging to S is absolutely integrable.

4.5.2 Proof of Existence

Define the norm and inner product of $X \in \mathbb{S}$ by

$$\|X\|^2 = \langle X, X \rangle = \int_0^\infty X^2(u)w(u)du, \tag{4.39}$$

where $w \in \mathbb{S}$. Combining any $X \in \mathbb{S}$ with its limit yields a Hilbert space that we denote again by $\mathbb{S}$ without confusions.

Let $g \in \mathbb{S}$ be a system function such that it transforms its input $X \in \mathbb{S}$ to the output by

$$y = (X \otimes g) \in \mathbb{S} \tag{4.40}$$

Denote the system by the operator L. Then, we purposely force the functionality of L such that it maps an element $X \in \mathbb{S}$ to another element $(X \otimes g) \in \mathbb{S}$. Note that L is linear. In fact, according to Lemma 4.11, we have

$$L(X \wedge g) = L(X) \wedge L(g). \tag{4.41}$$

In addition, from Lemma 4.12, we have

$$L(X + K) = L(X) + K. \tag{4.42}$$

Therefore, L is a linear mapping from $\mathbb{S}$ to $\mathbb{S}$.

Denote by **L** the space consisting of all such operators by

$$\mathbf{L}(\mathbb{S}, \mathbb{S}) = \mathbf{L}(\mathbb{S}) \tag{4.43}$$

Then, from Lemmas 4.11 and 4.12, one can easily see that $\mathbf{L}(\mathbb{S})$ is a linear space.

Lemma 4.18 (Archimedes Criterion)

For any positive real numbers $a > 0$ and $b > 0$, there exists positive integer $n \in \mathbf{Z}$ such that $na > b$ (Aleksandro et al. [24]).

Proof. An obvious property of a natural number is $\lim_{n \to \infty} n = \infty$. Thus, n is unbounded. In addition, if $na \le b$ for each $n \in \mathbf{Z}$, we would have a bounded n since $n \le b/a$. However, that is impossible.

Lemma 4.19 (Archimedes)

If $b \in \mathbf{R}$, there exists $n \in \mathbf{Z}$ such that $b < n$ (Bartle and Sherbert [25]).

Lemma 4.20

An operator $T : X \mapsto Y$ is invertible if and only if there exists constant $m > 0$ such that for all $x \in X$, $\|Tx\| \ge m\|x\|$, where X and Y are linear normed spaces (Istratescu [26]).

From the above discussions, we obtain the following theorem.

Theorem 4.3 (Existence) [27]

For $X, g \in \mathbb{S}$ and $X(0) \ne 0$ and $g(0) \ne 0$, if $L(X) = X \otimes g$ or $L_1(g) = g \otimes X$, then both L and L_1 are invertible. Consequently, the identity in the min-plus algebra exists.

Proof. Consider

$$\|LX\| = \sqrt{\|X \otimes g\|} = \sqrt{\int_0^\infty \left[\inf_{0 \le u \le t} \{ X(u) + g(t-u) \} \right]^2 w(u) \, du}. \quad (4.44)$$

Since

$$\inf_{0 \le u \le t} \{ X(u) + g(t-u) \} \ge \inf \{ X(u) \} = X(0) \quad (4.45)$$

and $X(u) \in \mathbb{S}$, we have

$$0 < X(0) \le X(u). \tag{4.46}$$

According to Lemmas 4.19 and 4.20, there exists $m > 0$ such that

$$X(0) \ge m^2 X(u). \tag{4.47}$$

Therefore,

$$\|LX\| \ge \sqrt{\int_0^\infty \left[\inf\{X(u)\}\right]^2 w(u)\, du} = \sqrt{\int_0^\infty \left[X(0)\right]^2 w(u)\, du}$$

$$\ge m\sqrt{\int_0^\infty X(u)^2 w(u)\, du} = m\|X\|. \tag{4.48}$$

Similarly, if $L_1 \in \mathbf{L}\,(\mathbb{S})$ is such that $L_1(g) = g \otimes X$, we have $\|L_1 g\| \ge m_1 \|g\|$ since $g(0) \ne 0$, where $m_1 > 0$ is a constant. Thus, according to Lemma 4.18, Theorem 4.3 holds.

4.6 THE CONDITION OF THE EXISTENCE OF MIN-PLUS DE-CONVOLUTION

In Theorem 4.3, we need the conditions of $X(0) \ne 0$ and $g(0) \ne 0$. Since $X(t)$ and $g(t)$ are wide sense increasing, we need in fact $X(0) > 0$ and $g(0) > 0$.

4.7 REPRESENTATION OF THE IDENTITY IN MIN-PLUS CONVOLUTION

Since the min-plus de-convolution exists when $X(0) \ne 0$ and $g(0) \ne 0$, there exists a unique identity in the min-plus convolution system. Express $\delta(t)$ by

$$\delta(t) = \frac{1}{2\pi} + \frac{1}{\pi} \sum_{k=-\infty}^{\infty} \cos(kt). \tag{4.49}$$

For the purpose of distinguishing the presented identity from the conventional one, we denote $I(t)$ as the identity in what follows instead of $I_1(t)$.

Theorem 4.4 (Representation)

The identity in the min-plus algebra is expressed by

$$I(t) = \lim_{T \to 0} \left[\frac{2}{T} + \frac{4}{T} \sum_{n=1}^{\infty} \cos\left(\frac{2n\pi t}{T}\right) \right]. \tag{4.50}$$

Proof. Take the following into account

$$\sum_{n=0}^{\infty} \delta(t - nT)(T > 0). \tag{4.51}$$

The identity in the discrete case is given by

$$I(k) = \sum_{n=0}^{\infty} \delta(k - nT). \tag{4.52}$$

The identity in the continuous case is taken as the limit expressed by

$$I(t) = \lim_{T \to 0} \sum_{n=0}^{\infty} \delta(t - nT). \tag{4.53}$$

Considering the Poisson's summation formula, we have

$$I(k) = \frac{2}{T} + \frac{4}{T} \sum_{n=1}^{\infty} \cos\left(\frac{2n\pi k}{T}\right). \tag{4.54}$$

In the limit case,

$$I(t) = \lim_{T \to 0} \left[\frac{2}{T} + \frac{4}{T} \sum_{n=1}^{\infty} \cos\left(\frac{2n\pi t}{T}\right) \right]. \tag{4.55}$$

This completes the proof.

If one uses the above representation, the contradictions previously given vanish.

REFERENCES

1. J. Lighthill, *An Introduction to Fourier Analysis and Generalized Functions*, Cambridge University Press, Cambridge, 1958.
2. J. Mikusinski, *Operational Calculus*, Pergamon Press, Oxford, 1959.
3. R. N. Bracewell, *The Fourier Transform and Its Applications*, 2nd Ed., McGraw-Hill, New York, 1978.
4. B. Gold and C. M. Rader, *Digital Processing of Signals*, McGraw-Hill, New York, 1969.
5. R. A. Gabel and R. A. Roberts, *Signals and Linear Systems*, John Wiley & Sons, New York, 1973.
6. W. H. Press, S. A. Teukolsky, W. T. Vetterling, and B. P. Flannery, *Numerical Recipes in C: the Art of Scientific Computing*, 2nd Ed., Cambridge University Press, Cambridge, 1992.
7. C. D. McGillem and G. R. Cooper, *Continuous and Discrete Signal and System Analysis*, Holt, Rinehart and Winston, Inc., New York, 1974.
8. G. A. Korn and T. M. Korn, *Mathematical Handbook for Scientists and Engineers*, McGraw-Hill, New York, 1961.
9. H. R. Zhang, *Elementary of Modern Algebra*, People's Education Press, Beijing, 1978. In Chinese.
10. K. F. Riley, M. P. Hobson, and S. J. Bence, *Mathematical Methods for Physics and Engineering*, Cambridge Press, Cambridge, 2006.
11. I. N. Bronshtein, K. A. Semendyayev, G. Musiol, and H. Muehlig, *Handbook of Mathematics*, Springer, New York, 2007.
12. J. Stillwell, *Mathematics and Its History*, 3rd Ed., Springer, New York, 2010.
13. D. C. Smith, An introduction to distribution theory for signals analysis: Part II the convolution, *Digi. Signal Process.*, 16(4) 2006, 419–444.
14. C. S. Chang, On deterministic traffic regulation and service guarantees: A systematic approach by filtering, *IEEE Trans. Inform. Theor.*, 44(3) 1998, 1097–1109.
15. J.-Y. Le Boudec, Application of network calculus to guaranteed service networks, *IEEE Trans. Inform. Theor.*, 44(3) 1998, 1087–1096.
16. A. Bouillard, B. Gaujal, S. Lagrange, and E. Thierry, Optimal routing for end-to-end guarantees using network calculus, *Perform. Eval.*, 65(11–12) 2008, 883–906.
17. Y.-M. Jiang, A basic stochastic network calculus, *ACM SIGCOMM Comp. Commun. Rev.*, 36(4) 2006, 123–134.
18. A. Burchard, J. Liebeherr, and S. D. Patek, A min-plus calculus for end-to-end statistical service guarantees, *IEEE Trans. Inform. Theor.*, 52(9) 2006, 4105–4114.
19. S. J. Golestani, Network delay analysis of a class of fair queueing algorithms, *IEEE J. Select. Areas Commun.*, 13(6) 1995, 1057–1070.
20. D. Starobinski, M. Karpovsky, and L. A. Zakrevski, Application of network calculus to general topologies using turn-prohibition, *IEEE/ACM Trans. Network.*, 11(3) 2003, 411–421.

21. K. Pyun, J. Song, and H.-K. Lee, The service curve service discipline for the rate-controlled EDF service discipline in variable-sized packet networks, *Comput. Commun.*, 29(18) 2006, 3886–3899.

22. M. Fidler, A survey of deterministic and stochastic service curve models in the network calculus, *IEEE Commun. Surveys Tutor.*, 12(1) 2010, 59–86.

23. S. Mao and S. S. Panwar, A survey of envelope processes and their applications in quality of service provisioning, *IEEE Commun. Surveys Tutor.*, 8(3) 2006, 2–20.

24. A. D. Aleksandro, et al., *Mathematics, Its Essence, Methods and Role,* Vol. 3, USSR Academy of Sciences, Moscow, 1952.

25. R. G. Bartle and D. R. Sherbert, *Introduction to Real Analysis*, 3rd Ed., John Wiley & Sons, New York, 2000.

26. V. I. Istratescu, *Introduction to Linear Operator Theory*, Marcel Dekker, New York/Basel, 1981.

27. M. Li and W. Zhao, Asymptotic identity in min-plus algebra: A report on CPNS, *Comput. Math. Methods Med.*, 2012 2012, Article ID 154038, 11 p.

CHAPTER 5

Noise and Systems of Fractional Order

Traffic is a class of fractional processes or fractional noise. It relates to the theory of noise and systems of fractional order. For this reason, we discuss the basics about fractional noise and fractional order systems in this chapter. There are two parts in this chapter. One is the concept of fractional derivatives and integrals explained in Section 5.1. The other contains four highlights: (1) representing the fractional Riemann-Liouville integral operator using the Mikusinski operator of fractional order (Section 5.2); (2) presenting an integral representation of the delta function of fractional order (Section 5.4); (3) giving the opinion that a fractional noise can be taken as a response to a linear system driven by fractional noise (Section 5.5); (4) suggesting that a fractional noise can be also considered as an output of a fractional system under the excitation of non-fractional noise (Section 5.6). Alternatively, a fractional noise can be taken as a response to a fractional order system driven by a fractional noise (Section 5.7).

5.1 DERIVATIVES AND INTEGRALS OF FRACTIONAL ORDER

Let $y(t)$ be a function differentiable any times for $t \in \mathbf{R}$ (the set of real numbers). Then,

DOI: 10.1201/9781003268802-5

$$\frac{dy(t)}{dt} = \lim_{\varepsilon \to 0} \frac{y(t) - y(t-\varepsilon)}{\varepsilon}. \tag{5.1}$$

For a positive integer n, one has

$$y^{(n)}(t) = \frac{d^n y(t)}{dt^n} = \lim_{\varepsilon \to 0} \frac{y^{(n-1)}(t) - y^{(n-1)}(t-\varepsilon)}{\varepsilon}. \tag{5.2}$$

Expanding the right side of (5.2) produces

$$\frac{d^n y(t)}{dt^n}$$

$$= \lim_{\varepsilon \to 0} \frac{y(t) - \binom{n}{1} y(t-\varepsilon) + \binom{n}{2} y(t-2\varepsilon) - \cdots + (-1)^n \binom{n}{n} y(t-n\varepsilon)}{\varepsilon^n} \tag{5.3}$$

where

$$\binom{n}{m} = \frac{n(n-1)\ldots(n-m+1)}{m!}. \tag{5.4}$$

When using the notion D^n for the derivative of $y(t)$ of order n, $y^{(n)}(t)$ is expressed by (Mikusinski [1])

$$y^{(n)}(t) = D^n y(t). \tag{5.5}$$

Similarly, the n times integral of $y(t)$ may be expressed by

$$y^{(-n)}(t) = D^{-n} y(t). \tag{5.6}$$

When considering the fractional derivative of $y(t)$ of order $v > 0$, one has (Letnikov [2, p. 109], [3])

$$y^{(v)}(t) = \frac{d^v y(t)}{dt^v}$$

$$= \lim_{\varepsilon \to 0} \frac{y(t) - \binom{v}{1} y(t-\varepsilon) + \binom{v}{2} y(t-2\varepsilon) - \cdots + (-1)^n \binom{v}{n} y(t-n\varepsilon)}{\varepsilon^v}. \tag{5.7}$$

A well-known example about (5.7) is $\dfrac{d^{\frac{1}{2}}t}{dt^{\frac{1}{2}}} = \dfrac{\sqrt{4t}}{\pi}$ (Letnikov [2], Leibniz [4],

Cajori [5, p. 419]).

According to Letnikov [3, p. 8], one has

$$\left[\lim_{h\to 0} \frac{d^{-\nu}y(t)}{dt^{-\nu}}\right]_{t_0}^{t} = \lim_{h\to 0} \sum_{r=0}^{n} h^{\nu}\binom{\nu}{r} y(t-rh)$$

$$= \frac{1}{1\cdot 2\ldots(\nu-1)} \int_{t_0}^{t} (t-u)^{\nu-1} f(u)du$$

$$= \frac{1}{\Gamma(\nu)} \int_{t_0}^{t} (t-u)^{\nu-1} f(u)du. \tag{5.8}$$

The above is well known today as the fractional integral of Riemann-Liouville (RL) type. Nowadays, it is rare to use the original limit like (5.7) and (5.8) to describe a fractional derivative or integral. Instead, one simply utilizes the definitions of fractional derivatives and integrals, such as the RL's (Liouville [6], Ross [7]) and the Weyl's (Weyl [8], Raina and Koul [9]). There are other types of definitions of fractional derivatives and integrals, see e.g., [10–21] but we mention the RL's definition and use the Weyl's in this book. The main contents of the theory of fractional calculus, such as the mean-value theorem, the Leibniz rule, the Taylor's series, refer to, e.g., Klafter et al. [10], Fabian [22], Osler [23–26], Kleinz and Osler [27], Davis [28], Ross [29].

Denote by $_0D_x^{-\alpha}$ the RL fractional integral operator of order $\alpha > 0$. Then (Miller and Ross [30, p. 10]), for a function $x(t)$, $t \in \mathbf{R}$, one has

$$_0D_x^{-\alpha}x(t) = \frac{1}{\Gamma(\alpha)} \int_0^t x(u)(t-u)^{\alpha-1}\, du. \tag{5.9}$$

Thus, the symbol $_0D_x^{\alpha}$ stands for the RL fractional derivative operator. Hence (Lavoie et al. [31, Eq. (5.1)]),

$$_0D_x^{\alpha}x(t) = \frac{1}{\Gamma(-\alpha)} \int_0^t \frac{x(u)}{(t-u)^{\alpha+1}}\, du. \tag{5.10}$$

Following Weyl [8], the Weyl fractional integral operator is denoted by $_tW_\infty^{-\alpha}$ in the form (Miller and Ross [30, p. 13])

$$_tW_\infty^{-\alpha}x(t) = \frac{1}{\Gamma(\alpha)} \int_t^\infty x(u)(u-t)^{\alpha-1}\,du. \qquad (5.11)$$

When using the Weyl fractional derivative operator $_tW_{-\infty}^\alpha$, one has (Lavoie et al. [31, p. 245], Rain and Koul [9]),

$$_tW_{-\infty}^\alpha x(t) = \frac{1}{\Gamma(-\alpha)} \int_{-\infty}^t \frac{x(u)}{(t-u)^{\alpha+1}}\,du. \qquad (5.12)$$

In general, different derivative operators may yield different results for a specific function. An example in this regard is the fractional derivatives of the elementary function e^{at} ($a<0$). To be precise (Lavoie et al. [31, p. 246]), on the one hand,

$$_0D_x^\alpha e^{at} = \frac{t^{-a}}{\Gamma(1-\alpha)}\,_1F_1(1;1-\alpha;\alpha t), \qquad (5.13)$$

where $_1F_1(\cdot)$ is the hypergeometric function. On the other hand,

$$_tW_{-\infty}^\alpha e^{at} = a^\alpha e^{at}. \qquad (5.14)$$

In this monograph, we use the fractional derivative of Weyl's unless otherwise stated. The notation $\dfrac{d^\alpha}{dt^\alpha}$ or $x^{(\alpha)}(t)$ is in the sense of Weyl fractional derivative.

Example 5.1

The fractional derivative of $\cos\omega t$ is given by (Miller and Ross [30, p. 248])

$$\frac{d^v \cos\omega t}{dt^v} = \omega^v \cos\left(\omega t - \frac{\pi v}{2}\right)$$

$$= \omega^v\left(\cos\omega t \cos\frac{\pi v}{2} + \sin\omega t \sin\frac{\pi v}{2}\right). \qquad (5.15)$$

Example 5.2

The fractional derivative of $\sin \omega t$ is in the form (Miller and Ross [30, p. 248])

$$\frac{d^\nu \sin \omega t}{dt^\nu} = \omega^\nu \sin\left(\omega t - \frac{\pi\nu}{2}\right)$$

$$= \omega^\nu \left(\sin \omega t \cos \frac{\pi\nu}{2} - \cos \omega t \sin \frac{\pi\nu}{2}\right). \qquad (5.16)$$

Note that (5.15) and (5.16) are consistent with those described by Fourier in Ref. [32, p. 437].

Example 5.3

The fractional derivative of $t^{-\lambda}$ is given by (Miller and Ross [30, p. 249])

$$\frac{d^\nu t^{-\lambda}}{dt^\nu} = \frac{\Gamma(\nu+\lambda)}{\Gamma(\lambda)} t^{-\nu-\lambda}. \qquad (5.17)$$

Example 5.4

The fractional derivative of t^λ is in the form (Miller and Ross [30, p. 249])

$$\frac{d^\nu t^\lambda}{dt^\nu} = \frac{\Gamma(\nu-\lambda)}{\Gamma(-\lambda)} t^{-\nu+\lambda}. \qquad (5.18)$$

Example 5.5

Let $X(\omega)$ be the Fourier transform of $x(t)$. Then (Uchaikin [21, p. 230], Lavoie et al. [31, Eq. (7.1)], Uchaikin [33,34], Li [35]), the Fourier transform of $x^{(\nu)}(t)$ is given by

$$F\left[x^{(\nu)}(t)\right] = \int_{-\infty}^{\infty} x^{(\nu)}(t) e^{-i\omega t}\, dt = (i\omega)^\nu X(\omega), \qquad (5.19)$$

where $i = \sqrt{-1}$.

5.2 MIKUSINSKI OPERATOR OF FRACTIONAL ORDER

A fractional operator of RL's can be expressed using the Mikusinski operator of fractional order (Li [36]). Let $a(t)$ and $b(t)$ belong to $C(0, \infty)$. Following the usage of Mikusinski's, we rewrite $a(t)$ and $b(t)$ by

$$a = \{a(t)\}, b = \{b(t)\}. \tag{5.20}$$

The convolution described by Mikusinski is then given by

$$ab = \{a(t)\}\{b(t)\} = \left\{\int_0^t a(t-\tau)b(\tau)d\tau\right\}. \tag{5.21}$$

The deconvolution, therefore, is expressed by

$$\frac{a}{b} = \frac{\{a(t)\}}{\{b(t)\}}. \tag{5.22}$$

Define $l = \{1\}$ such that

$$\{1\}\{a(t)\} = \left\{\int_0^t a(\tau)d\tau\right\}. \tag{5.23}$$

The representations (5.21) and (5.22) may be convenient to study the operations of the convolution and its inverse from a view of algebra. For instance, $C(0, \infty)$ is a commutative ring.

Let $a = \{1\}$ in (5.23). Then,

$$l^2 = \{1\}\{1\} = \left\{\int_0^t d\tau\right\} = \left\{\frac{t}{1}\right\}. \tag{5.24}$$

In the general case of $n = 1, \ldots,$ one has

$$l^n = \left\{\frac{t^{n-1}}{(n-1)!}\right\}, \tag{5.25}$$

where 0! = 1. The above l^n may be termed as a Mikusinski operator.

When one exerts l^n on $f(t) \in C(0, \infty)$, the following Cauchy formula results,

$$l^n\{f(t)\} = \left\{\int_0^t \frac{(t-\tau)^{n-1}}{(n-1)!} f(\tau)d\tau\right\}. \tag{5.26}$$

Considering the generalization of l^n in (5.25) for $v>0$ yields another Mikusinski operator given by

$$l^v = \left\{\frac{t^{v-1}}{(v-1)!}\right\} = \left\{\frac{t^{v-1}}{\Gamma(v)}\right\}. \tag{5.27}$$

Further, by taking into account $l^v\{f(t)\}$, we have

$$l^v\{f(t)\} = \left\{\int_0^t \frac{(t-\tau)^{v-1}}{\Gamma(v)} f(\tau)d\tau\right\}. \tag{5.28}$$

Releasing the usage of Mikusinski with respect to {}, we have

$$l^v f(t) = \int_0^t \frac{(t-\tau)^{v-1}}{\Gamma(v)} f(\tau)d\tau. \tag{5.29}$$

This completes the derivation because (5.29) is the definition of the RL fractional integral of order v.

5.3 FRACTIONAL DERIVATIVES: A CONVOLUTION VIEW

I would like to propose several theorems with respect to representations of fractional derivative from the point of view of convolution.

Theorem 5.1

Let $y^{(\alpha)}(t)$ be the fractional differential of $y(t)$ of order α. Then,

$$y^{(\alpha)}(t) = y(t) * \delta^{(\alpha)}(t). \tag{5.30}$$

Proof. Let $Y(\omega)$ be the Fourier transform of $y(t)$. The Fourier transform of $y^{(\alpha)}(t)$ is

$$F\left[y^{(\alpha)}(t)\right]=(i\omega)^{\alpha} Y(\omega). \tag{5.31}$$

Besides, the Fourier transform of the right side of (5.31) is, according to the convolution rule, in the form

$$F\left[y(t)*\delta^{(\alpha)}(t)\right]=Y(\omega)(i\omega)^{\alpha}. \tag{5.32}$$

From (5.31) and (5.32), we see that Theorem 5.1 holds.

Theorem 5.1 means that the fractional derivative of $y(t)$ of order α may be expressed by $y(t)$ convoluted with the fractional derivative of a delta function of order α. Also, Theorem 5.1 implies that $y^{(\alpha)}(t)$ may be expressed by $y(t)$ convoluted with a variable coefficient $\delta^{(\alpha)}(t)$.

Theorem 5.2

Let $y^{(\alpha)}(t)$ be the fractional differential of $y(t)$ of order α. For a positive integer n, we have

$$y^{(\alpha)}(t)= y^{(n)}(t)*\delta^{(\alpha-n)}(t). \tag{5.33}$$

Proof. Let $Y(\omega)$ be the Fourier transform of $y(t)$. Because

$$F\left[y^{(n)}(t)\right]=(i\omega)^{n} Y(\omega), \tag{5.34}$$

and

$$F\left[\delta^{(\alpha-n)}(t)\right]=(i\omega)^{\alpha-n}. \tag{5.35}$$

Based on the convolution rule, for the right side of (5.33), we have

$$F\left[y^{(n)}(t)*\delta^{(\alpha-n)}(t)\right]=(i\omega)^{n}(i\omega)^{\alpha-n} Y(\omega)=(i\omega)^{\alpha} Y(\omega). \tag{5.36}$$

Thus, Theorem 5.2 holds.

Theorem 5.2 says that $y^{(\alpha)}(t)$ may be expressed by an integer derivative $y^{(n)}(t)$ convoluted with the fractional derivative of a delta function of order $\alpha - n$. In other words, it also says that $y^{(\alpha)}(t)$ equals to an integer derivative $y^{(n)}(t)$ convoluted with a variable coefficient $\delta^{(\alpha-n)}(t)$.

Note that numerical computation of fractional integrals and derivatives is an interesting field in fractional calculus and its applications, see e.g., Li and Zeng [37], Li and Cai [38], Heydari [39,40], Heydari et al. [41], just mentioning a few. The research stated in this monograph, however, is in analytical style.

5.4 FRACTIONAL ORDER DELTA FUNCTION

We now give an integral representation of the fractional derivative of $\delta(t)$ of order $\nu \geq 0$.

Theorem 5.3 (Li [42])

The fractional derivative of $\delta(t)$ of order $\nu \geq 0$ is given by

$$\delta^{(\nu)}(t) = \frac{1}{\pi} \int_0^\infty \frac{d^\nu \cos \omega t}{dt^\nu} d\omega. \tag{5.37}$$

Proof: Since $\delta(t) = \dfrac{1}{\pi} \displaystyle\int_0^\infty \cos \omega t \, d\omega$, we have

$$\delta^{(\nu)}(t) = \frac{d^\nu \delta(t)}{dt^\nu} = \frac{1}{\pi} \frac{d^\nu}{dt^\nu} \int_0^\infty \cos \omega t \, d\omega. \tag{5.38}$$

As

$$\frac{d^\nu}{dt^\nu} \int_0^\infty \cos \omega t \, d\omega = \int_0^\infty \frac{d^\nu \cos \omega t}{dt^\nu} d\omega. \tag{5.39}$$

Theorem 5.3 holds.

Theorem 5.4

The fractional derivative of $\delta(t)$ of order $\nu \geq 0$ can be written by

$$\delta^{(\nu)}(t) = \frac{1}{\pi} \int_0^\infty \omega^\nu \cos\left(\omega t - \frac{\pi \nu}{2}\right) d\omega. \qquad (5.40)$$

Proof: Following Miller and Ross [30, p. 248], one has

$$\frac{d^\nu \cos \omega t}{dt^\nu} = \omega^\nu \cos\left(\omega t - \frac{\pi \nu}{2}\right). \qquad (5.41)$$

Replacing $\dfrac{d^\nu \cos \omega t}{dt^\nu}$ in (5.37) with the above yields (5.40).

5.5 LINEAR SYSTEMS DRIVEN BY FRACTIONAL NOISE

Denote by $h(t)$ the impulse response of a linear system L (Figure 5.1). The system response $y(t)$ under the excitation of $x(t)$ is given by

$$y(t) = x(t) * h(t), \qquad (5.42)$$

Let $x(t)$ be white noise $w(t)$. Then, $w^{(\nu)}(t)$ is a fractional white noise. Since

$$y^{(\nu)}(t) = w^{(\nu)}(t) * h(t), \qquad (5.43)$$

we see that the response $y^{(\nu)}(t)$ to a linear system $h(t)$ driven by a fractional white noise is a fractional noise.

5.6 FRACTIONAL SYSTEMS DRIVEN BY NON-FRACTIONAL NOISE

From (5.43), we have

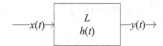

FIGURE 5.1 Linear system.

$$y^{(v)}(t) = w(t) * h^{(v)}(t), \tag{5.44}$$

where $h^{(v)}(t)$ stands for a fractional order system. Thus, we conclude that the response $y^{(v)}(t)$ to a fractional order system $h^{(v)}(t)$ excited by a white noise $w(t)$, which is a non-fractional noise, is a fractional noise.

5.7 FRACTIONAL SYSTEMS DRIVEN BY FRACTIONAL NOISE

Let $x(t) = w^{(v)}(t)$. Denote by $h^{(u)}(t)$ a system of order $u > 0$. Then, we have

$$y^{(v+u)}(t) = w^{(v)}(t) * h^{(u)}(t). \tag{5.45}$$

The above says that the response of a fractional system of order u driven by a fractional noise of order v is a fractional noise of order $u+v$, referring [42–51] for the literature regarding fractional noise and fractional order systems.

REFERENCES

1. J. Mikusinski, *Operational Calculus*, Pergamon Press, Oxford, 1959.
2. A. V. Letnikov, Historical development of the theory of differentiation of fractional order, *Moskow Matematicheskii Sbornik*, 3(2) 1868, 85–119. In Russian.
3. A. V. Letnikov, Theory of differentiation of fractional order, *Moskow Matematicheskii Sbornik*, 3(1) 1868, 1–68. In Russian.
4. G. W. Leibniz, *Letter from Hanover, Germany to G. F. A. L'Hospital*, September 30, 1695, in Math. Schriften, 1849 reprinted in 1962, Hildesheim, Germany (Olms Verlag), 2, pp. 301–302. (http://www.olms.com/).
5. F. Cajori, Leibniz, The master-builder of mathematical notations, *Isis*, 7(3) 1925, 412–429.
6. J. Liouville, Memoire sur le theoreme des complementaires, *Journal für die reine und angewandte Mathematik*, 11 1834, 1–19.
7. B. Ross, *Fractional Calculus and Its Applications*, Lecture Notes in Mathematics, vol. 457, Springer-Verlag, New York, 1975.
8. H. Weyl, Bemerkungen zum Begriff des Differentialquotienten gebrochener Ordnung, *Vierteljahrsschrift der Naturforschenden Gesellschaft in Zürich*, 62 1917, 296–302.
9. R. K. Raina and C. L. Koul, On Weyl fractional calculus, *Proc. Am. Math. Soc.*, 73(2) 1979, 188–192.
10. J. Klafter, S. C. Lim, and R. Metzler, *Fractional Dynamics: Recent Advances*, World Scientific, Singapore, 2012.
11. J. Sabatier and C. Farge, Comments on the description and initialization of fractional partial differential equations using Riemann-Liouville's and Caputo's definitions, *J. Comput. Appl. Math.*, 339 Sep 2018, 30–39.

12. A. Giusti, A comment on some new definitions of fractional derivative, *Nonlinear Dyn.*, 93(3) 2018, 1757–1763.
13. A. Giusti, Addendum to: A comment on some new definitions of fractional derivative, *Nonlinear Dyn.*, 94(2) 2018, 1547–1547.
14. J. Hristov, Derivatives with non-singular kernels from the Caputo-Fabrizio definition and beyond: Appraising analysis with emphasis on diffusion models, in *Frontiers in Fractional Calculus*, Editor, S. Bhalekar, Vol. 1, Bentham Science Publishers, New York, 2017, 270–342.
15. R. Khalil, M. Al Horani, A. Yousef, and M. Sababheh, A new definition of fractional derivative, *J. Comput. Appl. Math.*, 264 2014, 65–70.
16. G.-H. Gao, Z.-Z. Sun, and H.-Wei Zhang, A new fractional numerical differentiation formula to approximate the Caputo fractional derivative and its applications, *J. Comput. Phys.*, 259 2014, 33–50.
17. M. Mazandarani and M. Najariyan, Type-2 fuzzy fractional derivatives, *Commun. Nonlinear Sci. Num. Simul.*, 19(7) 2014, 2354–2372.
18. Z. Zheng, W. Zhao, and H. Dai, A new definition of fractional derivative, *Int. J. Non-Linear Mech.*, 108 2019, 1–6.
19. T. M. Atanackovic, S. Pilipovic, B. Stankovic, and D. Zorica, *Fractional Calculus With Applications in Mechanics*, John Wiley & Sons, New York, 2014.
20. M. Caputo and M. Fabrizio, The kernel of the distributed order fractional derivatives with an application to complex materials, *Fractal Fract.*, 1(1) 2017 (11 p).
21. V. V. Uchaikin, *Fractional Derivatives for Physicists and Engineers*, Vol. I, Springer, New York, 2013.
22. W. Fabian, Fractional calculus, *Math. Gazette*, 20(238) 1936, 88–92.
23. T. J. Osler, The integral analog of the Leibniz rule, *Math. Comput.*, 26(120) 1972, 903–915.
24. T. J. Osler, Fractional derivatives and Leibniz rule, *Am. Math. Mont.*, 78(6) 1971, 645–649.
25. T. J. Osler, Leibniz rule for fractional derivatives generalized and an application to infinite series, *SIAM J. Appl. Math.*, 18(3) 1970, 658–674.
26. T. J. Osler, An integral analogue of Taylor's series and its use in computing Fourier transforms, *Math. Comput.*, 26(118) 1972, 449–460.
27. M. Kleinz and T. J. Osler, A child's garden of fractional derivatives, *Coll. Math. J.*, 31(2) 2000, 82–88.
28. H. T. Davis, The application of fractional operators to functional equations, *Am. J. Math.*, 49(1) 1927, 123–142.
29. B. Ross, Fractional calculus, *Math. Magaz.*, 50(3) 1977, 115–122.
30. K. S. Miller and B. Ross, *An Introduction to the Fractional Calculus and Fractional Differential Equations*, John Wiley, New York, 1993.
31. J. L. Lavoie, T. J. Osler, and R. Tremblay, Fractional derivatives and special functions, *SIAM Rev.*, 18(2) 1976, 240–268.
32. J. Fourier, *The Analytic Theory of Heat*, University Press, Cambridge, London, 1878. Translated by A. Freeman, M. A.

33. V. V. Uchaikin, Relaxation processes and fractional differential equations, *Int. J. Theor. Phys.*, 42(1) 2003, 121–34.
34. V. V. Uchaikin, *Fractional Derivatives for Physicists and Engineers*, Vol. II, Springer, New York, 2013.
35. M. Li, Three classes of fractional oscillators, *Sym.-Basel*, 10(2) 2018, 91 p.
36. M. Li and W. Zhao, Essay on Fractional Riemann-Liouville integral operator versus Mikusinski's, *Math. Prob. Eng.*, 2013 2013, Article ID 635412, 3 p.
37. C. P. Li and F. H. Zeng, *Numerical Methods for Fractional Calculus*, Chapman and Hall/CRC, Boca Raton, FL, 2015.
38. C. P. Li and M. Cai, *Theory and Numerical Approximations of Fractional Integrals and Derivatives*, SIAM, Philadelphia, PA, 2019.
39. M. H. Heydari, A computational method for a class of systems of nonlinear variable-order fractional quadratic integral equations, *Appl. Num. Math.*, 153 2020, 164–178.
40. M. H. Heydari, Numerical solution of nonlinear 2D optimal control problems generated by Atangana-Riemann-Liouville fractal-fractional derivative, *Appl. Num. Math.*, 150 2020, 507–518.
41. M. H. Heydari, M. R. Hooshmandasl, C. Cattani, F. M. Maalek Ghaini, An efficient computational method for solving nonlinear stochastic Itô integral equations: Application for stochastic problems in physics, *J. Comput. Phys.*, 283 2015, 148–168.
42. M. Li, Integral representation of fractional derivative of delta function, *Fractal Fract.*, 4(3) 2020, 47.
43. M. Li, Fractal time series — A tutorial review, *Math. Prob. Eng.*, 2010 2010, Article ID 157264, 26 p, Doi:10.1155/2010/157264.
44. M. Li, X. Sun, and X. Xiao, Revisiting fractional Gaussian noise, *Phys. A*, 514 2019, 56–62.
45. M. D. Ortigueira and A. G. Batista, A Fractional linear system view of the fractional Brownian motion, *Nonlin. Dyn.*, 38(1–4) 2004, 295–303.
46. M. D. Ortigueira and J. Machado, Which derivative? *Fractal Fract.*, 1(1) 2017, 13 p.
47. M. D. Ortigueira and J. Machado, Fractional definite integral, *Fractal Fract.*, 1(1) 2017, 9 p.
48. R. Magin, M. D. Ortigueira, I. Podlubny, and J. Trujillo, On the fractional signals and systems, *Signal Process.*, 91(3) 2011, 350–371.
49. V. E. Tarasov, Fractional nonlinear dynamics of learning with memory, *Nonlinear Dyn.*, 100(2) 2020, 1231–1242.
50. V. E. Tarasov, S. S. Tarasova, Fractional and integer derivatives with continuously distributed lag, *Commun. Nonlinear Sci. Num. Simul.*, 70 May 2019, 125–169.
51. V. E. Tarasov, Generalized memory: Fractional calculus approach, *Fractal Fract.*, 2(4) 2018, 23.

CHAPTER 6

Fractional Gaussian Noise and Traffic Modeling

The fractional Gaussian noise (fGn for short) may be the earliest fractal model of traffic. When scientists introduced the fGn model of traffic, they realized that the fGn is not a model of accurately fitting the data of real traffic. However, the research about the fGn model of traffic may yet stand for a considerable advance in the theory of traffic because people began in any case studying traffic models from the point of view of fractal time series instead of conventional non-fractal time series, such as a Poisson type process. For that reason, we start our discussions on traffic modeling from the fGn model in this book. We first address the integral representation of the fGn and the fractional Brownian motion in Section 6.1, which are novel in the field. Traffic modeling using fGn is explained in Section 6.2. An approximation of the autocorrelation function of fGn is described in Section 6.3. The fractal dimension of fGn is given in Section 6.4. Finally, we discuss the problem statements regarding traffic modeling using fGn in Section 6.5.

6.1 FRACTIONAL GAUSSIAN NOISE

Theorem 6.1 (Li et al. [1])

Let $w(t)$ be a normalized white noise. Let $0 < H < 1$ be the Hurst parameter. Denote by $G(t)$ the fractional Gaussian noise (fGn). Then,

DOI: 10.1201/9781003268802-6

$$G(t) = \frac{\sqrt{V_H \sin(H\pi)\Gamma(2H+1)}}{-2\sin\left(\dfrac{(H-3/2)\pi}{2}\right)\Gamma\left(H-\dfrac{1}{2}\right)} \int_{-\infty}^{t} \frac{w(\tau)}{|t-\tau|^{\frac{3}{2}-H}} d\tau, \qquad (6.1)$$

where

$$V_H = \Gamma(1-2H)\frac{\cos\pi H}{\pi H}. \qquad (6.2)$$

Proof. Let $S_{fGn}(\omega)$ be the power spectrum density (PSD) of fGn. Denote by $C_{fGn}(t)$ the autocorrelation function (ACF) of fGn. Following the Wiener–Khinchin's relation (Chapter 1),

$$S_{fGn}(\omega) = F\big[C_{fGn}(t)\big], \qquad (6.3)$$

where F is the operator of the Fourier transform. According to Li and Lim [2],

$$S_{fGn}(\omega) = V_H \sin(H\pi)\Gamma(2H+1)|\omega|^{1-2H}. \qquad (6.4)$$

Since $S_{fGn}(\omega) \geq 0$, we have

$$\sqrt{S_{fGn}(\omega)} = \sqrt{F\big[C_{fGn}(t)\big]} = \sqrt{V_H \sin(H\pi)\Gamma(2H+1)}\,|\omega|^{\frac{1}{2}-H}. \qquad (6.5)$$

Denote by $\lambda = H - \dfrac{3}{2}$. Let

$$A(H) = \sqrt{V_H \sin(H\pi)\Gamma(2H+1)}. \qquad (6.6)$$

Then, we have

$$\sqrt{F\big[C_{fGn}(t)\big]} = A(H)|\omega|^{-1-\lambda}. \qquad (6.7)$$

Rewrite the above by

$$\sqrt{\mathrm{F}[C_{\mathrm{fGn}}(t)]} = \frac{-2\sin\left(\dfrac{\lambda\pi}{2}\right)\Gamma(\lambda+1)A(H)}{-2\sin\left(\dfrac{\lambda\pi}{2}\right)\Gamma(\lambda+1)}|\omega|^{-1-\lambda}. \tag{6.8}$$

Because (Gelfand and Vilenkin [3, Chapter 2])

$$\mathrm{F}\left(|t|^{\lambda}\right) = -2\sin(\lambda\pi/2)\Gamma(\lambda+1)|\omega|^{-\lambda-1}, \tag{6.9}$$

we have

$$\mathrm{F}^{-1}\left\{\sqrt{\mathrm{F}[C_{\mathrm{fGn}}(t)]}\right\} = \frac{A(H)}{-2\sin\left(\dfrac{\lambda\pi}{2}\right)\Gamma(\lambda+1)}|t|^{\lambda}$$

$$= \frac{A(H)}{-2\sin\left(\dfrac{(H-3/2)\pi}{2}\right)\Gamma(H-1/2)}|t|^{H-\frac{3}{2}}. \tag{6.10}$$

Following Li [4], we have

$$G(t) = w(t) * \mathrm{F}^{-1}\left\{\sqrt{\mathrm{F}[C_{\mathrm{fGn}}(t)]}\right\}$$

$$= \frac{\sqrt{V_H \sin(H\pi)\Gamma(2H+1)}}{-2\sin\left(\dfrac{(H-3/2)\pi}{2}\right)\Gamma\left(H-\dfrac{1}{2}\right)}\int_{-\infty}^{t}\frac{w(\tau)}{|t-\tau|^{\frac{3}{2}-H}}d\tau. \tag{6.11}$$

This finishes the proof.

Corollary 6.1

Let $w(t)$ be a normalized white noise. Let $0 < H < 1$ be the Hurst parameter. Denote by $B_H(t)$ the fractional Brownian motion. Then,

$$B_H(t) = \int_{-\infty}^{t} G(u)du. \tag{6.12}$$

The proof is straightforward and omitted.

6.2 FRACTIONAL GAUSSIAN NOISE IN TRAFFIC MODELING

The ACF of fGn is given by

$$C_{fGn}(\tau) = \frac{V_H \varepsilon^{2H}}{2}\left[\left(\left|\frac{\tau}{\varepsilon}\right|+1\right)^{2H} + \left|\left|\frac{\tau}{\varepsilon}\right|-1\right|^{2H} - 2\left|\frac{\tau}{\varepsilon}\right|^{2H}\right], \qquad (6.13)$$

where $\varepsilon > 0$ is the parameter utilized for smoothing $B_H(t)$ so that the smoothed one is differentiable (Mandelbrot and van Ness [5, pp. 427,428]). The above contains three subclasses of fGn. When $H \in (0.5, 1)$, $C_{fGn}(\tau)$ is positive and finite for all τ. It is non-integrable and the corresponding series is of long-range dependence (LRD). If $H \in (0, 0.5)$, the integral of $C_{fGn}(\tau)$ is zero and $C_{fGn}(0)$ diverges when $\varepsilon \to 0$. Hence, it is of short-range dependence when $H \in (0, 0.5)$. Moreover, $C_{fGn}(\tau)$ changes its sign and becomes negative for some τ proportional to ε in this parameter domain [5, p. 434]. It reduces to white noise when $H = 0.5$.

Practically, one uses $C_{fGn}(\tau)$ for $\varepsilon \to 0$. In that case,

$$C_{fGn}(\tau) = \frac{V_H}{2}\left[(|\tau|+1)^{2H} + ||\tau|-1|^{2H} - 2|\tau|^{2H}\right]. \qquad (6.14)$$

In the discrete case, denoting the lag by k, we have

$$C_{fGn}(k) = \frac{V_H}{2}\left[(|k|+1)^{2H} + ||k|-1|^{2H} - 2|k|^{2H}\right]. \qquad (6.15)$$

In the case of normalized ACF for the modeling purpose (Li et al. [6]), we use

$$C_{fGn}(k) = \frac{1}{2}\left[(|k|+1)^{2H} + ||k|-1|^{2H} - 2|k|^{2H}\right]. \qquad (6.16)$$

We use three sets of real traffic traces. The first set is about four real traffic traces recorded by the Bellcore (BC) in 1989. The second is about four traces measured at the Digital Equipment Corporation (DEC) in 1995. Both are available in Danzig et al. [7]. The third set is about four traces recorded by the MAWI (Measurement and Analysis on the WIDE Internet) Working

Group Traffic Archive (Japan) in 2019.[1] The file names for data at BC are pAug.TL, pOct.TL, Octext.TL, and OctExt4.TL, respectively. The data files at DEC are DEC-pkt-1.TCP, DEC-pkt-2.TCP, DEC-pkt-3.TCP, and DEC-pkt-4.TCP, respectively. The file names of the traffic traces at MAWI are MAWI-pkt-1.TCP, MAWI-pkt-2.TCP, MAWI-pkt-3.TCP, and MAWI-pkt-4.TCP, respectively. Tables 6.1–6.3 show the data information. The record length of those traces is enough for a satisfied ACF or PSD estimate as stated by Li [8].

Let $x(i)$ be the packet size of the ith packet ($i = 0, 1, \ldots$). Figures 6.1–6.3 indicate the plots of $x(i)$ of three sets of traces, respectively.

TABLE 6.1   Four Real Traffic Traces on the Ethernet at BC in 1989 [7]

Trace Name	Starting Time of Measurement	Duration	Number of packets
pAug.TL	11:25 AM, 29 Aug 89	52 minutes	1 million
pOct.TL	11:00 AM, 05 Oct 89	29 minutes	1 million
OctExt.TL	11:46 PM, 03 Oct 89	34.111 hours	1 million
OctExt4.TL	2:37 PM, 10 Oct 89	21.095 hours	1 million

TABLE 6.2   Four Wide-Area Real TCP Traffic Traces at DEC [7]

Trace Name	Record Date	Duration	Number of Packets
DEC-pkt-1.TCP	08 Mar 95	10–11 PM	3.3 million
DEC-pkt-2.TCP	08 Mar 95	2–3 AM	3.9 million
DEC-pkt-3.TCP	08 Mar 95	10–11 AM	4.3 million
DEC-pkt-4.TCP	08 Mar 95	2–3 PM	5.7 million

TABLE 6.3   Four Wide-Area TCP Traces Recorded by MAWI in 2019.

Trace Name	Starting Record Time	Duration (Minutes)	Number of Packets
MAWI-pkt-1.TCP	2:00 PM, 18 Apr 2019	6.77208	741,404
MAWI-pkt-2.TCP	2:00 PM, 19 Apr 2019	6.65965	742,638
MAWI-pkt-3.TCP	2:00 PM, 20 Apr 2019	12.55740	482,564
MAWI-pkt-4.TCP	2:00 PM, 21 Apr 2019	12.66541	576,495

---

[1] The data at MAWI are available via http://mawi.wide.ad.jp/mawi/.

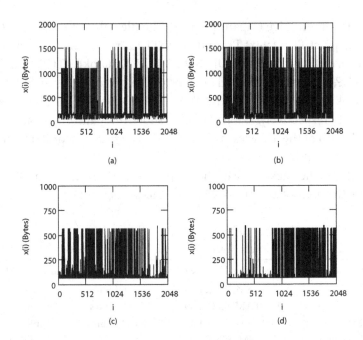

FIGURE 6.1   Plots of traces at BC in 1989. (a) pAug.TL. (b) pOct.TL. (c) OctExt. TL. (d) OctExt4.TL.

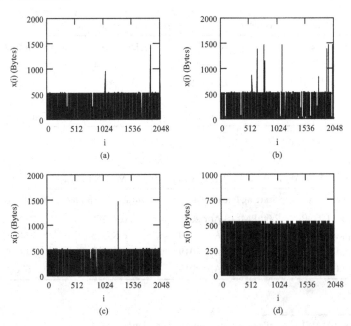

FIGURE 6.2   Plots of traces at DEC in 1995. (a) DEC-pkt-1.TCP. (b) DEC-pkt-2. TCP. (c) DEC-pkt-3.TCP. (d) DEC-pkt-4.TCP.

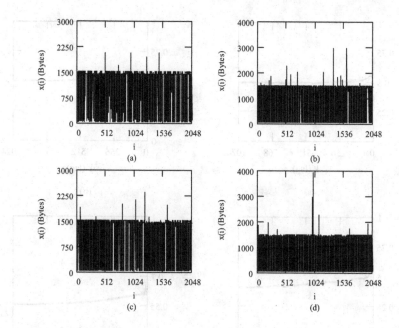

FIGURE 6.3   Plots of traces at MAWI in 2019. (a) MAWI-pkt-1.TCP. (b) MAWI-pkt-2.TCP. (c) MAWI-pkt-3.TCP. (d) MAWI-pkt-4.TCP.

The computation settings are as follows. Block size L is 2,048 and average counts $N = 30$. Section the series as $x(i)$, $i = (n-1)(L \times N), \ldots, n(L \times N)$ for $n = 1, \ldots, 30$. Denote the measured ACF by $r(k)$. Then, $r(k)$ is the average ACF of all 30 sections. Figures 6.4–6.6 illustrate the measured ACFs of three sets of traces.

Since there is a parameter H in $C_{fGn}(k)$, we denote it by $C_{fGn}(k; H)$. Denote by $M^2 = E\left\{\left[C_{fGn}(k;H) - r(k)\right]^2\right\} = \text{MSE}(H)$ the mean square error (MSE) of the ACF estimate with respect to $r(k)$. Then,

$$\frac{dM^2}{dH} = 0 \qquad (6.17)$$

produces a value of H, denoted by H_0. Thus, $\text{MSE}(H_0)$ corresponds to the minimum of M^2 so that $C_{fGn}(k; H_0)$ best fits $r(k)$, see Li et al. [6], [9,10]. Tables 6.4–6.6 give the modeling results expressed by H_0 and M^2. Figures 6.7–6.9 show the plots of $C_{fGn}(k; H_0)$ of three sets of traces. Fitting the data is shown in Figures 6.10–6.12.

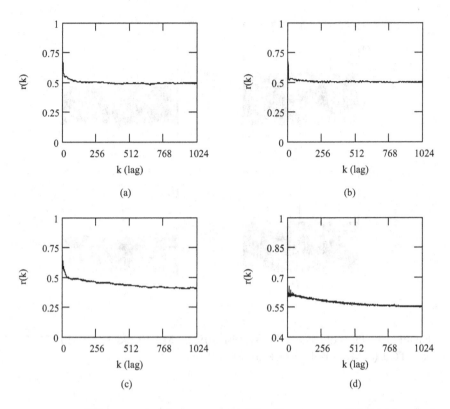

FIGURE 6.4   Illustrations of the measured ACFs of four traces at BC. (a) Measured ACF of pAug.TL. (b) Measured ACF of pOct.TL. (c) Measured ACF of OctExt.TL. (d) Measured ACF of OctExt4.TL.

The MSE for the test traces is in the magnitude order 10^{-3}–10^{-4}. In most cases, the magnitude order of the MSE using fGn modeling of traffic is about 10^{-3}, referring Li [11,12] and Li et al. [13] for the demonstrations of more real traffic traces.

We now explain that the results using the curve fitting are optimal with respect to fGn. To explain that, we define the norm of ACF by

$$\|r(k)\| = \sqrt{\langle r,r \rangle} = \sqrt{\sum_{k=0}^{N-1} |r(k)|}, \tag{6.18}$$

where N is the block size and $<r, r>$ is the inner product of r. Denote by $l_{2,\,N}$ the space that $r(k)$ belongs to in the form

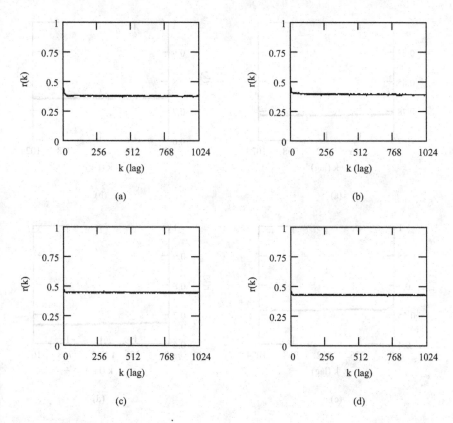

FIGURE 6.5 Illustrations of the measured ACFs of four traces at DEC.
(a) Measured ACF of DEC-pkt-1.TCP. (b) Measured ACF of DEC-pkt-2.TCP.
(c) Measured ACF of DEC-pkt-3.TCP. (d) Measured ACF of DEC-pkt-4.TCP.

$$l_{2,N} = \{r(k); \|r(k)\| < \infty\}. \tag{6.19}$$

Due to the finite block size, $\|r\| < \infty$. The space $l_{2,\,N}$ is an inner product space with finite dimensions. Thus, it is a Hilbert space according to Note 3.22.

Let $\mathbf{B}_{fGn}$ be the space that contains the ACFs of fGn with the same block size as measured ACF r. Thus,

$$\mathbf{B}_{fGn} = \{C_{fGn}(k); \|C_{fGn}(k)\| < \infty\}. \tag{6.20}$$

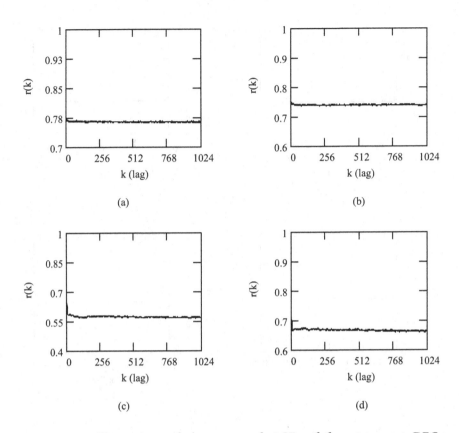

FIGURE 6.6 Illustrations of the measured ACFs of four traces at DEC. (a) Measured ACF of MAWI-pkt-1.TCP. (b) Measured ACF of MAWI-pkt-2.TCP. (c) Measured ACF of MAWI-pkt-3.TCP. (d) Measured ACF of MAWI-pkt-4.TCP.

TABLE 6.4   Modeling Results of Four Real Traffic Traces at BC

Trace Name	H_0	MSE (H_0)
pAug.TL	0.954	1.786×10^{-3}
pOct.TL	0.960	3.293×10^{-3}
OctExt.TL	0.948	6.531×10^{-4}
OctExt4.TL	0.963	8.229×10^{-4}

According to the optimal approximation in Hilbert space (see Chapter 3), for any measured ACF $r(k) \in l_{2, N}$, there exists a unique element $C_{fGn}(k; H_0) \in \mathbf{B}_{fGn}$ such that

$$\left\| C_{fGn}(k; H_0) - r(k) \right\| = \min. \tag{6.21}$$

TABLE 6.5   Modeling Results of Four Real Traffic Traces at DEC

Trace Name	H_0	MSE (H_0)
DEC-pkt-1.TCP	0.942	4.249×10^{-3}
DEC-pkt-2.TCP	0.937	2.491×10^{-3}
DEC-pkt-3.TCP	0.952	4.134×10^{-3}
DEC-pkt-4.TCP	0.949	4.099×10^{-3}

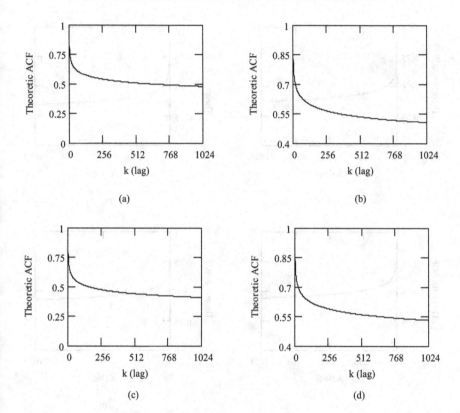

FIGURE 6.7   Plots of the theoretical fGn ACFs of four traces at BC. (a) $C_{fGn}(k; H_0)$ of pAug.TL. (b) $C_{fGn}(k; H_0)$ of pOct.TL. (c) $C_{fGn}(k; H_0)$ of OctExt.TL. (d) $C_{fGn}(k; H_0)$ of OctExt4.TL.

6.3 APPROXIMATION OF THE ACF OF FRACTIONAL GAUSSIAN NOISE

The function $C_{fGn}(\tau)$ can be considered as a second-order difference of $0.5(\tau)^{2H}$ (Mandelbrot [14,16], Li and Chi [15]). Doing the second-order difference of $0.5(\tau)^{2H}$, therefore, yields

TABLE 6.6   Modeling Results of Four Real Traffic Traces at MAWI

Trace Name	H_0	MSE (H_0)
MAWI-pkt-1.TCP	0.984	1.155×10^{-3}
MAWI-PKT-2.TCP	0.982	1.347×10^{-3}
MAWI-PKT-3.TCP	0.966	2.248×10^{-3}
MAWI-PKT-3.TCP	0.976	1.974×10^{-3}

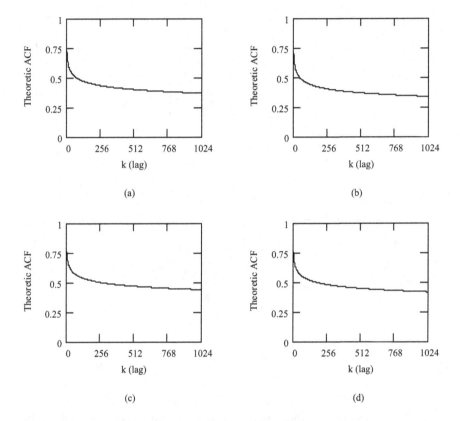

FIGURE 6.8   Plots of the theoretical $C_{\text{fGn}}(k; H_0)$ of four traces at DEC. (a) DEC-pkt-1.TCP. (b) DEC-pkt-2.TCP. (c) DEC-pkt-3.TCP. (d) DEC-pkt-4.TCP.

$$C_{\text{fGn}}(\tau) = \frac{1}{2}\left[\left(|\tau|+1\right)^{2H} + \left\||\tau|-1\right\|^{2H} - 2|\tau|^{2H} \right] \approx H(2H-1)|\tau|^{2H-2}. \qquad (6.22)$$

Mandelbrot noticed that the above approximation is quite well for $\tau > 10$. That might be conservative in a way. The approximation may be quite well when $\tau > 5$.

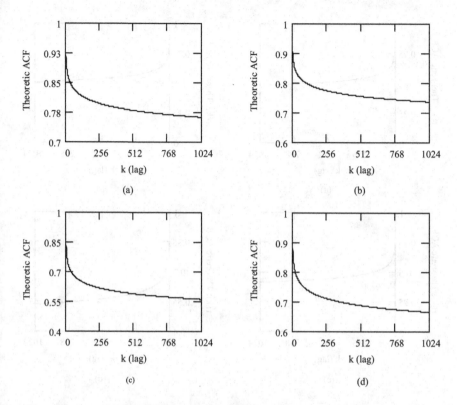

FIGURE 6.9 Plots of the theoretical ACF $C_{fGn}(k; H_0)$ of four traces at MAWI. (a) MAWI-pkt-1.TCP. (b) MAWI-pkt-2.TCP. (c) MAWI-pkt-3.TCP. (d) MAWI-pkt-4.TCP.

6.4 FRACTAL DIMENSION OF FRACTIONAL GAUSSIAN NOISE

Denote by D_{fGn} and H_{fGn} the fractal dimension and the Hurst parameter of fGn, respectively. The quantity H_{fGn} measures the LRD of fGn since it is in the case of $\tau \to \infty$, i.e., for large τ,

$$C_{fGn}(\tau) \sim H(2H-1)|\tau|^{2H-2}. \qquad (6.23)$$

Therefore, LRD is a global property of fGn. On the other hand, D_{fGn} is a measure to characterize the local property (local self-similarity, local roughness of fGn (Mandelbrot [16,17]). Since $C_{fGn}(\tau)$ is sufficiently smooth on $(0, \infty)$, we have

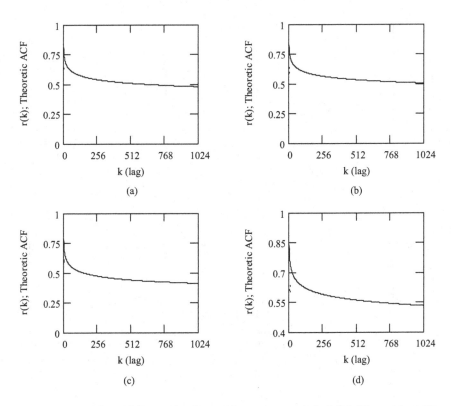

FIGURE 6.10 Plots of fitting the data of four traces at BC. Solid: Theoretic ACF. Dot: Measured ACF. (a) pAug.TL. (b) pOct.TL. (c) OctExt.TL. (d) OctExt4.TL.

$$C_{fGn}(0) - C_{fGn}(\tau) \sim c|\tau|^a, \text{ for } \tau \to 0, \tag{6.24}$$

where c is a constant and α is the fractal index of fGn. Following Hall and Roy [18], D_{fGn} is given by

$$D_{fGn} = 2 - \frac{\alpha}{2}. \tag{6.25}$$

Therefore, we have

$$D_{fGn} = 2 - H_{fGn}. \tag{6.26}$$

Thus, two measures, namely, D_{fGn} and H_{fGn}, happen to be linearly related.

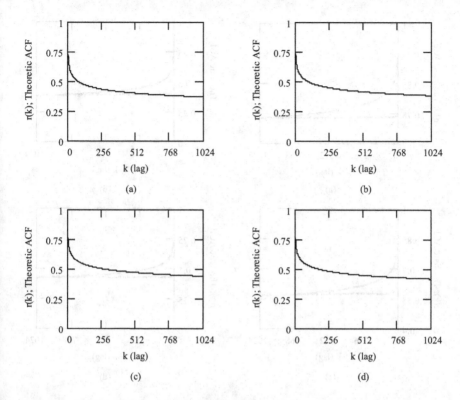

FIGURE 6.11 Plots of fitting the data of four traces at DEC. Solid: Theoretic ACF. Dot: Measured ACF. (a) DEC-pkt-1.TCP. (b) DEC-pkt-2.TCP. (c) DEC-pkt-3.TCP. (d) DEC-pkt-4.TCP.

6.5 PROBLEM STATEMENTS

In mathematics, the modeling results in Section 6.2 are optimal in Hilbert space. However, they are not satisfactory for small lags. As a matter of fact, scientists noticed that fGn cannot well fit real traffic (Paxson and Floyd [19], Tsybakov and Georganas [20]). From Figure 6.4, we see that fGn does not well fit traffic traces for small τ. However, the local behavior of traffic, local self-similarity (local roughness) is crucial to computer communications (Feldmann et al. [21]). Since D_{fGn} linearly relates to H_{fGn}, there only exists one fractal parameter, either D_{fGn} or H_{fGn}, in fGn. Obviously, both local and global properties of fGn cannot be measured by a single parameter. That is the limitation of fGn in traffic modeling.

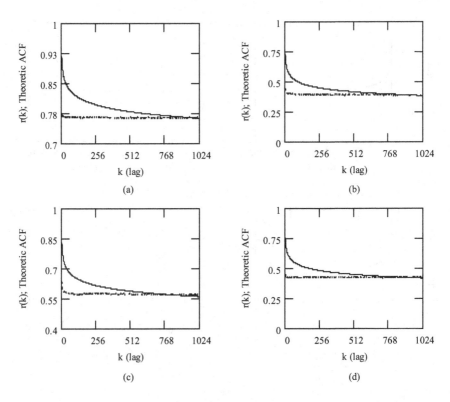

FIGURE 6.12 Plots of fitting the data of four traces at MAWI. Solid: Theoretic ACF. Dot: Measured ACF. (a) MAWI-pkt-1.TCP. (b) MAWI-pkt-2.TCP. (c) MAWI-pkt-3.TCP. (d) MAWI-pkt-4.TCP.

In the end, it is noted that the statistics of traffic data from the early data recorded by the BC in 1989 to the current ones by the MAWI Working Group Traffic Archive (Japan) remain the same, see Li [22,23] and Fontugne et al. [24]. Thus, the present results, including the problem statements, are available for the traffic data today.

REFERENCES

1. M. Li, X. Sun, and X. Xiao, Revisiting fractional Gaussian noise, *Phys. A*, 514 2019, 56–62.
2. M. Li and S. C. Lim, A rigorous derivation of power spectrum of fractional Gaussian noise, *Fluct. Noise Lett.*, 6(4) 2006, C33–C36.
3. I. M. Gelfand and K. Vilenkin, *Generalized Functions*; Vol. 1, Academic Press, New York, 1964.

4. M. Li, Generation of teletraffic of generalized Cauchy type, *Phys. Scr.*, 81(2) 2010, 025007 (10 p).
5. B. B. Mandelbrot and J. W. van Ness, Fractional Brownian motions, fractional noises and applications, *SIAM Rev.*, 10(4) 1968, 422–437.
6. M. Li, W. Zhao, W. Jia, D. Y. Long, and C.-H. Chi, Modeling autocorrelation functions of self-similar teletraffic in communication networks based on optimal approximation in Hilbert space, *Appl. Math. Model.*, 27(3) 2003, 155–168.
7. P. Danzig, J. Mogul, V. Paxson, and M. Schwartz, The internet traffic archive 2000, Ftp://ita.ee.lbl.gov/traces/ [dataset].
8. M. Li, Record length requirement of long-range dependent teletraffic, *Phys. A*, 472 2017, 164–187.
9. M. Li, P. Zhang, and J. Leng, Improving autocorrelation regression for the Hurst parameter estimation of long-range dependent time series based on golden section search, *Phys. A*, 445C 2016, 189–199.
10. M. Li and S. C. Lim, Modeling network traffic using generalized Cauchy process, *Phys. A*, 387(11) 2008, 2584–2594.
11. M. Li, Error order of magnitude for modeling autocorrelation function of interarrival times of network traffic using fractional Gaussian noise, *Proc. the 7th WSEAS Int. Conf. on Applied Computer and Applied Computational Science*, Hangzhou, China, April 6–8, 2008, 167–172.
12. M. Li, *Self-Similar Traffic - Its Modeling and Simulation*, PhD dissertation, City University of Hong Kong, Mar. 2002.
13. M. Li, C.-H. Chi, and D. Y. Long, Fractional Gaussian noise: A tool of characterizing traffic for detection purpose, *Springer LNCS 3309* 2004, 94–103.
14. B. B. Mandelbrot, Fast fractional Gaussian noise generator, *Water Resour. Res.*, 7(3) 1971, 543–553.
15. M. Li and C.-H. Chi, A correlation-based computational method for simulating long-range dependent data, *J. Franklin Inst.*, 340(6–7) 2003, 503–514.
16. B. B. Mandelbrot, *Gaussian Self-Affinity and Fractals*, Springer, Berlin, 2001.
17. B. B. Mandelbrot, *The Fractal Geometry of Nature*, W.H. Freeman, New York, 1982.
18. P. Hall and R. Roy, On the relationship between fractal dimension and fractal index for stationary stochastic processes, *Ann. Appl. Probab.*, 4(1) 1994, 241–253.
19. V. Paxson and S. Floyd, Wide area traffic: The failure of Poison modeling, *IEEE ACM Trans. Netw.*, 3(3) 1995, 226–244.
20. B. Tsybakov and N. D. Georganas, Self-similar processes in communications networks, *IEEE Trans. Inf. Theory*, 44(5) 1998, 1713–1725.
21. A. Feldmann, A. C. Gilbert, W. Willinger, and T. G. Kurtz, The changing nature of network traffic: Scaling phenomena, *ACM SIGCOMM Comp. Commun. Rev.*, 28(2) 1998, 5–29.

22. M. Li, Long-range dependence and self-similarity of teletraffic with different protocols at the large time scale of day in the duration of 12 years: Autocorrelation modeling, *Phys. Scr.*, 95(4) 2020, 065222, (15 p).

23. M. Li, Generalized fractional Gaussian noise and its application to traffic modeling, *Phys. A*, 579 2021, 1236137 (22 p).

24. R. Fontugne, P. Abry, K. Fukuda, D. Veitch, K. Cho, P. Borgnat, and H. Wendt, Scaling in Internet traffic: A 14 year and 3 day longitudinal study, with multiscale analyses and random projections, *IEEE/ACM Trans. Netw.*, 25(4) 2017, 2152–2165.

CHAPTER 7

Generalized Fractional Gaussian Noise and Traffic Modeling

As discussed in the last chapter, the limitation of fractional Gaussian noise (fGn) in traffic modeling is in the aspect of poorly fitting traffic at small time lags of autocorrelation function (ACF). Since the ACF of traffic at small lags designates a local behavior of traffic and characterizing the local behavior of traffic is critically important in applications, we desire a new ACF model that can be used to flexibly control the shape of ACF at small lags. For that reason, in this chapter, we introduce a novel type of fractional noise, called the generalized fractional Gaussian noise (gfGn). Its ACF is with two parameters. It is actually the fGn model equipped with fractional lag. With the fractional lag, the shape of the ACF of gfGn can be flexibly controlled, eliminating the limitation of fGn in traffic modeling. In this chapter, we introduce the gfGn in Section 7.1. Its application to traffic modeling is explained in Section 7.2. The results exhibit that the limitation of fGn in traffic modeling may release by using gfGn.

DOI: 10.1201/9781003268802-7

7.1 GENERALIZED FRACTIONAL GAUSSIAN NOISE

Let $x(t)$ be a random function. If its autocorrelation function (ACF) follows the one described in the theorem below, it is called the generalized fractional Gaussian noise (gfGn).

Theorem 7.1 (Li [1,2])

Let $0 < H < 1$ be the Hurst parameter. Let $0 < a \leq 1$ be a constant. Let $C_{\text{gfGn}}(\tau)$ be the ACF of gfGn. Then,

$$C_{\text{gf Gn}}(\tau) = \frac{V_H}{2}\left[\left(\left|\tau^a\right|+1\right)^{2H} + \left|\left|\tau^a\right|-1\right|^{2H} - 2\left|\tau^a\right|^{2H}\right], \tag{7.1}$$

where

$$V_H = \Gamma(1-2H)\frac{\cos \pi H}{\pi H}. \tag{7.2}$$

Proof. Denote by $B_H(t)$ the fractional Brownian motion (fBm). Then,

$$\mathrm{E}\left\{\left[B_H(t_2)-B_H(t_1)\right]^2\right\} = \mathrm{E}\left\{\left[B_H(t_2-t_1)-B_H(0)\right]^2\right\}$$

$$= \mathrm{E}\left\{\left[B_H(t_2-t_1)\right]^2\right\} = V_H(t_2-t_1)^{2H}. \tag{7.3}$$

Besides,

$$\mathrm{E}\left\{\left[B_H(t_2)-B_H(t_1)\right]^2\right\} = \mathrm{E}\left\{\left[B_H(t_2)\right]^2\right\} + \mathrm{E}\left\{\left[B_H(t_1)\right]^2\right\} - 2\mathrm{E}\left[B_H(t_2)B_H(t_1)\right]$$

$$= V_H(t_2)^{2H} + V_H(t_1)^{2H} - 2\rho\left[B_H(t_2), B_H(t_1)\right], \tag{7.4}$$

where $\rho[B_H(t_2), B_H(t_1)]$ is the ACF of fBm. It is given by

$$\rho\left[B_H(t_1), B_H(t_2)\right] = 0.5V_H\left[(t_2)^{2H} + (t_1)^{2H} - (t_2-t_1)^{2H}\right]. \tag{7.5}$$

Let (t_1, t_2) and (t_3, t_4) be two non-overlapping intervals. Then, the ACF of the increment process of $B_H(t)$ is given by

$$\rho\left\{\left[B_H(t_4)-B_H(t_3)\right], \left[B_H(t_2)-B_H(t_1)\right]\right\}$$

$$= \rho\left[B_H(t_4),B_H(t_2)\right]-\rho\left[B_H(t_4),B_H(t_1)\right]$$

$$- \rho\left[B_H(t_3),B_H(t_2)\right]+\rho\left[B_H(t_3),B_H(t_1)\right]$$

$$= 0.5V_H\left[(t_4-t_1)^{2H} +(t_3-t_2)^{2H} -(t_4-t_2)^{2H} -(t_3-t_1)^{2H}\right]. \quad (7.6)$$

Let $t_1=n$, $t_2=n+1$, $t_3=n+\tau^a$, $t_4=n+\tau^a+1$. Then, the above becomes

$$\rho\left\{\left[B_H(t_4)-B_H(t_3)\right], \left[B_H(t_2)-B_H(t_1)\right]\right\}$$

$$= 0.5V_H\left[(\tau^a+1)^{2H} -2(\tau^a)^{2H} +(\tau^a-1)^{2H}\right]. \quad (7.7)$$

This finishes the proof.

It is easily seen that $C_{\text{fGn}}(\tau)$ is a special case of $C_{\text{gfGn}}(\tau)$ for $a=1$. In fact,

$$C_{\text{gfGn}}(\tau)\big|_{a=1}=C_{\text{fGn}}(\tau). \quad (7.8)$$

In the discrete and normalized case,

$$C_{\text{gf Gn}}(k)= \frac{V_H}{2}\left[\left(|k^a|+1\right)^{2H} +\left\||k^a|-1\right\|^{2H} -2|k^a|^{2H}\right]. \quad (7.9)$$

Theorem 7.2 (Li [2,3])

Let $0<H<1$ be the Hurst parameter. Let $0<a\leq1$ be a constant. Let $S_{\text{gfGn}}(\omega)$ be the Fourier transform of $C_{\text{gfGn}}(\tau)$, i.e., the power spectrum density (PSD) of gfGn. Then

$S_{gfGn}(\omega) =$

$$
\begin{cases}
\sin(H\alpha\pi)\Gamma(2H\alpha+1)|\omega|^{-2H\alpha-1} \\
\quad +0.5\sum_{k=0}^{\infty}\dfrac{[(-1)^{k+1}-1]\Gamma(2H+k)\Gamma(\alpha k+1)}{\Gamma(2H)\Gamma(1+k)}\sin\left(\dfrac{\alpha k\pi}{2}\right)|\omega|^{-\alpha k-1}, \\
\qquad |\tau|<1, \sin(H\alpha\pi)\Gamma(2H\alpha+1)|\omega|^{-2H\alpha-1} \\
\quad +0.5\sum_{k=0}^{\infty}\dfrac{[(-1)^{k}-1]\Gamma(2H+k)\Gamma[(\alpha(2H-k)+1]}{\Gamma(2H)\Gamma(1+k)} \\
\quad \sin\left[\dfrac{\alpha(2H-k)\pi}{2}\right]|\omega|^{-\alpha(2H-k)-1}, \ |\tau|^{\alpha}>1.
\end{cases}
\tag{7.10}
$$

Proof. Write $C_{gfGn}(\tau)$ by

$$
C_{gfGn}(\tau) = 0.5[r_1(\tau) - 2r_2(\tau) + r_3(\tau)],
\tag{7.11}
$$

where $r_1 = \left(|\tau|^a+1\right)^{2H}$, $r_2 = \left(|\tau|^{\alpha}\right)^{2H}$, $r_3 = \left||\tau|^a-1\right|^{2H}$. Denote $S_m(\omega) = F(r_m)$ $(m=1, 2, 3)$. Then, $F[C_{gfGn}(\tau)]$ is given by

$$
S_{gfGn}(\omega) = 0.5\left[S_1(\omega) - 2S_2(\omega) + S_3(\omega)\right].
\tag{7.12}
$$

Since (Gelfand and Vilenkin [4, Chapter 2])

$$
F\left(|t|^{\lambda}\right) = -\sin\left(\dfrac{\lambda\pi}{2}\right)\Gamma(\lambda+1)|\omega|^{-\lambda-1}, \quad \text{where } \lambda \neq -1, -3, \dots
\tag{7.13}
$$

we have

$$
S_2(\omega) = -\sin(H\alpha\pi)\Gamma(2H\alpha+1)|\omega|^{-2H\alpha-1},
\tag{7.14}
$$

where $2H\alpha \neq -1, -3, \dots$ For $|\tau|^{\alpha} < 1$, we have

$$r_1(\tau)=\left(1+|\tau|^\alpha\right)^{2H}=\sum_{k=0}^{\infty}\binom{2H}{k}|\tau|^{\alpha k}=\sum_{k=0}^{\infty}\frac{\Gamma(2H+k)}{\Gamma(2H)\Gamma(1+k)}|\tau|^{\alpha k} \quad (7.15)$$

and

$$r_3(\tau)=\left(1-|\tau|^\alpha\right)^{2H}=\sum_{k=0}^{\infty}(-1)^k\binom{2H}{k}|\tau|^{\alpha k}=\sum_{k=0}^{\infty}\frac{(-1)^k\Gamma(2H+k)}{\Gamma(2H)\Gamma(1+k)}|\tau|^{\alpha k}.$$

$$(7.16)$$

However, when $|\tau|^\alpha>1$, we have

$$r_1(\tau)=\left(1+|\tau|^\alpha\right)^{2H}=|\tau|^{2H\alpha}\sum_{k=0}^{\infty}\binom{2H}{k}|\tau|^{-\alpha k}$$

$$=\sum_{k=0}^{\infty}\frac{\Gamma(2H+k)}{\Gamma(2H)\Gamma(1+k)}|\tau|^{\alpha(2H-k)} \quad (7.17)$$

and

$$r_3(\tau)=\left||\tau|^\alpha-1\right|^{2H}=|\tau|^{2H\alpha}\sum_{k=0}^{\infty}(-1)^k\binom{2H}{k}|\tau|^{-\alpha k}$$

$$=\sum_{k=0}^{\infty}\frac{(-1)^k\Gamma(2H+k)}{\Gamma(2H)\Gamma(1+k)}|\tau|^{\alpha(2H-k)}. \quad (7.18)$$

Therefore, when $|\tau|^\alpha<1$, S_1 and S_3 are given by

$$S_1(\omega)=\sum_{k=0}^{\infty}\frac{-\Gamma(2H+k)\Gamma(\alpha k+1)}{\Gamma(2H)\Gamma(1+k)}\sin\left(\frac{\alpha k\pi}{2}\right)|\omega|^{-\alpha k-1} \quad (7.19)$$

and

$$S_3(\omega)=\sum_{k=0}^{\infty}\frac{(-1)^{k+1}\Gamma(2H+k)\Gamma(\alpha k+1)}{\Gamma(2H)\Gamma(1+k)}\sin\left(\frac{\alpha k\pi}{2}\right)|\omega|^{-\alpha k-1}. \quad (7.20)$$

On the other side, for $|\tau|^{\alpha} > 1$, S_1 and S_3 are given by

$$S_1(\omega) = \sum_{k=0}^{\infty} \frac{-\Gamma(2H+k)\Gamma\left[\alpha(2H-k)+1\right]}{\Gamma(2H)\Gamma(1+k)} \sin\left[\frac{\alpha(2H-k)\pi}{2}\right]|\omega|^{-\alpha(2H-k)-1}$$

(7.21)

and

$$S_3(\omega) = \sum_{k=0}^{\infty} \frac{(-1)^{k+1}\Gamma(2H+k)\Gamma\left[\alpha(2H-k)+1\right]}{\Gamma(2H)\Gamma(1+k)}$$

$$\times \sin\left[\frac{\alpha(2H-k)\pi}{2}\right]|\omega|^{-\alpha(2H-k)-1}.$$

(7.22)

Considering (7.12), we see that the theorem holds.

Note that $S_{\text{gfGn}}(\omega)$ is divergent at $\omega = 0$ for $0 < 2H\alpha + 1 < 1$, which is the long-range dependence (LRD) condition reflected in the frequency domain. Recall $2H\alpha + 1 > 0$. Then, the cases of $2H\alpha + 1 < 1$ and $H \in (0.5, 1)$ imply $\alpha \in (0, 1]$. This explains the range of α in the ACF of gfGn from a view in the frequency domain.

7.2 TRAFFIC MODELING USING GENERALIZED FRACTIONAL GAUSSIAN NOISE

In the discrete case, denoting the lag by k, the normalized ACF of gfGn is

$$C_{gfGn}(k) = \frac{1}{2}\left[\left(|k^a|+1\right)^{2H} + \left\||k^a|-1\right\|^{2H} - 2|k^a|^{2H}\right].$$

(7.23)

For facilitating discussions and the sake of self-containing, we write the test data again in this chapter. We use three sets of real traffic traces. The first set about four real traffic traces was recorded by the Bellcore (BC) in 1989. The second set about four traces was measured at the Digital Equipment Corporation (DEC) in 1995. Both data are available in Danzig et al. [5]. The third set about four traces was recorded by the MAWI (Measurement and Analysis on the WIDE Internet) Working Group Traffic Archive (Japan) in 2019 [6]. The file names for data at BC are pAug.TL, pOct.TL, Octext. TL, and OctExt4.TL, respectively. The data at DEC are named DEC-pkt-1. TCP, DEC-pkt-2.TCP, DEC-pkt-3.TCP, and DEC-pkt-4.TCP, respectively.

The data files of the traces at MAWI are MAWI-pkt-1.TCP, MAWI-pkt-2. TCP, MAWI-pkt-3.TCP, and MAWI-pkt-4.TCP, respectively. Tables 7.1–7.3 give the data information. The record length of those traces is enough for a satisfied ACF or PSD estimate as analyzed by Li [7].

Denote by $x(i)$ the packet size of the ith packet ($i=0, 1, \ldots$). The plots of $x(i)$ at BC, DEC, and MAWI are shown in Figures 7.1–7.3, respectively.

The computation settings are as follows. Block size L is 2,048 and average counts $N=30$. Section the series as $x(i)$, $i=(n-1)(L \times N), \ldots, n(L \times N)$ for $n=1, \ldots, 30$. Denote the measured ACF by $r(k)$. Then, $r(k)$ is the average ACF of all 30 sections. Figures 7.4–7.6 demonstrate the measured ACFs of three sets of traces.

Since there is a pair of parameters (H, a) in $C_{\text{gfGn}}(k)$. We denote it by $C_{\text{gfGn}}(k; H, a)$. Denote by $M^2 = E\left\{\left[C_{\text{gfGn}}(k; H, a) - r(k)\right]^2\right\} = \text{MSE}(H, a)$ the mean square error (MSE) of the ACF estimate for $r(k)$. Then,

TABLE 7.1   Four Real Traffic Traces on the Ethernet at BC in 1989 [5]

Trace Name	Starting Time of Measurement	Duration	Number of Packets
pAug.TL	11:25 AM, 29 Aug 89	52 minutes	1 million
pOct.TL	11:00 AM, 05 Oct 89	29 minutes	1 million
OctExt.TL	11:46 PM, 03 Oct 89	34.111 hours	1 million
OctExt4.TL	2:37 PM, 10 Oct 89	21.095 hours	1 million

TABLE 7.2   Four Wide-Area TCP Traffic Traces at DEC in 1995 [5].

Trace Name	Record Date	Duration	Number of Packets
DEC-pkt-1.TCP	08 Mar 95	10–11 PM	3.3 million
DEC-pkt-2.TCP	08 Mar 95	2–3 AM	3.9 million
DEC-pkt-3.TCP	08 Mar 95	10–11 AM	4.3 million
DEC-pkt-4.TCP	08 Mar 95	2–3 PM	5.7 million

TABLE 7.3   Four Wide-Area TCP Traces Recorded by MAWI in 2019 [6]

Trace Name	Starting Record Time	Duration	Number of Packets
MAWI-pkt-1.TCP	2:00 PM, 18 Apr 2019	6.77208 minutes	741,404
MAWI-pkt-2.TCP	2:00 PM, 19 Apr 2019	6.65965 minutes	742,638
MAWI-pkt-3.TCP	2:00 PM, 20 Apr 2019	12.55740 minutes	482,564
MAWI-pkt-4.TCP	2:00 PM, 21 Apr 2019	12.66541 minutes	576,495

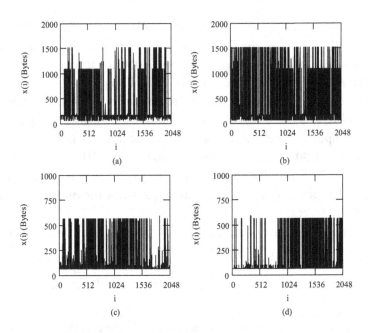

FIGURE 7.1   Plots of traces at BC in 1989. (a) pAug.TL. (b) pOct.TL. (c) OctExt. TL. (d) OctExt4.TL.

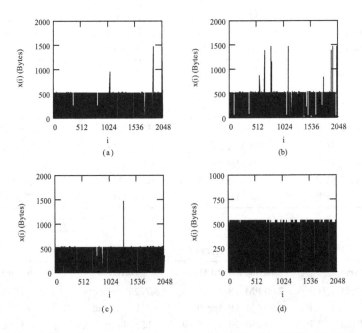

FIGURE 7.2   Plots of traces at DEC in 1995. (a) DEC-pkt-1.TCP. (b) DEC-pkt-2. TCP. (c) DEC-pkt-3.TCP. (d) DEC-pkt-4.TCP.

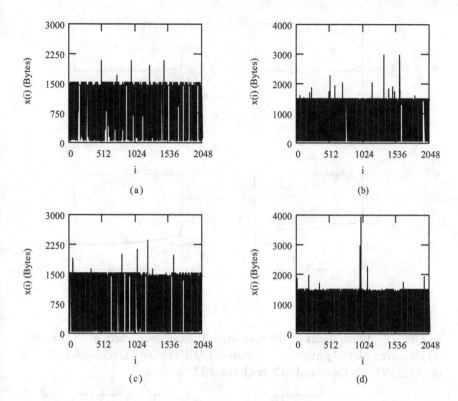

FIGURE 7.3 Plots of traces at MAWI in 2019. (a) MAWI-pkt-1.TCP. (b) MAWI-pkt-2.TCP. (c) MAWI-pkt-3.TCP. (d) MAWI-pkt-4.TCP.

$$\frac{\partial \text{MSE}(H,a)}{\partial H} = 0,$$

$$\frac{\partial \text{MSE}(H,a)}{\partial a} = 0,$$

(7.24)

yields a pair of values (H_{10}, a_0). Hence, $\text{MSE}(H_{10}, a_0)$ corresponds to the minimum of M^2 so that $C_{\text{gfGn}}(k; H_{10}, a_0)$ best fits $r(k)$. Tables 7.4–7.6 give the modeling results. Figures 7.7–7.9 indicate the illustrations of $C_{\text{gfGn}}(k; H_0, a_0)$ of three sets of traces. Fitting the data is shown in Figures 7.10–7.12. The results exhibit that MSE for the test traces is in the magnitude order 10^{-4}–10^{-6}, much better than the fractional Gaussian noise (fGn) model described in Chapter 6.

Consider the modeling results in Hilbert space. Define the norm of measured ACF by

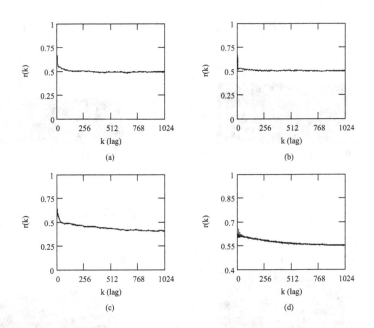

FIGURE 7.4 Illustrations of the measured ACFs of four traces at BC in 1989. (a) Measured ACF of pAug.TL. (b) Measured ACF of pOct.TL. (c) Measured ACF of OctExt.TL. (d) Measured ACF of OctExt4.TL.

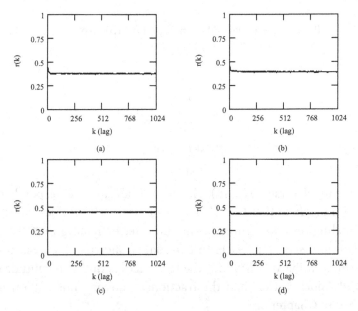

FIGURE 7.5 Illustrations of the measured ACFs of four traces at DEC in 1995. (a) Measured ACF of DEC-pkt-1.TCP. (b) Measured ACF of DEC-pkt-2.TCP. (c) Measured ACF of DEC-pkt-3.TCP. (d) Measured ACF of DEC-pkt-4.TCP.

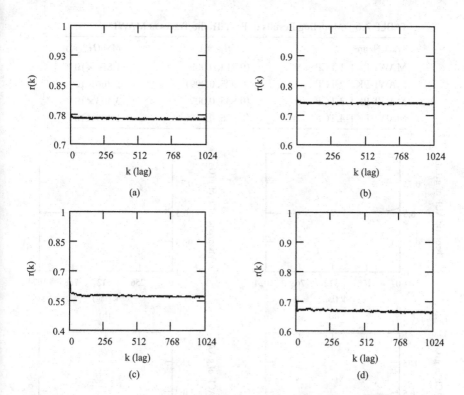

FIGURE 7.6   Illustrations of the measured ACFs of four traces at MAWI in 2019. (a) Measured ACF of MAWI-pkt-1.TCP. (b) Measured ACF of MAWI-pkt-2.TCP. (c) Measured ACF of MAWI-pkt-3.TCP. (d) Measured ACF of MAWI-pkt-4.TCP.

TABLE 7.4   Modeling Results of Four Traffic Traces at BC

Trace Name	(H_{10}, a_0)	$MSE(H_{10}, a_0)$
pAug.TL	(0.830, 0.053)	9.233×10^{-5}
pOct.TL	(0.823, 0.044)	1.535×10^{-4}
OctExt.TL	(0.840, 0.130)	2.513×10^{-4}
OctExt4.TL	(0.870, 0.074)	1.419×10^{-4}

TABLE 7.5   Modeling Results of Four Traffic Traces at DEC

Trace Name	(H_{10}, a_0)	$MSE(H_{10}, a_0)$
DEC-pkt-1.TCP	(0.750, 0.023)	7.946×10^{-5}
DEC-pkt-2.TCP	(0.750, 0.013)	6.924×10^{-5}
DEC-pkt-3.TCP	(0.780, 0.013)	6.322×10^{-5}
DEC-pkt-1.TCP	(0.771, 0.015)	2.135×10^{-5}

TABLE 7.6   Modeling Results of Four Traffic Traces at MAWI

Trace Name	(H_{10}, a_0)	$MSE(H_{10}, a_0)$
MAWI-PKT-1.TCP	(0.914, 0.009)	1.856×10^{-6}
MAWI-PKT-2.TCP	(0.905, 0.009)	5.266×10^{-6}
MAWI-PKT-3.TCP	(0.835, 0.009)	3.403×10^{-5}
MAWI-PKT-4.TCP	(0.876, 0.010)	1.489×10^{-5}

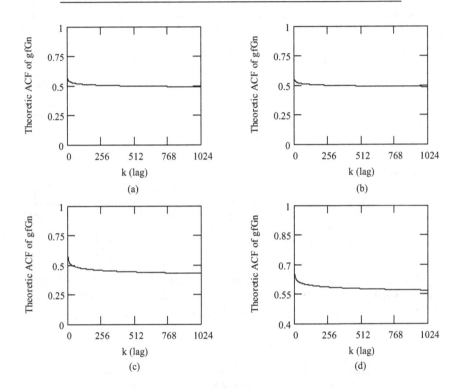

FIGURE 7.7   Plots of the theoretical ACFs of gfGn for four traces at BC. (a) $C_{gfGn}(k; H_{10}, a_0)$ of pAug.TL. (b) $C_{gfGn}(k; H_{10}, a_0)$ of pOct.TL. (c) $C_{gfGn}(k; H_{10}, a_0)$ of OctExt.TL. (d) $C_{gfGn}(k; H_{10}, a_0)$ of OctExt4.TL.

$$\|r(k)\| = \sqrt{\langle r, r \rangle} = \sqrt{\sum_{k=0}^{N-1} |r(k)|}, \qquad (7.25)$$

where N is the block size in computing the ACF estimate and $\langle r, r \rangle$ the inner product of r. Denote by $l_{2, N}$ the space that $r(k)$ belongs to in the form

$$l_{2,N} = \left\{ r(k); \|r(k)\| < \infty \right\}. \qquad (7.26)$$

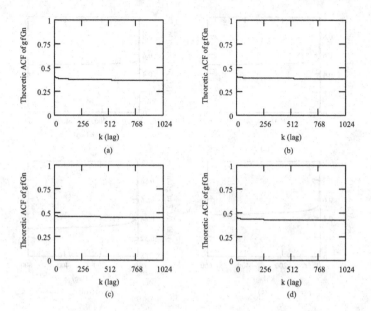

FIGURE 7.8 Plots of the theoretical ACFs of gfGn for four traces at DEC. (a) $C_{gfGn}(k; H_{10}, a_0)$ of DEC-pkt-1.TCP. (b) $C_{gfGn}(k; H_{10}, a_0)$ of DEC-pkt-2.TCP. (c) $C_{gfGn}(k; H_{10}, a_0)$ of DEC-pkt-3.TCP. (d) $C_{gfGn}(k; H_{10}, a_0)$ of DEC-pkt-4.TCP.

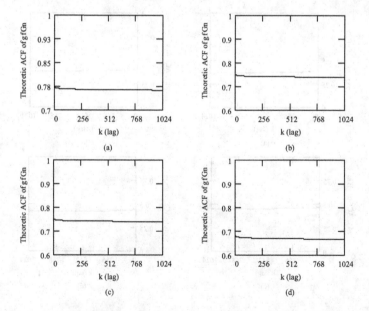

FIGURE 7.9 Plots of the theoretical ACFs of gfGn for four traces at MAWI. (a) $C_{gfGn}(k; H_{10}, a_0)$ of MAWI-pkt-1.TCP. (b) $C_{gfGn}(k; H_{10}, a_0)$ of MAWI-pkt-2.TCP. (c) $C_{gfGn}(k; H_{10}, a_0)$ of MAWI-pkt-3.TCP. (d) $C_{gfGn}(k; H_{10}, a_0)$ of MAWI-pkt-4.TCP.

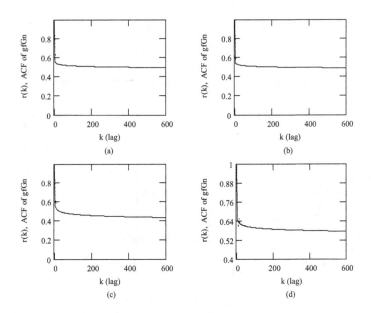

FIGURE 7.10   Plots of fitting the data of four traces at BC. Solid: Theoretic ACF of gfGn. Dot: Measured ACF $r(k)$. (a) pAug.TL. (b) pOct.TL. (c) OctExt.TL. (d) OctExt4.TL.

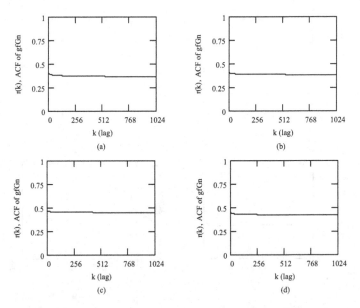

FIGURE 7.11   Plots of fitting the data of four traces at DEC. Solid: Theoretic ACF of gfGn. Dot: Measured ACF $r(k)$. (a) DEC-pkt-1.TCP. (b) DEC-pkt-2.TCP. (c) DEC-pkt-3.TCP. (d) DEC-pkt-4.TCP.

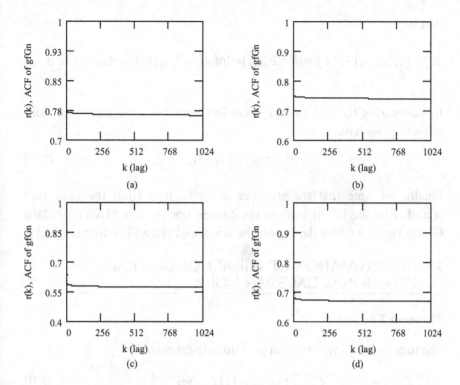

FIGURE 7.12 Plots of fitting the data of four traces at MAWI. Solid: Theoretic ACF of gfGn. Dot: Measured ACF $r(k)$. (a) MAWI-pkt-1.TCP. (b) MAWI-pkt-2. TCP. (c) MAWI-pkt-3.TCP. (d) MAWI-pkt-4.TCP.

Due to the finite block size, $\|r\| < \infty$. Thus, $l_{2, N}$ is an inner product space, moreover, Euclidean, and Hilbert space, accordingly.

Let $\mathbf{B}_{\text{gfGn}}$ be the space that contains the ACFs of gfGn with the same block size as measured ACF r. Thus,

$$\mathbf{B}_{\text{gfGn}} = \left\{ C_{\text{gfGn}}(k); \| C_{\text{gfGn}}(k) \| < \infty \right\}. \tag{7.27}$$

Based on the optimal approximation in Hilbert space (see Chapter 3), for any measured ACF $r(k) \in l_{2, N}$, there exists a unique element $C_{\text{gfGn}}(k; H_0, a_0)$ $\in \mathbf{B}_{\text{gfGn}}$ such that

$$\| C_{\text{gfGn}}(k; H_0, a_0) - r(k) \| = \min, \tag{7.28}$$

that is,

$$\left\| C_{\text{gfGn}}\left(k;H_0,a_0\right)-r(k)\right\| = d\left(r,\mathbf{B}_{\text{gfGn}}\right) = \inf d\left(r,C_{\text{gfGn}}(k)\right) \text{ for } C_{\text{gfGn}}(k) \in \mathbf{B}_{\text{gfGn}}.$$
(7.29)

By comparing the results with those in Chapter 6 with respect to traffic modeling, we have

$$d\left(r,\mathbf{B}_{\text{gfGn}}\right) \leq d\left(r,\mathbf{B}_{\text{fGn}}\right).$$
(7.30)

Finally, we note that the statistics of traffic data from the early data recorded by the BC in 1989 to the current ones by the MAWI Working Group Traffic Archive (Japan) are the same, see Li [8] and Fontugne et al. [9].

7.3 APPROXIMATION OF THE ACF OF GENERALIZED FRACTIONAL GAUSSIAN NOISE

Theorem 7.3

The function $C_{\text{gfGn}}(\tau)$ can be approximately expressed by

$$C_{\text{gfGn}}(\tau) \approx V_H H(2H-1)|\tau|^{2aH-2a}.$$
(7.31)

Proof. The right side of (7.1) is the finite second-order difference of $0.5V_H\left|\tau^a\right|^{2H}$ in terms of τ^a. Approximating it by the second-order difference results in

$$\frac{V_H}{2}\left[\left(\left|\tau^a\right|+1\right)^{2H}+\left\|\tau^a\right|-1\right|^{2H}-2\left|\tau^a\right|^{2H}\right] \approx \frac{\partial^2 0.5V_H\left|\tau^a\right|^{2H(t)}}{\partial\left(\tau^a\right)^2}$$

$$= V_H H(2H-1)\left|\tau^a\right|^{2H-2} = V_H H(2H-1)|\tau|^{2aH-2a}.$$
(7.32)

The proof is finished.

Note that, for $0.5<H<1$, we have

$$\int_{-\infty}^{\infty}\left|\tau^a\right|^{2H-2}d\tau^a = \infty.$$
(7.33)

Thus, the LRD condition of gfGn is $0.5<H<1$.

7.4 FRACTAL DIMENSION OF GENERALIZED FRACTIONAL GAUSSIAN NOISE

Consider the ACF for small lags. When $\tau \to 0$, we have

$$C_{gfGn}(0) - C_{gfGn}(\tau) \sim c|\tau|^{2aH}. \tag{7.34}$$

Thus, the fractal index of gfGn is $2aH$. Let D_{gfGn} and H_{gfGn} be the fractal dimension and the Hurst parameter of gfGn, respectively. Then,

$$D_{gfGn} = 2 - aH_{gfGn}. \tag{7.35}$$

As can be seen from (6.26), D_{fGn} and H_{fGn} are linearly related or coupled. However, D_{gfGn} and H_{gfGn} are coupled with the parameter a. If calling a the coupling factor between D_{gfGn} and H_{gfGn}, the coupling between them is weaker than that between D_{fGn} and H_{fGn} unless $a = 1$.

In the end of this chapter, we summarize the values of the Hurst parameter and the fractional dimension of the traffic traces for the fGn model and gfGn one in Tables 7.7–7.9, respectively. Those exhibit that the fGn model overestimates the LRD of traffic and underestimates the local self-similarity (roughness) of traffic in general.

TABLE 7.7 Summary of H and D of Four Traffic Traces at BC with fGn and gfGn and Comparisons

Trace Name	(H_{fGn}, D_{fGn})	(H_{gfGn}, D_{gfGn})	$H_{fGn} > H_{gfGn}$	$D_{fGn} < D_{gfGn}$
pAug.TL	(0.954, 1.046)	(0.830, 1.956)	Yes	Yes
pOct.TL	(0.960, 1.040)	(0.823, 1.964)	Yes	Yes
OctExt.TL	(0.948, 1.052)	(0.840, 1.891)	Yes	Yes
OctExt4.TL	(0.963, 1.037)	(0.870, 1.936)	Yes	Yes

TABLE 7.8 Summary of H and D of Four Traffic Traces at DEC with fGn and gfGn and Comparisons

Trace Name	(H_{fGn}, D_{fGn})	(H_{gfGn}, D_{gfGn})	$H_{fGn} > H_{gfGn}$	$D_{fGn} < D_{gfGn}$
DEC-pkt-1.TCP	(0.942, 1.058)	(0.750, 1.983)	Yes	Yes
DEC-pkt-2.TCP	(0.937, 1.063)	(0.750, 1.983)	Yes	Yes
DEC-pkt-3.TCP	(0.948, 1.052)	(0.780, 1.990)	Yes	Yes
DEC-pkt-1.TCP	(0.949, 1.051)	(0.771, 1.988)	Yes	Yes

TABLE 7.9   Summary of H and D of Four Traffic Traces at MAWI with fGn and gfGn and Comparisons

Trace Name	(H_{fGn}, D_{fGn})	(H_{gfGn}, D_{gfGn})	$H_{fGn} > H_{gfGn}$	$D_{fGn} < D_{gfGn}$
MAWI-PKT-1.TCP	(0.984, 1.016)	(0.914, 1.992)	Yes	Yes
MAWI-PKT-2.TCP	(0.982, 1.018)	(0.905, 1.992)	Yes	Yes
MAWI-PKT-3.TCP	(0.966, 1.034)	(0.835, 1.992)	Yes	Yes
MAWI-PKT-4.TCP	(0.976, 1.024)	(0.876, 1.991)	Yes	Yes

REFERENCES

1. M. Li, Modeling autocorrelation functions of long-range dependent teletraffic series based on optimal approximation in Hilbert space-a further study, *Appl. Math. Model.*, 31(3) 2007, 625–631.
2. M. Li, Generalized fractional Gaussian noise and its application to traffic modeling, *Phys. A*, 579 2021, 1236137, 22 pp.
3. M. Li, Power spectrum of generalized fractional Gaussian noise, *Adv. Math. Phys.*, 2013 2013, Article ID 315979, 3 p.
4. I. M. Gelfand and K. Vilenkin, *Generalized Functions*; Vol. 1, Academic Press, New York, 1964.
5. P. Danzig, J. Mogul, V. Paxson, and M. Schwartz, The internet traffic archive 2000, Ftp://ita.ee.lbl.gov/traces/ [dataset].
6. The data at MAWI are available via http://mawi.wide.ad.jp/mawi.
7. M. Li, Record length requirement of long-range dependent teletraffic, *Phys. A*, 472 2017, 164–187.
8. M. Li, Long-range dependence and self-similarity of teletraffic with different protocols at the large time scale of day in the duration of 12 years: Autocorrelation modeling, *Phys. Scr.*, 95(4) 2020, 065222, (15 p).
9. R. Fontugne, P. Abry, K. Fukuda, D. Veitch, K. Cho, P. Borgnat, and H. Wendt, Scaling in Internet Traffic: A 14 year and 3 day longitudinal study, with multiscale analyses and random projections, *IEEE/ACM Trans. Netw.*, 25(4) 2017, 2152–2165.

CHAPTER 8

Generalized Cauchy Process and Traffic Modeling

We addressed the fractional Gaussian noise (fGN), the generalized fractional Gaussian noise (gfGn), and their applications to traffic modeling in Chapters 6 and 7, respectively. For either fGn or gfGn, the fractal dimension is coupled with the Hurst parameter. In this chapter, we discuss the generalized Cauchy (GC) process and its application to traffic modeling. A similar point between gfGn and GC process is that both are equipped with two parameters. The difference between the two is that the fractal dimension and the Hurst parameter of the GC model are decoupled. That is the particularity of the GC process model. Conventionally, a GC process designates a process the probability density function (PDF) of which follows the GC's PDF. In this book, the term GC process means that it is a process of the autocorrelation function which obeys the function form of the GC's PDF. We explain the theory of the GC process and its application to traffic modeling in this chapter.

DOI: 10.1201/9781003268802-8

8.1 MEANING OF GENERALIZED CAUCHY PROCESS IN THE BOOK

We rewrite the Cauchy probability density function (PDF) mentioned in Chapter 1 below:

$$p(x) = \frac{1}{\pi \alpha} \frac{1}{1 + \left(\dfrac{x - \xi}{\alpha}\right)^2}, \tag{8.1}$$

where α and ξ are shape and location parameters, respectively. Letting $\alpha = 1$ and $\xi = 1$ yields its simplification in the form

$$p(x) = \frac{1}{\pi} \frac{1}{1 + x^2}. \tag{8.2}$$

When the PDF of x follows (8.1) or (8.2), it is called a Cauchy random function or Cauchy process. There are several generalizations of the standard Cauchy PDF, see e.g., Lubashevsky [1], Konno and Tamura [2], Konno and Watanabe [3], and Lacaze [4]. If x obeys a generalized Cauchy (GC) PDF, it is conventionally called a GC process as can be seen from [1–4].

In geo-statistics, scientists use the function form of the Cauchy PDF for an autocorrelation function (ACF) $r(\tau) = E[x(t)x(t + \tau)]$ so that

$$r(\tau) = \frac{1}{\pi a} \frac{1}{1 + \left(\dfrac{\tau}{a}\right)^2}, \tag{8.3}$$

where a is the scale factor. When the ACF of a random variable x follows the above, it is called a process or random function in the Cauchy family so as to distinguish the Cauchy process based on PDF, see e.g., Chiles and Delfiner [5], Webster and Oliver [6], and Wackernagel [7]. If the ACF of x follows the generalization of the above, for instance,

$$r(\tau) = \frac{1}{\pi a} \frac{1}{1 + \left(\dfrac{\tau}{a}\right)^b}, \quad b > 0, \tag{8.4}$$

It is called a random process in the Cauchy class or the Cauchy class process (Chiles and Delfiner [5]).

In this book, the meaning of a Cauchy process and a generalized one is based on the function form of ACF instead of PDF.

8.2 HISTORICAL VIEW

Without the generality losing, we let $a = 1$ in what follows. The function in (8.4) is a power one with one parameter. In the study of traffic modeling, in June 2000, we generalized it to be an ACF with two parameters in the form

$$r(\tau) = \left(1 + \tau^{\alpha}\right)^{2H-2}, \quad \left(0 < \alpha \le 1, 0.5 < H < 1\right), \tag{8.5}$$

see Li et al. [8, p. 483]. In December 2000, Gneiting [9] proposed his ACF with two parameters in the form

$$r(\tau) = \left(1 + \left|\frac{\tau}{c}\right|^{\alpha}\right)^{-\beta/\alpha}, \quad \left(c > 0, 0 < \alpha \le 2, \beta > 0\right). \tag{8.6}$$

Late in 2004, Gneiting and Schlather wrote the above by

$$r(\tau) = \left(1 + |\tau|^{\alpha}\right)^{-\beta/\alpha}, \quad \left(0 < \alpha \le 2, \beta > 0\right), \tag{8.7}$$

see Gneiting and Schlather [10]. In 2006, the above was written by (Lim and Li [11])

$$r(\tau) = \left(1 + |\tau|^{\alpha}\right)^{-\beta}, \quad \left(0 < \alpha \le 2, \beta > 0\right). \tag{8.8}$$

In what follows, we use (8.7) unless otherwise stated.

8.3 GC PROCESS

Let $x(t)$ be a random process. If its ACF is in the form

$$C_{GC}(\tau) = \psi^2 \left(1 + |\tau|^{\alpha}\right)^{-\beta/\alpha}, \quad \left(0 < \alpha \le 2, \beta > 0\right), \tag{8.9}$$

where ψ^2 is the strength of $x(t)$, it is called GC process (Lim and Li [11], Li and Lim [12], Li [12–16], Li and Li [17]). Without losing the generality, we let $\psi^2 = 1$ in what follows. Thus,

$$C_{GC}(\tau) = \left(1 + |\tau|^{\alpha}\right)^{-\beta/\alpha}, \quad \left(0 < \alpha \le 2, \beta > 0\right). \tag{8.10}$$

Since

$$\lim_{\tau \to \infty} C_{GC}(\tau) = |\tau|^{-\beta}, \tag{8.11}$$

the condition of the GC process to be of long-range dependence (LRD) is

$$0 < \beta < 1. \tag{8.12}$$

Let

$$\beta = 2 - 2H, \tag{8.13}$$

where H is the Hurst parameter. Then, the LRD condition of the GC process is

$$0.5 < H < 1. \tag{8.14}$$

On the other hand, if

$$\beta > 1, \tag{8.15}$$

the GC process is of short-range dependence.

Because $C_{GC}(\tau)$ is sufficiently smooth on $(0, \infty)$ and

$$C_{GC}(0) - C_{GC}(\tau) \sim |\tau|^{\alpha}, \tag{8.16}$$

where α is the fractal index of the GC process (Hall and Roy [18]), the fractal dimension of the GC process is given by

$$D = 2 - \frac{\alpha}{2}. \tag{8.17}$$

Therefore, $C_{GC}(\tau)$ can be rewritten by

$$C_{GC}(\tau) = \left(1 + |\tau|^{4-2D}\right)^{-\frac{1-H}{2-D}}. \tag{8.18}$$

Let $S_{GC}(\omega)$ be the power spectrum density (PSD) of the GC process. Then,

$$S_{GC}(\omega) = \sum_{k=0}^{\infty} \frac{(-1)^k \Gamma\left[\left(\frac{\beta}{\alpha}\right)+k\right]}{\Gamma\left(\frac{\beta}{\alpha}\right)\Gamma(1+k)} I_1(\omega) * Sa(\omega)$$

$$+ \sum_{k=0}^{\infty} \frac{(-1)^k \Gamma\left[\left(\frac{\beta}{\alpha}\right)+k\right]}{\Gamma\left(\frac{\beta}{\alpha}\right)\Gamma(1+k)} \left[\pi I_2(\omega) - I_2(\omega) * Sa(\omega)\right], \quad (8.19)$$

where

$$I_1(\omega) = F\left(|\tau|^{\alpha k}\right) = \int_{-\infty}^{\infty} |\tau|^{\alpha k} e^{-i\omega\tau} \, d\tau,$$

$$I_2(\omega) = F\left[|\tau|^{-(\beta+\alpha k)}\right] = \int_{-\infty}^{\infty} |\tau|^{-(\beta+\alpha k)} e^{-i\omega\tau} \, d\tau, \quad (8.20)$$

$$Sa(\omega) = \frac{\sin\omega}{\omega}.$$

In fact, consider the binomial series for $|x| < 1$ in the form

$$(1+x)^\nu = \sum_{k=0}^{\infty} \binom{\nu}{k} x^k = \sum_{k=0}^{\infty} \frac{\Gamma(\nu+k)}{\Gamma(\nu)\Gamma(1+k)} x^k, \quad (8.21)$$

where ν is a real number and $\binom{\nu}{k}$ is the binomial coefficient. The ACF of the GC process can be expanded as

$$C_{GC}(\tau) = \left\{ \sum_{k=0}^{\infty} \frac{(-1)^k \Gamma\left[(\beta/\alpha)+k\right]}{\Gamma(\beta/\alpha)\Gamma(1+k)} |\tau|^{\alpha k} \right\} \left[u(\tau+1) - u(\tau-1)\right]$$

$$+ \left\{ \sum_{k=0}^{\infty} \frac{(-1)^k \Gamma\left[(\beta/\alpha)+k\right]}{\Gamma(\beta/\alpha)\Gamma(1+k)} |\tau|^{-(\beta+\alpha k)} \right\} \left[u(\tau-1) + u(-\tau-1)\right], \quad (8.22)$$

where $u(\tau)$ is the unit step function. If $|\tau| < 1$, replacing ν and x in (8.21) by $-\beta/\alpha$ and $|\tau|^{\alpha}$, respectively, yields

$$C_{\mathrm{GC}}(\tau) = \left(1+|\tau|^{\alpha}\right)^{-\beta/\alpha} = \sum_{k=0}^{\infty} \frac{(-1)^{k}\,\Gamma\left[(\beta/\alpha)+k\right]}{\Gamma(\beta/\alpha)\Gamma(1+k)}|\tau|^{\alpha k}. \qquad (8.23)$$

Truncating the right side of the above with $[u(\tau + 1) - u(\tau - 1)]$ produces the first term on the right side of (8.22). On the other side, for $|\tau| > 1$, we have

$$C_{\mathrm{GC}}(\tau) = \left(1+|\tau|^{\alpha}\right)^{-\beta/\alpha} = |\tau|^{-\beta}\left(1+|\tau|^{-\alpha}\right)^{-\beta/\alpha}. \qquad (8.24)$$

Thus, when $|\tau| > 1$,

$$C_{\mathrm{GC}}(\tau) = \left\{ \sum_{k=0}^{\infty} \frac{(-1)^{k}\,\Gamma\left[(\beta/\alpha)+k\right]}{\Gamma(\beta/\alpha)\Gamma(1+k)}|\tau|^{-(\beta+\alpha k)} \right\}. \qquad (8.25)$$

Truncating the right side of the above by $\left[u(\tau-1)+u(-\tau-1)\right]$ produces the second term on the right side of (8.22).

Since, for $\lambda \neq -1, -3, \ldots,$

$$\mathrm{F}\left(|t|^{\lambda}\right) = -2\sin\left(\lambda\pi/2\right)\Gamma(\lambda+1)|\omega|^{-\lambda-1}, \qquad (8.26)$$

we have

$$\mathrm{F}\left(|\tau|^{\alpha k}\right) = -2\sin\left(\alpha k\pi/2\right)\Gamma(\alpha k+1)|\omega|^{-\alpha k-1} \triangleq I_1(\omega). \qquad (8.27)$$

Besides,

$$\mathrm{F}\left(|\tau|^{-(\beta+\alpha k)}\right) = 2\sin\left[(\beta+\alpha k)\pi/2\right]\Gamma\left[1-(\beta+\alpha k)\right]|\omega|^{(\beta+\alpha k)-1} \triangleq I_2(\omega). \qquad (8.28)$$

Therefore,

$$F\left\{\left[\sum_{k=0}^{\infty}\frac{(-1)^{k}\Gamma\big[(\beta/\alpha)+k\big]}{\Gamma(\beta/\alpha)\Gamma(1+k)}|\tau|^{\alpha k}\right]\big[u(\tau+1)-u(\tau-1)\big]\right\}$$

$$=\frac{1}{2\pi}\left\{\sum_{k=0}^{\infty}\frac{(-1)^{k}\Gamma\big[(\beta/\alpha)+k\big]}{\Gamma(\beta/\alpha)\Gamma(1+k)}F\big(|\tau|^{\alpha k}\big)\right\}*F\big[u(\tau+1)-u(\tau-1)\big]$$

$$=\left\{\sum_{k=0}^{\infty}\frac{(-1)^{k}\Gamma\big[(\beta/\alpha)+k\big]}{\pi\Gamma(\beta/\alpha)\Gamma(1+k)}I_{1}(\omega)\right\}*\mathrm{Sa}(\omega)$$

$$=\sum_{k=0}^{\infty}\frac{(-1)^{k}\Gamma\big[(\beta/\alpha)+k\big]}{\pi\Gamma(\beta/\alpha)\Gamma(1+k)}I_{1}(\omega)*\mathrm{Sa}(\omega), \qquad (8.29)$$

which is the first term of the right side of (8.19).

On the other side, taking the Fourier transform of the second term on the right side of (8.22) yields

$$F\left\{\left[\sum_{k=0}^{\infty}\frac{(-1)^{k}\Gamma\big[(\beta/\alpha)+k\big]}{\Gamma(\beta/\alpha)\Gamma(1+k)}|\tau|^{-(\beta+\alpha k)}\right]\big[u(\tau-1)+u(-\tau-1)\big]\right\}$$

$$=\frac{1}{2\pi}\left\{\sum_{k=0}^{\infty}\frac{(-1)^{k}\Gamma\big[(\beta/\alpha)+k\big]}{\Gamma(\beta/\alpha)\Gamma(1+k)}F\big[|\tau|^{-(\beta+\alpha k)}\big]\right\}*F\big[u(\tau-1)+u(-\tau-1)\big]$$

$$=\left\{\sum_{k=0}^{\infty}\frac{(-1)^{k}\Gamma\big[(\beta/\alpha)+k\big]}{2\pi\Gamma(\beta/\alpha)\Gamma(1+k)}I_{2}(\omega)\right\}*\big[2\pi\delta(\omega)-2\mathrm{Sa}(\omega)\big]$$

$$=\sum_{k=0}^{\infty}\frac{(-1)^{k}\Gamma\big[(\beta/\alpha)+k\big]}{\pi\Gamma(\beta/\alpha)\Gamma(1+k)}\big[\pi I_{2}(\omega)-I_{2}(\omega)*\mathrm{Sa}(\omega)\big]. \qquad (8.30)$$

The above is the second term on the right side of (8.19) (Li and Lim [19]).

If $\omega \to 0$, we have

$$S_{\mathrm{GC}}(\omega)=\int_{-\infty}^{\infty}|\tau|^{-\beta}e^{-i\omega\tau}\,d\tau=2\sin(\beta\pi/2)\Gamma(1-\beta)|\omega|^{\beta-1}$$

$$=2\sin\big[(H-1)\pi\big]\Gamma(3-2H)|\omega|^{2H-3}, \qquad \omega\to 0. \qquad (8.31)$$

Thus, the GC process $x(t)$ is of LRD when $0.5<H<1$ or $0<\beta<1$. In that case, $S_{GC}(\omega)$ is a type of $1/f$ noise, which reflects the LRD property of the GC process in the frequency domain. The LRD property of the GC process only relies on H or β.

On the other side,

$$S_{GC}(\omega) = \int_{-\infty}^{\infty} \left(1-|\tau|^{\alpha}\right)e^{-i\omega\tau}\,d\tau = 2\pi\delta(\omega) - \int_{-\infty}^{\infty} |\tau|^{\alpha}\,e^{-i\omega\tau}\,d\tau$$

$$= -\int_{-\infty}^{\infty} |\tau|^{\alpha}\,e^{-i\omega\tau}\,d\tau = 2\sin(\alpha\pi/2)\Gamma(\alpha+1)|\omega|^{-\alpha-1}$$

$$= 2\sin\left[(2-D)\pi\right]\Gamma(5-2D)|\omega|^{2D-5}, \quad \omega\to\infty. \tag{8.32}$$

Since $S_{GC}(\omega)$ for $\omega \to \infty$, $\delta(\omega)$ is neglected in the above. As $1\le D<2$, the PSD of the GC process for $\omega \to \infty$ is also a kind of $1/f$ noise but it merely relates to D or α, irrelevant of H.

8.4 TRAFFIC MODELING USING THE GC PROCESS

Using the discrete ACF of the GC process, we write

$$C_{GC}(k) = \left(1+|k|^{\alpha}\right)^{-\beta/\alpha}, \quad (0<\alpha\le 2, \beta>0). \tag{8.33}$$

Alternatively,

$$C_{GC}(k) = \left(1+|k|^{4-2D}\right)^{-\frac{1-H}{2-D}}. \tag{8.34}$$

Use the same three sets of real traffic traces used in Chapters 6 and 7 at the Bellcore (BC) in 1989 (Danzig et al. [20]), the Digital Equipment Corporation (DEC) in 1995 (Danzig et al. [20]), and the MAWI (Measurement and Analysis on the WIDE Internet) in 2019 [21]. The file names of the data at BC are pAug.TL, pOct.TL, Octext.TL, and OctExt4. TL, respectively. The data files at DEC are named DEC-pkt-1.TCP, DEC-pkt-2.TCP, DEC-pkt-3.TCP, and DEC-pkt-4.TCP, respectively. The data files of the traces at MAWI are MAWI-pkt-1.TCP, MAWI-pkt-2.TCP,

MAWI-pkt-3.TCP, and MAWI-pkt-4.TCP, respectively. Tables 8.1–8.3 summarize the data information. The record length of those traces is enough for a satisfied ACF or PSD estimate as explained by Li [15].

Denote by $x(i)$ the packet size of the ith packet ($i = 0, 1,...$). The plots of $x(i)$ at BC are shown in Figure 8.1. Those at DEC are in Figure 8.2, and the plots of data at MAWI are in Figure 8.3.

The computation settings are as follows. Block size L is 2,048 and average counts $N = 30$. Section the series as $x(i)$, $i = (n - 1)(L \times N), ..., n(L \times N)$ for $n = 1, ..., 30$. Denote the measured ACF by $r(k)$. Then, $r(k)$ is the average ACF of all 30 sections. Figures 8.4–8.6 indicate the measured ACFs of three sets of traces.

Since there is a pair of parameters (D, H) in $C_{GC}(k)$. We denote it by $C_{GC}(k; H, D)$. Denote by $M^2 = E\{[C_{GC}(k; H, D) - r(k)]^2\} = \text{MSE}(D, H)$ the mean square error (MSE) of the ACF estimate for $r(k)$. Then,

TABLE 8.1   Four Real Traffic Traces on the Ethernet [20]

Trace Name	Starting Time of Measurement	Duration	Number of Packets
pAug.TL	11:25 AM, 29 Aug 89	52 minutes	1 million
pOct.TL	11:00 AM, 05 Oct 89	29 minutes	1 million
OctExt.TL	11:46 PM, 03 Oct 89	34.111 hours	1 million
OctExt4.TL	2:37 PM, 10 Oct 89	21.095 hours	1 million

TABLE 8.2   Four Wide-Area TCP Traffic Traces at DEC in 1995 [20]

Trace Name	Record Date	Duration	Number of Packets
DEC-pkt-1.TCP	08 Mar 95	10–11 PM	3.3 million
DEC-pkt-2.TCP	08 Mar 95	2–3 AM	3.9 million
DEC-pkt-3.TCP	08 Mar 95	10–11 AM	4.3 million
DEC-pkt-4.TCP	08 Mar 95	2–3 PM	5.7 million

TABLE 8.3   Four Wide-Area TCP Traces Recorded by MAWI in 2019 [21]

Trace Name	Starting Record Time	Duration (Minutes)	Number of Packets
MAWI-pkt-1.TCP	2:00 PM, 18 Apr 2019	6.77208	741,404
MAWI-pkt-2.TCP	2:00 PM, 19 Apr 2019	6.65965	742,638
MAWI-pkt-3.TCP	2:00 PM, 20 Apr 2019	12.55740	482,564
MAWI-pkt-4.TCP	2:00 PM, 21 Apr 2019	12.66541	576,495

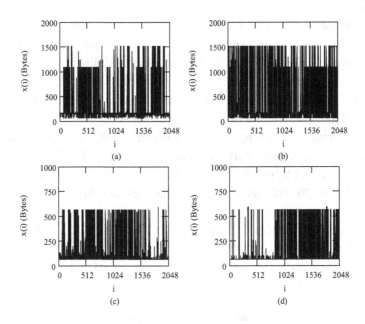

FIGURE 8.1   Plots of traces at BC in 1989. (a) pAug.TL. (b) pOct.TL. (c) OctExt. TL. (d) OctExt4.TL.

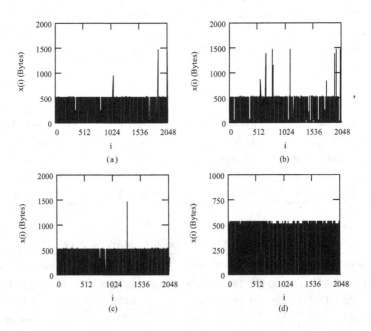

FIGURE 8.2   Plots of traces at DEC in 1995. (a) DEC-pkt-1.TCP. (b) DEC-pkt-2. TCP. (c) DEC-pkt-3.TCP. (d) DEC-pkt-4.TCP.

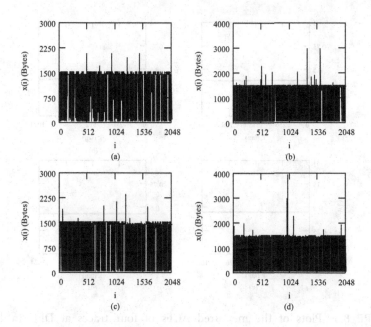

FIGURE 8.3   Plots of traces at MAWI in 2019. (a) MAWI-pkt-1.TCP. (b) MAWI-pkt-2.TCP. (c) MAWI-pkt-3.TCP. (d) MAWI-pkt-4.TCP.

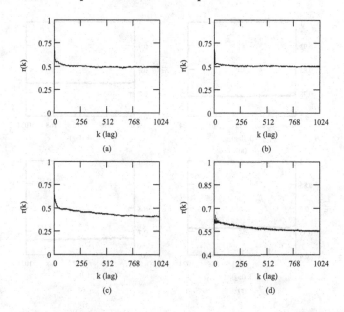

FIGURE 8.4   Illustrations of the measured ACFs of four traces at BC in 1989. (a) Measured ACF of pAug.TL. (b) Measured ACF of pOct.TL. (c) Measured ACF of OctExt.TL. (d) Measured ACF of OctExt4.TL.

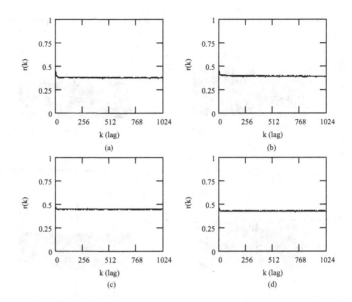

FIGURE 8.5 Plots of the measured ACFs of four traces at DEC in 1995.
(a) Measured ACF of DEC-pkt-1.TCP. (b) Measured ACF of DEC-pkt-2.TCP.
(c) Measured ACF of DEC-pkt-3.TCP. (d) Measured ACF of DEC-pkt-4.TCP.

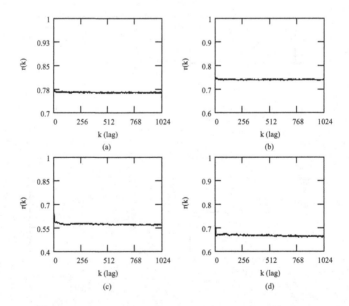

FIGURE 8.6 Plots of the measured ACFs of four traces at MAWI in 2019.
(a) Measured ACF of MAWI-pkt-1.TCP. (b) Measured ACF of MAWI-pkt-2.TCP.
(c) Measured ACF of MAWI-pkt-3.TCP. (d) Measured ACF of MAWI-pkt-4.TCP.

$$\frac{\partial \mathrm{MSE}(D,H)}{\partial D} = 0,$$

$$\frac{\partial \mathrm{MSE}(D,H)}{\partial H} = 0,$$

(8.35)

yields a pair of values (D_0, H_0), corresponding to $\mathrm{MSE}(D_0, H_0)$, which is the minimum of M^2, so that $C_{\mathrm{GC}}(k; D_0, H_0)$ best fits $r(k)$. Tables 8.4–8.6 list the modeling results for three sets of traces, respectively.

Figures 8.7–8.9 indicate the illustrations of $C_{\mathrm{GC}}(k; D_0, H_0)$ of four traces. Fitting the data is shown in Figures 8.10–8.12. The results exhibit that MSE for the test traces is in the magnitude order 10^{-4}–10^{-6}, much better than the fractional Gaussian noise (fGn) model described in Chapter 6.

We study the modeling in Hilbert space. Define the norm of measured ACF by

$$\|r(k)\| = \sqrt{\langle r, r \rangle} = \sqrt{\sum_{k=0}^{N-1} |r(k)|},$$

(8.36)

TABLE 8.4   Modeling Results of Four Real Traffic Traces at BC

Trace Name	(D_0, H_0)	MSE (D_0, H_0)
pAug.TL	(1.825, 0.725)	8.411×10^{-4}
pOct.TL	(1.939, 0.875)	6.352×10^{-4}
OctExt.TL	(1.900, 0.920)	2.726×10^{-4}
OctExt4.TL	(1.961, 0.966)	9.933×10^{-4}

TABLE 8.5   Modeling Results of Four Traffic Traces at DEC

Trace Name	(D_0, H_0)	MSE (D_0, H_0)
DEC-pkt-1.TCP	(1.988, 0.985)	6.093×10^{-5}
DEC-pkt-2.TCP	(1.988, 0.985)	3.629×10^{-5}
DEC-pkt-3.TCP	(1.944, 0.993)	5.283×10^{-5}
DEC-pkt-1.TCP	(1.944, 0.993)	1.825×10^{-5}

TABLE 8.6   Modeling Results of Four Traffic Traces at MAWI

Trace Name	(D_0, H_0)	MSE (D_0, H_0)
MAWI-PKT-1.TCP	(1.995, 0.998)	1.660×10^{-6}
MAWI-PKT-2.TCP	(1.995, 0.998)	9.083×10^{-6}
MAWI-PKT-3.TCP	(1.995, 0.998)	2.436×10^{-6}
MAWI-PKT-4.TCP	(1.995, 0.997)	1.531×10^{-5}

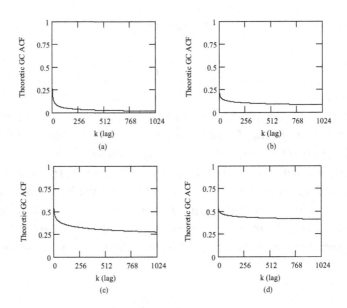

FIGURE 8.7 Plots of the theoretical GC ACFs for four traces. (a) $C_{GC}(k; D_0, H_0)$ of pAug.TL. (b) $C_{GC}(k; D_0, H_0)$ of pOct.TL. (c) $C_{GC}(k; D_0, H_0)$ of OctExt.TL. (d) $C_{GC}(k; D_0, H_0)$ of OctExt4.TL.

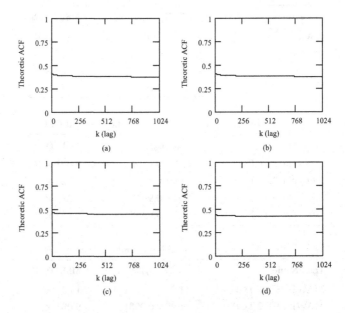

FIGURE 8.8 Plots of the theoretical ACFs of GC for four traces at DEC. (a) $C_{GC}(k; D_0, H_0)$ of DEC-pkt-1.TCP. (b) $C_{GC}(k; D_0, H_0)$ of DEC-pkt-2.TCP. (c) $C_{GC}(k; D_0, H_0)$ of DEC-pkt-3.TCP. (d) $C_{GC}(k; D_0, H_0)$ of DEC-pkt-4.TCP.

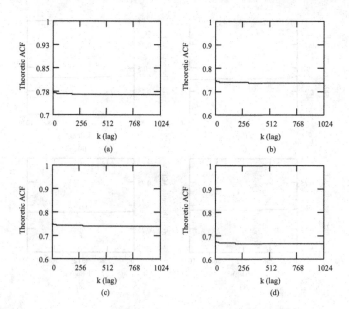

FIGURE 8.9 Plots of the theoretical GC ACFs for four traces at MAWI. (a) $C_{GC}(k;\ D_0, H_0)$ of MAWI-pkt-1.TCP. (b) $C_{GC}(k;\ D_0, H_0)$ of MAWI-pkt-2.TCP. (c) $C_{GC}(k;\ D_0, H_0)$ of MAWI-pkt-3.TCP. (d) $C_{GC}(k;\ D_0, H_0)$ of MAWI-pkt-4.TCP.

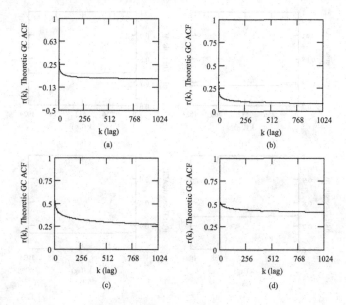

FIGURE 8.10 Plots of fitting the data of four traces at BC. Solid: Theoretic GC ACF. Dot: Measured ACF $r(k)$. (a) pAug.TL. (b) pOct.TL. (c) OctExt.TL. (d) OctExt4.TL.

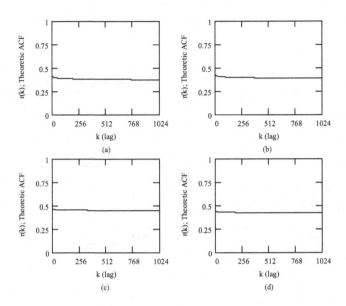

FIGURE 8.11   Plots of fitting the data of four traces at DEC. Solid: Theoretic GC ACF. Dot: Measured ACF $r(k)$. (a) DEC-pkt-1.TCP. (b) DEC-pkt-2.TCP. (c) DEC-pkt-3.TCP. (d) DEC-pkt-4.TCP.

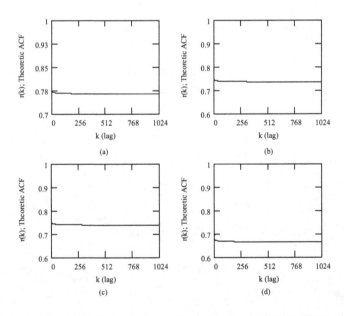

FIGURE 8.12   Plots of fitting the data of four traces at MAWI. Solid: Theoretic GC ACF. Dot: Measured ACF $r(k)$. (a) MAWI-pkt-1.TCP. (b) MAWI-pkt-2.TCP. (c) MAWI-pkt-3.TCP. (d) MAWI-pkt-4.TCP.

where N is the block size in computing the ACF estimate and $<r, r>$ is the inner product of r. Denote by $l_{2,N}$ the space that $r(k)$ belongs to in the form

$$l_{2,N} = \{r(k); \|r(k)\| < \infty\}. \tag{8.37}$$

Due to the finite block size, $\|r\| < \infty$ is a consequence. Thus, $l_{2,N}$ is an inner product space, moreover, Euclidean, and Hilbert space, accordingly.

Let $\mathbf{B}_{GC}$ be the space that contains the ACFs of the GC process with the same block size as measured ACF r. Thus,

$$\mathbf{B}_{GC} = \{C_{GC}(k); \|C_{GC}(k)\| < \infty\}. \tag{8.38}$$

Based on the optimal approximation in Hilbert space (see Chapter 3), for any measured ACF $r(k) \in l_{2,N}$, there exists a unique element $C_{GC}(k; D_0, H_0) \in \mathbf{B}_{GC}$ such that

$$\|C_{GC}(k; D_0, H_0) - r(k)\| = \min, \tag{8.39}$$

that is,

$$\|C_{GC}(k; D_0, H_0) - r(k)\| = d(r, \mathbf{B}_{GC}) = \inf d(r, C_{GC}(k)) \tag{8.40}$$
$$\text{for } C_{GC}(k) \in \mathbf{B}_{GC}.$$

By comparing the results with those in Chapter 6 for traffic modeling using fGn, we see that

$$d(r, \mathbf{B}_{GC}) \leq d(r, \mathbf{B}_{fGn}). \tag{8.41}$$

The statistics of traffic data from the early data recorded by the BC in 1989 to the current ones by the MAWI Working Group Traffic Archive (Japan) remain the same, see Li [16] and Fontugne et al. [22]. Finally, we note that Li [23] described the above results and compared them with those using the models of fGn and GC with the approximation in Hilbert space. The values of H and D based on the fGn model and GC one and the comparisons are summarized in Tables 8.7–8.9. These tables suggest that $D_{fGn} < D_{GC}$ for three sets of traces. That is obvious because the fGn

TABLE 8.7   Summary of H and D of Four Traffic Traces at BC with fGn and GC and Comparisons

Trace Name	(H_{fGn}, D_{fGn})	(H_{GC}, D_{GC})	$H_{fGn} > H_{GC}$	$D_{fGn} < D_{GC}$
pAug.TL	(0.954, 1.046)	(0.725, 1.825)	Yes	Yes
pOct.TL	(0.960, 1.040)	(0.875, 1.939)	Yes	Yes
OctExt.TL	(0.948, 1.052)	(0.900, 1.920)	Yes	Yes
OctExt4.TL	(0.963, 1.037)	(0.961, 1.966)	Yes	Yes

TABLE 8.8   Summary of H and D of Four Traffic Traces at DEC with fGn and GC and Comparisons

Trace Name	(H_{fGn}, D_{fGn})	(H_{GC}, D_{GC})	$H_{fGn} > H_{GC}$	$D_{fGn} < D_{GC}$
DEC-pkt-1.TCP	(0.942, 1.058)	(0.985, 1.988)	No	Yes
DEC-pkt-2.TCP	(0.937, 1.063)	(0.985, 1.983)	No	Yes
DEC-pkt-3.TCP	(0.948, 1.052)	(0.993, 1.994)	No	Yes
DEC-pkt-1.TCP	(0.949, 1.051)	(0.993, 1.994)	No	Yes

TABLE 8.9   Summary of H and D of Four Traffic Traces at MAWI with fGn and GC and Comparisons

Trace Name	(H_{fGn}, D_{fGn})	(H_{GC}, D_{GC})	$H_{fGn} > H_{GC}$	$D_{fGn} < D_{GC}$
MAWI-PKT-1.TCP	(0.984, 1.016)	(0.998, 1.995)	No	Yes
MAWI-PKT-2.TCP	(0.982, 1.018)	(0.998, 1.995)	No	Yes
MAWI-PKT-3.TCP	(0.966, 1.034)	(0.998, 1.995)	No	Yes
MAWI-PKT-4.TCP	(0.976, 1.024)	(0.997, 1.995)	No	Yes

model underestimates the local self-similarity (roughness) of traffic. For the traces at BC, we have $H_{fGn} > H_{GC}$. However, $H_{fGn} < H_{GC}$ is for the traces at DEC and MAWI.

REFERENCES

1. A. Lubashevsky, Truncated Lévy flights and generalized Cauchy processes, *Eur. Phys. J. B*, 82(2) 2011, 189–195.
2. H. Konno and Y. Tamura, A generalized Cauchy process having cubic non-linearity, *Rep. Math. Phys.*, 67(2) 2011, 179–195.
3. H. Konno and F. Watanabe, Maximum likelihood estimators for generalized Cauchy processes, *J. Math. Phys.*, 48(10) 2007, 103303, 19 p.
4. B. Lacaze, A stochastic model for propagation through tissue, *IEEE Trans. Ultrason. Ferroelectr. Freq. Control*, 56(10) 2009, 2180–2186.
5. J.-P. Chiles and P. Delfiner, *Geostatistics, Modeling Spatial Uncertainty*, Wiley, New York, 1999.

6. R. Webster and M. A. Oliver, *Geostatistics for Environmental Scientists*, Wiley, Chichester, 2007.
7. H. Wackernagel, *Multivariate Geostatistics: An Introduction with Applications*, 3rd. Edition, Springer Netherlands, 2005.
8. M. Li, W. Jia, and W. Zhao, A whole correlation structure of asymptotically self-similar traffic in communication networks, *Proc., IEEE WISE'2000*, 19–20 June 2000, Hong Kong, 461–466.
9. T. Gneiting, Power-law correlations, related models for long-range dependence and their simulation, *J. Appl. Prob.*, 37(4) Dec. 2000, 1104–1109.
10. T. Gneiting and M. Schlather, Stochastic models that separate fractal dimension and Hurst effect, *SIAM Rev.*, 46(2) 2004, 269–282.
11. S. C. Lim and M. Li, A generalized Cauchy process and its application to relaxation phenomena, *J. Phys. A: Math. General*, 39(12) 2006, 2935–2951.
12. M. Li and S. C. Lim, Modeling network traffic using generalized Cauchy process, *Phys. A*, 387(11) 2008, 2584–2594.
13. M. Li, Generation of teletraffic of generalized Cauchy type, *Phys. Scr.*, 81(2) 2010, 025007 (10 p).
14. M. Li, Fractal time series — A tutorial review, *Math. Prob. Eng.*, 2010 2010, Article ID 157264, 26 p, doi:10.1155/2010/157264.
15. M. Li, Record length requirement of long-range dependent teletraffic, *Phys. A*, 472 2017, 164–187.
16. M. Li, Long-range dependence and self-similarity of teletraffic with different protocols at the large time scale of day in the duration of 12 years: Autocorrelation modeling, *Phys. Scr.*, 95(4) 2020, 065222, (15 p).
17. M. Li and J.-Y. Li, Generalized Cauchy model of sea level fluctuations with long-range dependence, *Phys. A*, 484 2017, 309–335.
18. P. Hall and R. Roy, On the relationship between fractal dimension and fractal index for stationary stochastic processes, *Ann. Appl. Probab.*, 4(1) 1994, 241–253.
19. M. Li and S. C. Lim, Power spectrum of generalized Cauchy process, *Telecommun. Syst.*, 43(3–4) 2010, 219–222.
20. P. Danzig, J. Mogul, V. Paxson, and M. Schwartz, The internet traffic archive, 2000, Ftp://ita.ee.lbl.gov/traces/ [dataset].
21. The data at MAWI are available via http://mawi.wide.ad.jp/mawi.
22. R. Fontugne, P. Abry, K. Fukuda, D. Veitch, K. Cho, P. Borgnat, and H. Wendt, Scaling in Internet traffic: A 14 year and 3 day longitudinal study, with multiscale analyses and random projections, *IEEE/ACM Trans. Netw.*, 25(4) 2017, 2152–2165.
23. M. Li, Evidence of a two-parameter correlation of Internet traffic, in *Internet Policies and Issues*, Volume 8, B. G. Kutais, editor, Nova Science Publishers, New York, 2011, pp. 103–140.

CHAPTER 9

Traffic Bound of Generalized Cauchy Type

In Chapters 6–8, we addressed three stochastic models for traffic modeling. Stochastic models are needed in some applications, such as the infrastructure design of computer communication networks. However, stochastic models are not enough in real-time communications, such as admission control or traffic delay, where the computations of traffic must be run in a split second. In those cases, the model of autocorrelation function or power spectrum density is too complicated. Hence, a traffic model with simple computations is greatly desired. In the field, according to the theory of network calculus, bounded models of traffic are promising. Purely from a view of mathematics, it is easy to describe a bound of traffic because the inequality $x(t) < B$ always holds as long as B is sufficiently large. The difficulty in the aspect of bounding models of traffic is to find a tight traffic bound so that it may be accepted by researchers in the community of computer communications. In this chapter, we introduce a traffic bound of the generalized Cauchy (GC) type. It is tighter than the conventional bound by taking into account the fractal dimension and the Hurst parameter based on the GC model of traffic.

DOI: 10.1201/9781003268802-9

9.1 PROBLEM STATEMENTS AND RESEARCH AIM

There are two tracks on traffic modeling. One is about statistical models as some of them are discussed in Chapters 6–8. The other is about bounded models, see e.g., Li and Borgnat [1] and Michiel and Laevens [2]. Statistical models are desired in the performance analysis of network systems (Tsybakov and Georganas [3], Masugi and Takuma [4]), traffic pattern monitoring (Li [5,6]), and so on. In some applications, however, statistical models may be very difficult, if not impossible, to be used. For instance, when performing admission control of whether to accept or reject a connection request, one has to make a decision as quickly as possible. Consequently, a simple model for that purpose is demanded. That is a reason why a traffic bound is taken as a traffic model in the field of computer science. Another crucial application of bounded models of traffic is in the aspect of guaranteed traffic delay in real-time communications.

Note that a server serves arrival traffic on an interval-by-interval basis. Therefore, from a viewpoint of serve performance of a server, one is interested in accumulated traffic. Let $x(t)$ be an instantaneous traffic time series. Denote by $X(t)$ the accumulated traffic in the time interval $[0, t]$. Then,

$$X(t) = \int_0^t x(t)dt. \qquad (9.1)$$

A server serves $X(t)$ rather than $x(t)$ (McDysan [7], Stalling [8], Thomopoulos [9]).

A well-known traffic bound was proposed by Cruz [10]. It is given by

$$X(t) = \int_0^t x(t)dt \le \sigma + \rho t, \qquad (9.2)$$

where is σ a burstiness measure of $X(t)$. It is in the form

$$\lim_{t \to 0} X(t) = \lim_{t \to 0} \int_0^t x(t)dt \le \sigma. \qquad (9.3)$$

Another parameter ρ is a measure of the long-term average rate of $X(t)$. It is expressed by

$$\lim_{t \to \infty} \frac{X(t)}{t} = \lim_{t \to \infty} \frac{1}{t} \int_0^t x(t) dt \le \rho. \qquad (9.4)$$

Locally, i.e., for small t, the statistics of $X(t)$ is similar to that of $x(t)$. Globally, i.e., for large t, the statistics of $X(t)$ is asymptotically similar to that of $x(t)$ due to the local self-similarity and globally asymptotical self-similarity of traffic. However, using a pair of quantities (σ, ρ), $X(t)$ is modeled by a bound in the form

$$X(t) \le \sigma + \rho t. \qquad (9.5)$$

The pair (σ, ρ) is termed traffic shaper (Cruz [10]). Whatever $X(t)$ is, one replaces $X(t)$ with its bound $\sigma + \rho t$. Thus, if the service quality of $\sigma + \rho t$ can be assured, the service quality of $X(t)$ is guaranteed, accordingly.

For facilitating the discussions, we call (σ, ρ) of traffic Cruz bound. The key advantage of Cruz bound is its simplicity. It is only with two parameters. Whatever length of $X(t)$ is, one can quickly estimate its model (σ, ρ). Such an advantage is based on the sacrifice of more network resources. As a matter of fact, when a server services $\sigma + \rho t$ instead of $X(t)$, more resources are consumed. If we consider the end-to-end transmission of $X(t)$, at the input port of each server, we have to assign more resources for each arrival traffic at each input of a server along the end-to-end transmission line. The total sacrificed resources may be large such that such a strategy of traffic modeling may be physically unacceptable. This is a bottleneck of using Cruz bound in practice.

In order to relieve the bottleneck, people tried to find a bound that is tighter than the Cruz one. Note that another advantage of Cruz bound is that it is irrelevant to the statistics of $X(t)$. Methodologically, however, that advantage is also its defect because it abandons the appropriate use of the statistics of $X(t)$ to achieve a tighter bound of $X(t)$ with less resources sacrificed. By taking into account statistics, a probability bound of $X(t)$ was proposed by Parekh and Gallager [11] and Yaron and Sidi [12]. It is given by

$$\Pr \left\{ \int_0^t x(u) du \ge \sigma + \rho t \right\} \le A e^{-v\sigma}, \qquad (9.6)$$

where A and v are positive constants, $\Pr(\cdot)$ is a probability density function.

The above bound does not take the fractal properties of traffic into account, namely, the fractal dimension D and the Hurst parameter H. Therefore, its practical use cannot but be purely academic. In addition, the above takes into account a loosened bound $\sigma + \rho t$ so that the probability of $X(t) \geq \sigma + \rho t$ may be overestimated.

Mathematically, since $\max[\Pr(\cdot)] = 1$ and $\max[\exp(-\nu\sigma)] = 1$, the quantity A is unnecessary. In order to solve that problem, the following was presented (Starobinski and Sidi [13])

$$\Pr\left\{\int_s^t x(u)\,du \geq \sigma + \rho(t-s)\right\} \leq f(\sigma), \tag{9.7}$$

where $f(\sigma)$ is an abstract function in terms of σ. Nevertheless, it also considers the probability regarding $X(t) \geq \sigma + \rho t$. In order to improve Cruz bound, Li and Knightly [14] suggested a probability bound without the relation to (σ, ρ). It is given by

$$\Pr\left\{X(t+\tau) - X(t) \leq G^\delta(\tau)\right\} > 1 - \delta, \tag{9.8}$$

where $G^\delta(\tau)$ is an abstract function. Since its function form is unknown and it is unrelated to D and H of $X(t)$, its practical application is merely academic.

Our aim in this chapter is to introduce a bound of $X(t)$ by taking D and H into account for the purpose of tightening the Cruz bound.

9.2 UPPER BOUND OF THE GENERALIZED CAUCHY PROCESS

Let $x(t)$ be a GC random variable. Denote by $C_{GC}(\tau)$ its autocorrelation function (ACF). Then, with probability one, we have

$$\lim_{\tau \to \infty} C_{GC}(\tau) = |\tau|^{2H-2}. \tag{9.9}$$

On the other hand, with probability one,

$$C_{GC}(0) - C_{GC}(\tau) \sim |\tau|^{4-2D}. \tag{9.10}$$

Denote by ν the index of local self-similarity of $x(t)$. For $0 < \nu \leq 2$, it is given by

$$x(rt_0)-x(t)=r^v[x(t_0)-x(t)], \quad |t_0-t|\to 0, \tag{9.11}$$

see Lim and Li [15, p. 2937]. We call the above quantity r small-scale factor since the above equation is in the case of $|t_0-t| \to 0$. A less common description of the above is equivalently described as follows. A Gaussian stationary process is said to be locally self-similar of order v if its ACF $C_{GC}(t) = \text{cov}\{x(0), x(t)\}$ satisfies, for $t \to 0$,

$$C_{GC}(t)=1-A|t|^v\left[1+O\left(|t|^\alpha\right)\right], \tag{9.12}$$

where $A>0$ and $\alpha>0$, see Chan et al. [16], Kent and Wood [17], and Hall and Wood [18]. Thus, v characterizes the local behavior of traffic and so does D, where

$$D=2-v/2. \tag{9.13}$$

Theorem 9.1

Let $x(t)$ be the locally self-similar random function of index v. Then, its burstiness bound can be represented by $r^{-v-1}\sigma$.

Proof: In the case of $t \to 0_+$, according to (9.11), one has

$$\int_0^t [x(ru)-x(u_0)]du = \int_0^t r^v[x(u)-x(u_0)]du$$

$$= \int_0^t \left\{[r^v x(u)]-r^v[x(u_0)]\right\}du$$

$$= \int_0^t r^v x(u)du - \int_0^t r^v x(u_0)du. \tag{9.14}$$

Because $r^v x(u_0)$ and $x(ru_0)$ are constants, we have, for $t \to 0_+$,

$$\int_0^t r^v x(u_0)du=0, \quad \int_0^t x(ru_0)du=0. \tag{9.15}$$

Therefore, we have

$$\int_0^t x(ru)\,du = \int_0^t r^v x(u)\,du. \tag{9.16}$$

The above implies

$$\int_0^t x(u)\,du = r^{-v}\int_0^t x(ru)\,du = r^{-v-1}\int_0^t x(ru)\,d(ru). \tag{9.17}$$

When $t \to 0_+$, we have

$$\int_0^{0+} x(u)\,du = r^{-v-1}\int_0^{0+} x(ru)\,d(ru) \le r^{-v-1}\sigma. \tag{9.18}$$

Thus, we write

$$\int_0^{0+} x(u)\,du \le r^{2D-5}\sigma \triangleq \sigma'. \tag{9.19}$$

This finishes the proof.

Denote two real numbers by $a > 0$ and $0 < H < 1$. If $x(t)$ is such that it has the same statistical distribution with $a^{-H}x(at)$ for all $t > 0$, we say that $x(t)$ is a self-similar series with the self-similar degree H. This is written by

$$x(t) =_d a^{-H}x(at),\ t > 0, \tag{9.20}$$

where $=_d$ denotes equality in joint finite distribution and a is a large-scale factor.

Theorem 9.2

For large t, the bound of the long-term average rate of traffic can be represented by $a^{-H}\rho$.

Proof: Taking into account long-range dependence (LRD) that is a global property of a time series, σ is neglected for large t. In this case, according to (9.20), we have

$$\lim_{t \to \infty} \frac{\int_0^t x(u)\,du}{t} = a^{-H} \lim_{t \to \infty} \frac{\int_0^t x(au)\,du}{t}. \qquad (9.21)$$

On the other hand, following (9.4), we have

$$a^{-H} \lim_{t \to \infty} \frac{\int_0^t x(au)\,du}{t} = a^{-H} \lim_{t \to \infty} \frac{\int_0^t x(au)\,dau}{at} \leq a^{-H}\rho \triangleq \rho'. \qquad (9.22)$$

This completes the proof.

Theorem 9.3

Let $x(t)$ be a traffic series. Let D and H be its fractional dimension and the Hurst parameter, respectively. For $r \geq 1$ and $a \geq 1$, the following holds,

$$\int_0^t x(u)\,du = X(t) \leq r^{2D-5}\sigma + a^{-H}\rho. \qquad (9.23)$$

Proof: According to Theorem 9.1, we have

$$\int_0^{0+} x(u)\,du \leq r^{2D-5}\sigma.$$

On the other side, following (9.21) and (9.22), we have

$$\int_{0+}^t x(u)\,du \leq a^{-H}\rho t. \qquad (9.24)$$

Since

$$\int\limits_{0}^{t} x(u)\,du = \int\limits_{0}^{0_+} x(u)\,du + \int\limits_{0_+}^{t} x(u)\,du, \tag{9.25}$$

we have (9.23). The proof completes.

From Theorem 9.3, one may write the bound of $X(t)$ by

$$\int\limits_{0}^{t} x(u)\,du = X(t) \leq \sigma' + \rho' = r^{2D-5}\sigma + a^{-H}\rho, \tag{9.26}$$

where σ' and ρ' are expressed by (9.19) and (9.22), respectively. We write

$$\sigma' = \sigma'(\sigma, r, D),$$
$$\rho' = \rho'(\rho, a, H). \tag{9.27}$$

Theorem 9.1 implies that the burstiness bound σ' relates to D that characterizes the local self-similarity (irregularity) of traffic and r that is a small-time scale from a fractal view. Theorem 9.2 explains that the bound of the long-term average rate ρ' relates to H that is used to measure the LRD and a that is a large-time scale of traffic in fractal.

For facilitating the discussions, we call $\sigma' + \rho'$ Li's bound of traffic $X(t)$. It is tighter than the Cruz one in general. Note that the case $r=1$ or $a=1$ is trivial. The selected value of r is greater than 1. Since a is a large-scale factor, it may be selected to be much greater than 1. For example, assume $D=1.8$, $H=0.8$, $r=2$, and $a=10$. Then,

$$\sigma' = \sigma'(\sigma;1.8,2) = 0.379\sigma,$$
$$\rho' = \rho'(\rho;0.8,10) = 0.158\rho. \tag{9.28}$$

The above example exhibits that the present bound (σ', ρ') can be used to flexibly tighten the Cruz one (σ, ρ). We note that Cruz bound (σ, ρ) is a special case of Li's (σ', ρ') because $\sigma'(\sigma;H,1) = \sigma$ and $\rho'(\rho;D,1) = \rho$.

9.3 DISCUSSIONS

Note that the traffic bound (9.5), i.e., (σ, ρ), was introduced by Cruz from the point of view of physics instead of mathematics. To be precise, Cruz used a pair of parameters (σ, ρ) to force the bound of (9.5) on $X(t)$. Therefore, in the field, the Cruz bound (9.5) is often called the traffic shaper. In this chapter, however, the derivation of Li's bound (9.23) or (9.26) takes the Cruz one (9.5) as a mathematical bound of $X(t)$. Therefore, I have to present a proof that (9.5) is also a mathematical bound of $X(t)$. There are a number of methods of proof. One is given as follows.

Consider $x(t)$ be the packet size, e.g., the packet data length, at t. Let x_{min} and x_{max} be the minimum size and maximum one of a packet, respectively. Both are restricted by protocols and IEEE standard. Thus, for traffic series $x(t)$, there is an inequality in the form $0 \leq x_{min} \leq x(t) \leq x_{max}$. Therefore, for any traffic $x(t)$, we have

$$\int_0^t x(t)dt = \int_0^{0+} x(t)dt + \int_{0+}^t x(t)dt. \tag{9.29}$$

Besides,

$$\int_{0+}^t x(t)dt \leq \int_0^t x_{max}\,dt = x_{max}t. \tag{9.30}$$

In addition, for any $\sigma \geq 0$, it is obvious that

$$\int_0^{0+} x(t)dt \leq \sigma. \tag{9.31}$$

When denoting x_{max} by ρ in (9.30), therefore, we have

$$\int_0^t x(t)dt = \int_0^{0+} x(t)dt + \int_{0+}^t x(t)dt \leq \sigma + \rho t. \tag{9.32}$$

The above proves that (9.5) is a mathematical bound of $X(t)$.

Note the above implies that the traffic shaper (9.5) proposed by Cruz in [10] happens to be a mathematical bound of $X(t)$. The advance of Li's bound is that it is tighter than the Cruz one by taking into account D and H of $x(t)$. However, there is a mathematical problem explained below with respect to either Cruz bound or Li's bound.

Because of $0 \leq x(t) \leq x_{max}$, $x(t) \neq \delta(t)$, where $\delta(t)$ is the delta function.

Thus, it is quite natural to see that $\int_{0}^{0_+} x(t)dt = 0$ according to any theory of integrals. However, (9.31) is never trivial. On the contrary, it is critically important to characterize the local property of $X(t)$ in the field of traffic engineering and theory. How to explain the burstiness bound (9.31) is a challenging problem.

Given a traffic series $x(t)$, its D and H are known. However, how to determine the values of (σ', ρ') in Li's bound is an open problem [19]. The author will give a solution to it in Chapter 11.

REFERENCES

1. M. Li and P. Borgnat, Foreword to the special issue on traffic modeling, its computations and applications, *Telecommun. Syst.*, 43(3-4) 2010, 145-146.
2. H. Michiel and K. Laevens, Teletraffic engineering in a broad-band era, *Proc. IEEE*, 85(12) 1997, 2007-2033.
3. B. Tsybakov and N. D. Georganas, Self-similar traffic and upper bounds to buffer-overflow probability in an ATM queue, *Perform. Eval.*, 32(1) 1998, 57-80.
4. M. Masugi and T. Takuma, Multi-fractal analysis of IP-network traffic for assessing time variations in scaling properties, *Phys. D*, 225(2) 2007, 119-126.
5. M. Li, An approach to reliably identifying signs of DDOS flood attacks based on LRD traffic pattern recognition, *Comput. Secur.*, 23(7) 2004, 549-558.
6. M. Li, Change trend of averaged Hurst parameter of traffic under DDOS flood attacks, *Comput. Secur.*, 25(3) 2006, 213-220.
7. D. McDysan, *QoS & Traffic Management in IP & ATM Networks*, McGraw-Hill, New York, 2000.
8. W. Stallings, *Data and Computer Communications*, 7th Ed., Macmillan, New York, 2006.
9. N. T. Thomopoulos, *Fundamentals of Queuing Systems*, Springer, New York, 2012.
10. L. Cruz, A calculus for network delay, Part I: Network elements in isolation; Part II: Network analysis, *IEEE Trans. Inform. Theory*, 37(1) 1991, 114-131, 132-141.
11. A. K. Parekh and R. G. Gallager, A generalized processor sharing approach to flow control in integrated services networks-the single-node case, *IEEE/ACM Trans. Net.*, 1(3) 1993, 344-357.
12. O. Yaron and M. Sidi, Performance and stability of communication networks via robust exponential bounds, *IEEE/ACM Trans. Net.*, 1(3) 1993, 372-385.

13. D. Starobinski and M. Sidi, Stochastically bounded burstiness for communication networks, *IEEE Trans. Inform. Theor.*, 46(1) 2000, 206–212.
14. C. Li and E. Knightly, Schedulability criterion and performance analysis of coordinated schedulers, *IEEE/ACM Trans. Net.*, 13(2) 2005, 276–287.
15. S. C. Lim and M. Li, A generalized Cauchy process and its application to relaxation phenomena, *J. Phys. A: Math. General*, 39(12) 2006, 2935–2951.
16. G. Chan, P. Hall, and D. S. Poskitt, Periodogram-based estimators of fractal properties, *Ann. Stat.*, 23(5) 1995, 1684–1711.
17. J. T. Kent and A. T. Wood, Estimating the fractal dimension of a locally self-similar Gaussian process by using increments, *J. Roy. Stat. Soc. B*, 59(3) 1997, 679–699.
18. P. Hall and A. Wood, On the performance of box-counting estimators of fractal dimension, *Biometrika*, 80(1) 1993, 246–252.
19. M. Li and W. Zhao, Representation of a stochastic traffic bound, *IEEE Trans. Paral Distrib. Syst.*, 21(9) 2010, 1368–1372.

CHAPTER 10

Fractal Traffic Delay Bounds

From the point of view of stochastic processes, we explained the generalized Cauchy (GC) process and its application to traffic modeling in Chapter 8. In addition, based on the GC process and the Cruz bound of traffic, we introduced the traffic bound of GC type in Chapter 9. In the aspect of algebra, we proposed the representation of the identity in the min-plus convolution system. This provides a foundation to discuss an interesting topic in computer communications, that is, traffic delay bounds. In this chapter, the research background of traffic delay bounds is described in Section 10.1. We address the fractal traffic delay bounds in Section 10.2. Discussion is given in Section 10.3.

10.1 BACKGROUND

Computation of delay bound of traffic plays a role in the quality of service in computer communications or cyber physical systems, see for example [1–18]. We explain our research on fractal delay bounds of traffic, which are tighter than conventional non-fractal ones.

Denote by $x(t)$ the instantaneous arrival traffic time series. The unit of $x(t)$ is byte when it is taken as the packet size of a packet arriving at time t. Its size is restricted by

$$0 \le x_{\min} \le x(t) \le x_{\max}, \tag{10.1}$$

where $x_{\min}$ and $x_{\max}$ are specified by protocols and IEEE standard without technical reason. For instance, without considering the Ethernet preamble, header, or Cyclic Redundancy Check (CRC), the Ethernet protocol forces all packets to have $x_{\min} = 64$ bytes and $x_{\max} = 1,518$ bytes (Stalling [19]).

Denote by S a server. Usually, it simultaneously serves a number of connections within a time interval $[0, t]$. Let $x_j(t)$ be the instantaneous arrival traffic from the jth connection ($j = 1, 2, ..., J$). Denote by $X_j(t)$ the accumulated amount of $x_j(t)$ in $[0, t]$. It is given by

$$X_j(t) = \int_0^t x_j(u)\, du. \tag{10.2}$$

Generally, S serves $X_j(t)$ on an interval-by-interval basis for $j = 1, 2, ..., J$ (Stalling [19]).

Let $Y_j(t)$ be departure traffic of S that is driven by $X_j(t)$. Let $d_j(t)$ be the delay that $X_j(t)$ suffers from S. Then,

$$Y_j(t) = X_j\big(t - d_j(t)\big). \tag{10.3}$$

Since $d_j(t)$ is random [20–22] and $X_j(t)$ is of fractal [11,23], delay computation is a difficulty.

In order to overcome this difficulty, people pay attention to finding a bound of $d_j(t)$ for $j = 1, 2, ..., J$ within $[0, t]$ instead of obtaining instantaneous $d_j(t)$ for each connection. Denote by d_m a bound of $d_j(t)$ for all connections ($j = 1, 2, ..., J$) within $[0, t]$. Then, if we can assure $d_j(t) \le d_m$ for $j = 1, 2, ..., J$ in $[0, t]$, the quality of service of $X_j(t)$ in delay for all connections ($j = 1, 2, ..., J$) within $[0, t]$ can be guaranteed. Thus, the research issue of delay bound is essential in computer communications.

Note d_m relates to a service time length of S that serves $X_j(t)$ while the service time length relates to the size of $X_j(t)$. Since traffic is a fractal time series, $X_j(t)$ is random. Thus, instead of directly computing $X_j(t)$, people concern with a bound of $X_j(t)$ for $j = 1, 2, ..., J$ in $[0, t]$. Denote by X_m a bound of $X_j(t)$ for all connections ($j = 1, 2, ..., J$) within $[0, t]$. Then, as long as S serves X_m with a guaranteed d_m in $[0, t]$, it is assured for S to serve $X_j(t)$

with a guaranteed d_m for any connection $j = 1, 2, ..., J$ within $[0, t]$. This research way, shortly speaking, implies that one has to research arrival traffic bound in order to study traffic delay bound, according to the theory of network calculus introduced by Cruz [24].

Without the generality loss, we omit the subscript j for $X_j(t)$ or $d_j(t)$ in what follows. Write the general form of accumulated arrival traffic in $[0, t]$ by

$$X(t) = \int_0^t x(u)\,du. \tag{10.4}$$

The network calculus pays attention to two key properties of traffic [1–3,24–26]. One property of traffic is called burstiness in the field. It is a *local property* of traffic [24–26]. Cruz used a symbol σ to characterize it in the form, see [1–3,11–14,24–26].

$$\lim_{t \to 0} \int_0^t x(u)\,du \le \sigma, \tag{10.5}$$

The parameter σ serves as a measure of burstiness, reflecting a local property of traffic because it is obtained under the condition of $[0, t] \to [0, 0]$. The other property of traffic is the long-term average rate given by

$$\lim_{t \to \infty} \frac{\int_0^t x(u)\,du}{t} \le \rho. \tag{10.6}$$

The parameter ρ characterizes a *global property* of traffic as it is attained under the condition of $[0, t] \to [0, \infty]$.

Combining (10.5) with (10.6) yields an inequality for representing a bound of $X(t)$ in the form

$$\int_0^t x(u)\,du = X(t) \le \sigma + \rho t. \tag{10.7}$$

The above is called (σ, ρ) traffic shaper. We call it the Cruz model of traffic for the memento of Cruz. The unit of σ is byte×sec while that of ρ byte when $x(t)$ stands for the packet size. It is worth noting that the two parameters σ and ρ are independent of each other.

Let $Y(t)$ be the departure traffic from a server S. Let $\otimes$ be the min-plus convolution operator. According to the theory addressed in Chapter 4, there exists an identity (Theorem 4.3) in the min-plus convolution system. Thus, we denote by $S(t)$ a service curve of S so that

$$X(t) \otimes S(t) = Y_{XS}(t) \le Y(t), \tag{10.8}$$

where $Y_{XS}(t)$ is the departure traffic of S. Therefore,

$$Y_{XS}(t) \le Y(t) = \sigma + \rho(t-d), \tag{10.9}$$

where d is the delay with the unit sec. Consequently, one has a delay bound in the form

$$d = d(t) \le \frac{\sigma + \rho t - Y_{XS}(t)}{\rho} \triangleq d_{\text{Cruz1}}. \tag{10.10}$$

We use the subscript Cruz for d_{Cruz1} to imply that it is based on the Cruz bound (σ, ρ). Note that $d_{\text{Cruz1}} \ge 0$ due to (10.9).

The quantity d_{Cruz1} in (10.10) is irrelevant to the statistics of traffic. That is a significant advantage of network calculus. It implies that delay computation is simple without the statistics of traffic consideration. However, the simple computation of delay bound in (10.10) is at the cost of sacrifice of network resources because arrival traffic bound (10.7) is loose. The sacrifice of network resources may be such that the theory of network calculus [24] is difficult to be practically applied. Consequently, tighter bounds of $X(t)$ are desired.

In addition to (10.7), there are three probabilistic models in the aspect of bounds of $X(t)$. One is the exponential bound [27,28]. It is in the form

$$\Pr\left\{ \int_0^t x(u)\,du \ge \sigma + \rho t \right\} \le A e^{-v\sigma}, \tag{10.11}$$

where A and v are constants and $\Pr(\cdot)$ is the probability. Clearly, (10.11) requires $v \ge 0$ and $A \ge 0$. Let $v\sigma = \sigma_v$. Then, (10.11) may be rewritten by

$$\Pr\left\{ \int_0^t x(u)\,du \ge \frac{\sigma_v}{v} + \rho t \right\} \le A e^{-\sigma_v}. \tag{10.12}$$

Since the maximum of $\Pr(\cdot)$ is 1 and $e^{-v\sigma} \in [0,1]$, A has to be 1 in the above. Thus, the above becomes

$$\Pr\left\{\int_0^t x(u)\,du \geq \frac{\sigma_v}{v} + \rho t\right\} \leq e^{-\sigma_v}. \tag{10.13}$$

Note that the probabilistic bound $e^{-v\sigma}$ may only be a hypothesis. On this track, therefore, a generalized form of (10.12) was proposed in [29]. It is given by

$$\Pr\left\{\int_s^t x(u)\,du \geq \sigma + \rho(t-s)\right\} \leq f(\sigma). \tag{10.14}$$

The above bounding function $f(\sigma)$ is only a hypothesis too. Its concrete form lacks.

In the field, a probabilistic bound of $X(t)$ is presented in [5] in the form

$$\Pr\left\{X(t+\tau) - X(t) \leq G^\delta(\tau)\right\} > 1 - \delta, \tag{10.15}$$

where $G^\delta(\tau)$ is a non-negative function if the above holds and δ is positive infinitesimal. When τ is small enough, it reflects the local property. For large τ, it reflects the global property. Nevertheless, a concrete form of $G^\delta(\tau)$ is lacking.

One thing in common with respect to (10.11), (10.14), and (10.15) is that they lack in considering fractal properties of traffic, namely, long-range dependence and self-similarity, referring to [30–56] for fractal time series and traffic. As a matter of fact, finding a tighter bound of $X(t)$ becomes a bottleneck work to study a tighter delay bound of traffic. In this regard, the last chapter, see also [49], mentioned a fractal bound of $X(t)$ in the form

$$\int_0^t x(u)\,du \leq r^{2D-5}\sigma + a^{-H}\rho t, \tag{10.16}$$

where $r \geq 1$ is the small time scale factor and $a \geq 1$ is the large time scale factor. Because of $r \geq 1$ and $a \geq 1$, the above is tighter than the conventional one (10.7). We write the above traffic bound by $\left(r^{2D-5}\sigma, a^{-H}\rho\right)$. Because it is obtained with (10.17), we call it a fractal bound of $X(t)$. It reduces to the conventional bound (10.7) when $r=a=1$. Obviously, for $r>1$ and $a>1$, $\left(r^{2D-5}\sigma, a^{-H}\rho\right)$ is tighter than (σ, ρ). As a matter of fact,

$$\int_0^t x(u)du \le r^{2D-5}\sigma + a^{-H}\rho t \le \sigma + \rho t, \tag{10.17}$$

where $0<r^{2D-5}\le 1$ and $0<a^{-H}\le 1$ for $r>1$ and $a>1$ because $1\le D<2$ and $0.5<H<1$. All D, H, r, and a are dimensionless. For facilitating discussions, we write

$$\sigma_1 = r^{2D-5}\sigma \le \sigma, \quad \rho_1 = a^{-H}\rho \le \rho. \tag{10.18}$$

Based on the above, we address four fractal traffic delay bounds that are tighter than the corresponding non-fractal ones.

10.2 FRACTAL DELAY BOUNDS

10.2.1 Fractal Delay Bound 1

Considering (10.10) and (10.17) (see also [57,58]), we obtain a delay bound given by

$$d(t) \le \frac{\sigma_1 + \rho_1 t - Y_{XS}(t)}{\rho_1} \triangleq d_{\text{fractal1}}. \tag{10.19}$$

We call $d_{\text{fractal 1}}$ the fractal bound 1 of traffic delay. The subscript "fractal" is used to imply that it relates to the fractal parameters D and H. Note that d_{Cruz1} is a special case of $d_{\text{fractal 1}}$ for $r=a=1$.

Since $\sigma_1 + \rho_1 t \ge Y_{XS}(t)$, we have $d_{\text{fractal1}} \ge 0$. By comparing (10.19) with (10.10), we obtain the following inequality

$$d_{\text{fractal 1}} \le d_{\text{Cruz 1}}. \tag{10.20}$$

10.2.2 Fractal Delay Bound 2

Practically, one may be often interested in a delay bound for $[0, t]$, where t is small [24]. For example, admission control requires delay computation [8,9,11]. Since H measures the global property of $x(t)$, we may ignore it in (10.19) by letting $a=1$ when focusing on the local behavior of traffic delay. In doing so, we propose a bound of $X(t)$ in the form

$$X(t) \le r^{2D-5}\sigma + \rho t. \tag{10.21}$$

Therefore, based on the above, we bring forward the fractal delay bound 2 in the form

$$d(t) \le \frac{\sigma_1 + \rho t - Y_{\mathrm{XS}}(t)}{\rho} \triangleq d_{\mathrm{fractal2}}. \tag{10.22}$$

Because $0 < r^{2D-5} < 1$, we have $\sigma_1 + \rho t \le \sigma + \rho t$. Thus, we attain the inequality

$$d_{\mathrm{fractal2}} \le d_{\mathrm{Cruz1}}. \tag{10.23}$$

The conventional bound d_{Cruz1} is also a special case of d_{fractal2} for $r = 1$.

10.2.3 Fractal Delay Bound 3

When focusing on local behavior of delay, we may further neglect $Y_{\mathrm{SX}}(t)$ in (10.19) for the purpose of simplifying computation in practice. In that case, we denote a non-fractal delay bound by d_{Cruz2}. It is given by

$$d(t) \le \frac{\sigma + \rho t}{\rho} \triangleq d_{\mathrm{Cruz2}}. \tag{10.24}$$

Similarly, by ignoring $Y_{\mathrm{SX}}(t)$ in (10.22), we present the fractal delay bound 3 in the form

$$d(t) \le \frac{\sigma_1 + \rho t}{\rho} \triangleq d_{\mathrm{fractal3}}. \tag{10.25}$$

From the above, we see that d_{fractal3} reduces to d_{Cruz2} if $r = 1$. Since $\sigma_1 + \rho t \le \sigma + \rho t$, we attain an inequality expressed by

$$d_{\mathrm{fractal3}} \le d_{\mathrm{Cruz2}}. \tag{10.26}$$

10.2.4 Fractal Delay Bound 4

Let ε be the positive infinitesimal. By letting $t = \varepsilon$, we introduce a non-fractal delay bound d_{Cruz3} in the form

$$d(\varepsilon) \le \frac{\sigma + \rho \varepsilon}{\rho} = \frac{\sigma}{\rho} \triangleq d_{\mathrm{Cruz3}}. \tag{10.27}$$

On the other side, by letting $t=\varepsilon$ in (10.25), we put forward the fractal delay bound 4

$$d(\varepsilon) \le \frac{\sigma_1 + \rho\varepsilon}{\rho} = \frac{\sigma_1}{\rho} = \frac{r^{2D-5}\sigma}{\rho} \triangleq d_{\text{fractal4}}. \tag{10.28}$$

The fractal bound d_{fractal4} takes non-fractal one d_{Cruz3} as a special case for $r=1$. Because $r^{2D-5}\sigma \le \sigma$, we present an inequality given by

$$d_{\text{fractal4}} \le d_{\text{Cruz3}}. \tag{10.29}$$

10.3 DISCUSSION

Consider $t=\varepsilon$ for the purpose of exhibiting that a fractal delay bound is tighter than its corresponding non-fractal one. Define a delay-bound ratio of d_{fractal4} to d_{Cruz3}. It is given by

$$\lambda = \frac{d_{\text{fractal4}}}{d_{\text{Cruz3}}} = r^{2D-5}. \tag{10.30}$$

Figure 10.1 shows the plots of λ. It shows $\lambda < 1$ for $r > 1$ and $D \in (1, 2)$. Note that traffic has highly local irregularity with around $D \in (1.90, 1.97)$ [50,52]. Thus, traffic has the property of $\lambda < 1$. From Figure 10.1, we see that a smaller D corresponds to a smaller value of d_{fractal4} and $D=1$ corresponds to the smallest d_{fractal4} for a fixed r. Contrarily, a larger D implies a larger d_{fractal4} for a given r. That is natural as D measures the local self-similarity

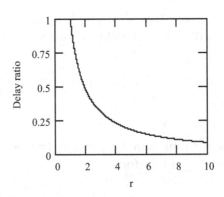

FIGURE 10.1   Plots of delay-bound ratio λ for $D=1.97$ (solid line), 1.90 (dot line), 1.00 (dash line), and $1 \le r \le 10$.

(irregularity) of $x(t)$. A larger D means a stronger local irregularity. Thus, from a view of (10.30), we see that fractal delay bound $d_{fractal4}$ is proportional to D of arrival traffic.

REFERENCES

1. Y.-M. Jiang and Y. Liu, *Stochastic Network Calculus*, Springer, New York, 2008.
2. Y.-M. Jiang, Per-domain packet scale rate guarantee for expedited forwarding, *IEEE/ACM Trans. Net.*, 14(3) 2006, 630–643.
3. Y.-M. Jiang, A basic stochastic network calculus, *ACM SIGCOMM Comput. Commun. Rev.*, 36(4) 2006, 123–134.
4. C. Huang, F. Li, T. Ding, Y.-M. Jiang, J. Guo, and Y. Liu, A bounded model of the communication delay for system integrity protection schemes, *IEEE Trans. Power Deliv.*, 31(4) 2016, 1921–1933.
5. C. Li and E. Knightly, Schedulability criterion and performance analysis of coordinated multihop schedulers, *IEEE/ACM Trans. Net.*, 13(2) 2005, 276–287.
6. C. Li, A. Burchard, and J. Liebeherr, A network calculus with effective bandwidth, *IEEE/ACM Trans. Net.*, 15(6) 2007, 1442–1452.
7. S. Wang, D. Xuan, R. Bettati, and W. Zhao, Providing absolute differentiated services for real-time applications in static-priority scheduling networks, *IEEE/ACM Trans. Net.*, 12(2) 2004, 326–339.
8. X. Jia, A distributed algorithm of delay bounded multicast routing for multimedia applications in wide area networks, *IEEE/ACM Trans. Net.*, 6(6) 1998, 828–837.
9. X. Jia, W. Zhao, and J. Li, An integrated routing and admission control mechanism for real-time multicast connections in ATM networks, *IEEE Trans. Commun.*, 49(9) 2001, 1515–1519.
10. M. Akselrod and M. Fidler, Statistical delay bounds for automatic repeat request protocols with pipelining, *Perform. Eval.*, 135 2019, 102029.
11. H. Michiel and K. Laevens, Teletraffic engineering in a broad-band era, *Proc. IEEE*, 85(12) 1997, 800–819.
12. V. Firoiu, J.-Y. Le Boudec, D. Towsley, and Z.-L. Zhang, Theories and models for Internet quality of service, *Proc. IEEE*, 90(9) 2002, 1565–1591.
13. M. Fidler and A. Rizk, A guide to the stochastic network calculus, *IEEE Commun. Surv. Tutor.*, 17(1) 2015, 92–105.
14. M. Fidler, A survey of deterministic and stochastic service curve models in the network calculus, *IEEE Commun. Surv. Tutor.*, 12(1) 2010, 59–86.
15. S. Mao and S. S. Panwar, A survey of envelope processes and their applications in quality of service provisioning, *IEEE Commun. Surv. Tutor.*, 8(3) 2006, 2–20.
16. K. Wang, F. Ciucu, C. Lin, and H. L. Steven, A stochastic power network calculus for integrating renewable energy sources into the power grid, *IEEE J. Select. Areas Commun.*, 30(6) 2012, 1037–1048.

17. M. Fidler, B. Walker, and Y.-M. Jiang, Non-asymptotic delay bounds for multi-server systems with synchronization constraints, *IEEE Trans. Parallel Distrib. Syst.*, 29(7) 2018, 1545–1559.

18. Z. Li, Y.-M. Jiang, Y. Gao, P. Li, L. Sang, and D. Yang, Delay and delay-constrained throughput performance of a wireless-powered communication system, *IEEE Access*, 5 2017, 21620–21631.

19. W. Stallings, *Data and Computer Communications*, 4th Ed., Macmillan, New York, 1994.

20. D. L. Mills, *Computer Network Time Synchronization*, 2nd Ed., CRC Press, New York, 2011.

21. R. Jain and S. Routhier, Packet trains-measurements and a new model for computer network traffic, *IEEE J. Select. Areas Commun.*, 4(6) 1986, 986–995.

22. L. Lei, J. Lu, Y.-M. Jiang, X. Shen, X. Li, Y. Zhong, and Z. Lin, Chuang, Stochastic delay analysis for train control services in next-generation high-speed railway communications system, *IEEE Trans. Intel. Trans. Syst.*, 17(1) 2016, 48–64.

23. R. Fontugne, P. Abry, K. Fukuda, D. Veitch, K. Cho, P. Borgnat, H. Wendt, Scaling in Internet traffic: A 14 year and 3 day longitudinal study, with multiscale analyses and random projections, *IEEE/ACM Trans. Net.*, 25(4) 2017, 2152–2165.

24. R. L. Cruz, A calculus for network delay, part I: Network elements in isolation, part II: Network analysis, *IEEE Trans. Inform. Theor.*, 37(1) 1991, 114–141.

25. J. Y. Le Boudec, Application of network calculus to guaranteed service networks, *IEEE Trans. Inform. Theor.*, 44(3) 1998, 1087–1096.

26. J.-Yves L.-Boudec and T. Patrick, *Network Calculus, A Theory of Deterministic Queuing Systems for the Internet*, Springer, New York, 2001.

27. O. Yaron and M. Sidi, Performance and stability of communication networks via robust exponential bounds, *IEEE/ACM Trans. Net.*, 1(3) 1993, 372–385.

28. A. K. Parekh and R. G. Gallager, A generalized processor sharing approach to flow control in integrated services networks: The single-node case, *IEEE/ACM Trans. Net.*, 1(3) 1993, 372–385.

29. D. Starobinski and M. Sidi, Stochastically bounded burstiness for communication networks, *IEEE Trans. Inform. Theor.*, 46(1) 2000, 206–212.

30. M. Li, Generalized fractional Gaussian noise and its application to traffic modeling, *Physica A*, 579, 1 Oct. 2021, 1236137 (22 pp).

31. M. Lelarge, Z. Liu, and C. H. Xia, Asymptotic tail distribution of end-to-end delay in networks of queues with self-similar cross traffic, *Proc. INFOCOM 2004*, 7–11 Mar. 2004, Hong Kong, China, pp. 2352–2363.

32. G. Mayor and J. Silvester, Time scale analysis of an ATM queueing system with long-range dependent traffic, *Proc. INFOCOM 1997*, 7–11 April 1997, Kobe, Japan, pp. 205–212.

33. J. Liebeherr, A. Burchard, and F. Ciucu, Delay bounds in communication networks with heavy-tailed and self-similar traffic, *IEEE Trans. Inform. Theor.*, 58(2) 2012, 1010–1024.

34. B. Tsybakov and N. D. Georganas, On self-similar traffic in ATM queues: Definitions, overflow probability bound and cell delay distribution, *IEEE/ACM Trans. Net.*, 5(3) 1997, 397–409.

35. A. Erramilli, O. Narayan, and W. Willinger, Experimental queuing analysis with long-range dependent packet traffic, *IEEE/ACM Trans. Net.*, 4(2) 1996, 209–223.

36. M. Pinchas, Symbol error rate for non-blind adaptive equalizers applicable for the SIMO and fGn case, *Math. Prob. Eng.*, 2014 2014, Article ID 606843, 11 p.

37. M. Pinchas, Cooperative multi PTP slaves for timing improvement in an fGn environment, *IEEE Commun. Lett.*, 22(7) 2018, 1366–1369.

38. M. M. Meerschaert, E. Nane, and Y. M. Xiao, Large deviations for local time fractional Brownian motion and applications, *J. Math. Anal. Appl.*, 346(2) 2008, 432–445.

39. A. Ayache, D. Wu, and Y. M. Xiao, Joint continuity of the local times of fractional Brownian sheets, *Annales de Institut Henri Poincare – Probabilities et Statistiques*, 44(3) 2008, 727–748.

40. J. Lévy-Véhel, Beyond multifractional Brownian motion: New stochastic models for geophysical modeling, *Nonlinear Proc. Geophys.*, 20(5) 2013, 643–655.

41. B. B. Mandelbrot, *Gaussian Self-Affinity and Fractals*, Springer, New York, 2001.

42. J. Beran, R. Shernan, M. S. Taqqu, and W. Willinger, Long-range dependence in variable bit-rate video traffic, *IEEE Trans. Commun.*, 43(2–4) 1995, 1566–1579.

43. B. Tsybakov and N. D. Georganas, Self-similar processes in communications networks, *IEEE Trans. Inform. Theor.*, 44(5) 1998, 1713–1725.

44. M. Li, X. Sun, and X. Xiao, Revisiting fractional Gaussian noise, *Phys. A*, 514 2019, 56–62.

45. V. Paxson and S. Floyd, Wide area traffic: The failure of Poison modeling, *IEEE/ACM Trans. Network.*, 3(3) 1995, 226–244.

46. M. Li, Fractal time series — A tutorial review, *Math. Prob. Eng.*, 2010 2010, Article ID 157264, 26 p.

47. T. Gneiting and M. Schlather, Stochastic models that separate fractal dimension and the Hurst effect, *SIAM Rev.*, 46(2) 2004, 269–282.

48. S. C. Lim and M. Li, Generalized Cauchy process and its application to relaxation phenomena, *J. Phys. A: Math. General*, 39(12) 2006, 2935–2951.

49. M. Li and W. Zhao, Representation of a stochastic traffic bound, *IEEE Trans. Paral. Distrib. Syst.*, 21(9) 2010, 1368–1372.

50. M. Li, Long-range dependence and self-similarity of teletraffic with different protocols at the large time scale of day in the duration of 12 years: Autocorrelation modeling, *Phys. Scr.*, 96(6) 2020, 065222 (15 p).

51. M. Li, Multi-fractional generalized Cauchy process and its application to teletraffic, *Phys. A*, 550, 2020.

52. M. Li and S. C. Lim, Modeling network traffic using generalized Cauchy process, *Phys. A*, 387(11) 2008, 2584–2594.

53. M. Li, Record length requirement of long-range dependent teletraffic, *Phys. A*, 472 2017, 164–187.

54. M. Li and J.-Y. Li, Generalized Cauchy model of sea level fluctuations with long-range dependence, *Phys. A*, 484 2017, 309–335.

55. J. T. Kent and A. T. Wood, Estimating the fractal dimension of a locally self-similar Gaussian process by using increments, *J. Roy. Statist. Soc.*, 59(3) 1997, 679–699.

56. G. Chan, P. Hall, and D. S. Poskitt, Periodogram-based estimators of fractal properties, *Ann. Statist.*, 23(5) 1995, 1684–1711.

57. M. Li, W. Zhao, and C. Cattani, Delay bound: Fractal traffic passes through servers, *Math. Prob. Eng.*, 2013 2013, Article ID 157636, 15 p.

58. M. Li and A. Wang, Fractal teletraffic delay bounds in computer networks, *Phys. A*, 557 2020, 124903 (13 p).

CHAPTER 11

Computations of Scale Factors

The contributions in this chapter are in six aspects. First, we propose the formulas to compute the small-scale factor r and large-scale one a of traffic in Theorems 11.1 and 11.2, respectively. Second, we put forward the asymptotic expressions of r for $t \to 0$ and a for $t \to \infty$ in Theorems 11.3 and 11.4, respectively. Third, we present the formulas of the minimum of r and a in Corollaries 11.1 and 11.2, as well as the minimum of the asymptotic values of r when $t \to 0$ and a if $t \to \infty$ in Corollaries 11.3 and 11.4, respectively. Fourth, we bring forward the approximations of the fractal bound of traffic in Theorem 11.5 and Corollary 11.5, respectively. Fifth, the applications of the present computations of two scale factors to traffic bound and traffic delay bound are explained with real traffic traces. Finally, we propose the formula for the maximum of a fractal delay bound in Corollary 11.6.

11.1 BACKGROUND[1]

Let $x[t(i)]$ be the packet size of the ith packet ($i = 0, 1, 2, \ldots$) at the time $t(i)$, where $t(i)$ is a timestamp sequence of teletraffic (traffic for short) in computer networks (Li et al. [1]). Without causing confusion, we use $x(i)$ as a discrete sequence of traffic to denote the packet size of the ith packet

---

[1] Theorems 11.1 and 11.2 give a solution to the open problem regarding the computation of r and a.

DOI: 10.1201/9781003268802-11

and $x(t)$ as a continuous traffic sequence to represent the packet size of a packet at t.

Denote by $X(t)$ the accumulated arrival traffic in the time interval $[0, t]$. It is given by

$$X(t) = \int_0^t x(u)\,du. \tag{11.1}$$

In computer communications, a server serves $X(t)$ on an interval-by-interval basis (Stalling [2], Inme and Saito [3]). Let us consider the transmission of $X(t)$ from source A to destination B. When $X(t)$ arrives at B from A, it suffers from delay d. Accordingly, traffic at B is $X(t-d)$ as indicated by Figure 11.1.

In real-time communications, one says that the transmission of $X(t)$ from A to B is successful if

$$d \leq d_{\text{bound}} \tag{11.2}$$

can be guaranteed, where d_{bound} is a predetermined value of delay bound. Otherwise, the transmission fails (Gibson [4], Kleinrock [5]). Consequently, the computation of traffic delay bound plays a role in computer communications ([2–5], Cerf and Kirstein [6], Mills [7]).

Research exhibit that traffic $x(t)$ is a fractal time series, see e.g., Paxson and Floyd [8], Tsybakov and Georganas [9], Li [10–22], Li and Borgnat [23], Li and Lim [24], and Lim and Li [25,26–39]. Besides, d is a random function ([7], Tobagi et al. [40], Wong [41], Tejado et al. [42], Yue et al. [43]). Thus, computing delay bound is a tough issue in computer communications. In this regard, Cruz introduced a bound of $X(t)$ in the form

$$\int_0^t x(u)\,du = X(t) \leq \sigma + \rho t, \tag{11.3}$$

where σ and ρ are non-negative constants for computing delay bound of traffic (Cruz [44], Le Boudec [45], Le Boudec and Patrick [46], Jiang and

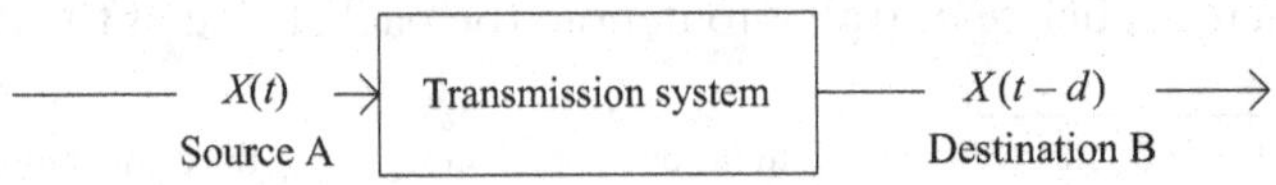

FIGURE 11.1 Traffic $X(t)$ transmitted from source A to destination B.

Liu [47]). The unit of σ is byte × second while that of ρ is byte when the unit of $x(t)$ is byte. Let

$$A(t) = \sigma + \rho t. \tag{11.4}$$

We call $A(t)$ the Cruz bound of $X(t)$ for simplicity (Li and Wang [48]). It is denoted by (σ, ρ) for short [44–48].

For a given $X(t)$, σ characterizes its burstiness, which is a deterministically local property of traffic because σ is attained under the condition of $t \to 0$ [44]. In fact, σ satisfies

$$\lim_{t \to 0} A(t) = \sigma. \tag{11.5}$$

Although $A(t)$ relies on σ and ρ in general, for the small time scale of $t \to 0$, ρ in (11.4) may be ignored. On the other hand, ρ measures the long-term average rate of $X(t)$ since

$$\lim_{t \to \infty} \frac{X(t)}{t} = \lim_{t \to \infty} \frac{\int_0^t x(u)\,du}{t} \leq \rho. \tag{11.6}$$

The long-term average rate is a deterministically global property of traffic since ρ is obtained in the case of $t \to \infty$. Although $A(t)$ generally depends on ρ and σ, σ in (11.4) may be ignored if $t \to \infty$. As a matter of fact,

$$\lim_{t \to \infty} A(t) = \rho t. \tag{11.7}$$

Denote by $S(t)$ the service curve of a server. Let $\otimes$ be the operation of min-plus convolution. Denote by $X(t)$ and $Y_{XS}(t)$ the arrival traffic and departure one of the server, respectively (Figure 11.2).

According to the theory of network calculus [44–47], one has

$$Y_{XS}(t) = X(t) \otimes S(t). \tag{11.8}$$

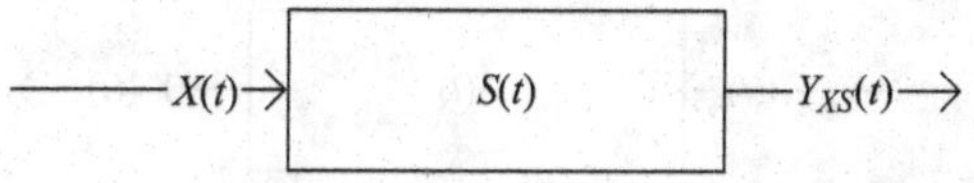

FIGURE 11.2   Input and output of a server.

Note that $X(t) \geq 0$, $S(t) \geq 0$, and $Y_{XS}(t) \geq 0$. Besides, they are non-negative and increasing in the wide sense [44–49]. Because of the server mechanism (buffering, service time, etc.), one has

$$Y_{XS}(t) \leq X(t). \tag{11.9}$$

Taking into account delay d that $X(t)$ suffers from $S(t)$, we have

$$Y_{XS}(t) = X(t-d). \tag{11.10}$$

Since $X(t)$ is of fractal, $Y_{XS}(t)$ is of fractal too. That is a difficulty to apply (11.8) to practice for computing a bound of d. In order to overcome this difficulty, one utilizes the bound of $X(t)$, namely, $A(t)$, as an arrival traffic, instead of $X(t)$ [44–47]. In this way, one has

$$Y_{AS}(t) = A(t) \otimes S(t), \tag{11.11}$$

as shown in Figure 11.3.

Again, due to server mechanism, we have

$$Y_{AS}(t) \leq A(t) = \sigma + \rho t. \tag{11.12}$$

However, based on $A(t)$, one has

$$Y_{AS}(t) = A(t-d) = \sigma + \rho(t-d). \tag{11.13}$$

Following [44–48], from (11.13), one has a bound of d in the form

$$d \leq \frac{\sigma + \rho t - Y_{AS}(t)}{\rho} = d_{\text{Cruz1}}. \tag{11.14}$$

Because d_{Cruz1} is obtained based on $A(t)$, $d \leq d_{\text{Cruz1}}$ can be assured for any $X(t)$.

FIGURE 11.3   Input and output of a server based on arrival traffic bound $A(t)$.

There are two advantages with respect to (11.14) in computing delay bound. One is that (11.14) is simple in computation. The other is that the computation of d_{Cruz1} is irrelevant to statistics of traffic. It attracts the interest of researchers, see e.g., [49–62]. Nonetheless, its simplicity is based on sacrificing network resources since $A(t)$ is loose. Accordingly, d_{Cruz1} may be loose such that it may be very difficult to be applicable. Thus, tighter bounds of arrival traffic $X(t)$ are greatly desired.

11.2 PROBLEM STATEMENT

In order to attain a tighter bound of $X(t)$, [63–67] reported their research results, see Chapters 9 and 10. However, they lack in considering the fractal properties, namely, local self-similarity and long-range dependence, of traffic. Our previous work [68] presents a stochastic bound of traffic with the consideration of fractal properties of traffic. It is given by

$$\int_0^t x(u)du = X(t) \leq r^{2D-5}\sigma + a^{-H}\rho t, \qquad (11.15)$$

where $1 \leq D < 2$ and $0.5 < H < 1$ are, respectively, the fractal dimension and the Hurst parameter of $x(t)$, r is the small-scale factor, and a is the large-scale one. Both r and a are dimensionless. From the point of view of physics, r is the burstiness scale factor while a is the long-term average rate scale factor. The right side of (11.15) stands for a fractal bound of $X(t)$ since it contains the fractal parameters D and H. For facilitating the discussions, we call it Li's bound of $X(t)$ for the simplicity in Chapter 9.

There are two key points of Li's bound (11.15). On the one side, it introduces the scale factors r and a for a bound of traffic. On the other side, fractal parameters D and H are separately combined with r and a. Let

$$\sigma_1 = r^{2D-5}\sigma, \quad \rho_1 = a^{-H}\rho. \qquad (11.16)$$

Denote by (σ_1, ρ_1) Li's bound of $X(t)$ in (11.15). Then, we see that it takes the conventional Cruz bound (σ, ρ) as a special case when $r = a = 1$. As $r \geq 1$ and $a \geq 1$, we have

$$\sigma_1 = r^{2D-5}\sigma \leq \sigma, \qquad (11.17)$$

$$\rho_1 = a^{-H}\rho \leq \rho. \qquad (11.18)$$

When writing

$$X(t) \leq A_1(t) = \sigma_1 + \rho_1 t, \tag{11.19}$$

we see that

$$A_1(t) \leq A(t). \tag{11.20}$$

The above implies that $A_1(t)$ is tighter than $A(t)$. Consequently, we have the input–output relationship given by

$$Y_{A_1 S}(t) = A_1(t) \otimes S(t). \tag{11.21}$$

Figure 11.4 shows the input and output of a server based on $A_1(t)$.

Again, due to server mechanism, we have

$$Y_{A_1 S}(t) \leq A_1(t). \tag{11.22}$$

However, with the help of $A_1(t)$, we have

$$Y_{A_1 S}(t) = A_1(t-d) = \sigma_1 + \rho_1(t-d). \tag{11.23}$$

From the above, we obtain a delay bound based on $A_1(t)$ in the form

$$d(t) \leq \frac{\sigma_1 + \rho_1 t - Y_{A_1 S}(t)}{\rho_1} = d_{\text{fractal1}}. \tag{11.24}$$

Following [48], we have

$$d_{\text{fractal1}} \leq d_{\text{Cruz1}}. \tag{11.25}$$

Thus, a delay bound based on $A_1(t)$ is tighter than that based on $A(t)$.

FIGURE 11.4 Input and output of a server based on arrival traffic bound $A_1(t)$.

In order to compute $A_1(t)$ and or the fractal delay bound in (11.24) for a given arrival traffic $x(t)$ and a service curve $S(t)$, we have to know the values of six parameters, namely, D, H, σ, ρ, r, and a. The literature regarding the estimations of D and H is rich [11–15,17,19,22,38,69–75]. The computations of σ and ρ are simple. However, how to compute the scale factors r and a is a problem that remains open. This chapter gives a solution to the open problem.

11.3 RESEARCH THOUGHTS FOR PROBLEM SOLVING

The research thoughts consist of the following two ideas.

11.3.1 Idea 1

Since it is impossible to get two variables r and a directly from one inequality (11.15), we propose the first idea to compute r and a separately. Because σ is the conservative value of σ_1 while ρ is the conservative one of ρ_1, we may simplify the right side of (11.15) by letting $\rho_1 = \rho$ so that

$$\int_0^t x(u)\,du \leq r^{2D-5}\sigma + \rho t = \sigma_1 + \rho t. \tag{11.26}$$

The above is an inequality with only one unsolved variable r. After r is solved, another variable a can be solved readily.

11.3.2 Idea 2

In order to solve r from (11.26), we need a boundary. In this regard, we suggest that r and a are departure traffic dependent. As a matter of fact, since departure traffic is the output of a server that serves the arrival traffic $X(t)$, it is reasonable to consider departure traffic as a boundary with respect to (11.26) for solving r.

11.4 RESULTS

We shall derive the computation formulas for r and a and the asymptotic formulas for r when $t \to 0$ and a for $t \to \infty$, respectively.

11.4.1 Computation Formulas of r and a

Now, we propose a theorem below for the computation of r.

Theorem 11.1

The small-scale factor r is given by

$$r \geq \left[\frac{Y_{A_1 S}(t) - \rho t}{\sigma} \right]^{\frac{1}{2D-5}}, \quad t > 0. \tag{11.27}$$

Proof. With Idea 1, letting $\rho_1 = \rho$ in (11.24) yields

$$d \leq \frac{\sigma_1 + \rho t - Y_{A_1 S}(t)}{\rho}. \tag{11.28}$$

Because $d \geq 0$, we have a boundary of $\sigma_1 + \rho t$ in the form

$$\sigma_1 + \rho t - Y_{A_1 S}(t) \geq 0. \tag{11.29}$$

Using (11.17), we have

$$r^{2D-5} \sigma + \rho t - Y_{A_1 S}(t) \geq 0. \tag{11.30}$$

The above implies

$$r^{2D-5} \geq \frac{Y_{A_1 S}(t)}{\sigma + \rho t}. \tag{11.31}$$

Since $A_1(t)$ and $Y_{A_1 S}(t)$ are defined for $t > 0$, we have (11.27) from the above.

Theorem 11.1 implies that the small-scale factor r is associated with the burstiness parameter σ, the long-term average rate ρ, the local self-similarity measure D, and the departure traffic $Y_{A_1 S}(t)$.

Corollary 11.1

Denote by $r_{\min}$ the minimum of r. Then,

$$r_{\min} = \left[\frac{Y_{A_1 S}(t) - \rho t}{\sigma} \right]^{\frac{1}{2D-5}}, \quad t > 0. \tag{11.32}$$

Proof. The proof is straightforward from Theorem 11.1.

Now, we consider the computation formula of a.

Theorem 11.2

Let a be the large-scale factor under the condition that r is known. Then,[2]

$$a^{-1} \geq \left[\frac{Y_{A_1S}(t) - r_{\min}^{2D-5}\sigma}{\rho t} \right]^{\frac{1}{H}}, \quad t > 0. \tag{11.33}$$

Proof. Considering $d \geq 0$ in (11.24), we have

$$\sigma_1 + \rho_1 t - Y_{A_1S}(t) \geq 0. \tag{11.34}$$

That is,

$$r^{2D-5}\sigma + a^{-H}\rho t - Y_{A_1S}(t) \geq 0. \tag{11.35}$$

Replacing r with $r_{\min}$ in the above produces

$$r_{\min}^{2D-5}\sigma + a^{-H}\rho t - Y_{A_1S}(t) \geq 0. \tag{11.36}$$

As $A_1(t)$ and $Y_{A_1S}(t)$ are for $t>0$, we obtain (11.33) from the above.

Theorem 11.2 implies that the large-scale factor a relates to σ, D, ρ, H, and $Y_{A_1S}(t)$.

Corollary 11.2

Let $a_{\min}$ be the minimum of a. Then,

$$a_{\min}^{-1} = \left[\frac{Y_{A_1S}(t) - r_{\min}^{2D-5}\sigma}{\rho t} \right]^{\frac{1}{H}}, \quad t > 0. \tag{11.37}$$

Proof. The proof is straightforward from Theorem 11.2.

From (11.37), we have

$$a_{\min} = \frac{1}{\left[\dfrac{Y_{A_1S}(t) - r_{\min}^{2D-5}\sigma}{\rho t} \right]^{\frac{1}{H}}}, \quad t > 0. \tag{11.38}$$

---

[2] For simplicity, we give the formula for a^{-1}.

11.4.2 Asymptotic Computation Formulas of r and a

In practice, we are interested in r for small t and a for large t.

Theorem 11.3

Let r for $t \to 0$ be r_0. Then,

$$r_0 \geq \left[\frac{Y_{A_1 S}(0)}{\sigma} \right]^{\frac{1}{2D-5}}. \tag{11.39}$$

Proof. Considering $\lim_{t \to 0} \rho t = 0$ and $Y_{A_1 S}(0)$ in (11.27) produces (11.39).

The formula (11.39) exhibits that r_0 relies only on parameters to characterize the local properties of traffic, namely, D and σ, and the local value of departure traffic $Y_{A_1 S}(0)$.

Corollary 11.3

Denote by $r_{0 \min}$ the minimum of r_0. Then,

$$r_{0 \min} = \left[\frac{Y_{A_1 S}(0)}{\sigma} \right]^{\frac{1}{2D-5}}. \tag{11.40}$$

Proof. The proof is straightforward from Theorem 11.3.

Theorem 11.4

Let a^{-1} for $t \to \infty$ be a_∞^{-1}. Then,

$$a_\infty^{-1} \geq \lim_{t \to \infty} \left[\frac{Y_{A_1 S}(t)}{\rho t} \right]^{\frac{1}{H}}. \tag{11.41}$$

Proof. When $t \to \infty$, (11.19) reduces to

$$\lim_{t \to \infty} A_1(t) = \lim_{t \to \infty} \rho_1 t = \lim_{t \to \infty} a_\infty^{-H} \rho t. \tag{11.42}$$

Besides, (11.24) becomes the following when $t \to \infty$

$$d \le \frac{\rho_1 t - Y_{A_1 S}(t)}{\rho} = \frac{a_\infty^{-H} \rho t - Y_{A_1 S}(t)}{\rho}, \quad t \to \infty. \tag{11.43}$$

As $d \ge 0$, we have

$$a_\infty^{-H} \rho t - Y_{A_1 S}(t) \ge 0, \quad t \to \infty. \tag{11.44}$$

Thus, we obtain (11.41) from (11.44).

Theorem 11.4 implies that a_∞^{-1} depends only on the parameters to measure the global properties of traffic, namely, H and ρ, and the departure traffic when $t \to \infty$, that is, $Y_{A_1 S}(\infty)$.

Corollary 11.4

Let $a_{\infty \min}^{-1}$ be the minimum of a_∞^{-1}. Then,

$$a_{\infty \min}^{-1} = \lim_{t \to \infty} \left[\frac{Y_{A_1 S}(t)}{\rho t} \right]^{\frac{1}{H}}. \tag{11.45}$$

Proof. The proof is omitted since it is straightforward from Theorem 11.4.

Example 11.1

Suppose that $Y_{A_1 S}(t)$ is the affine function in the form [46, p. 128]

$$Y_{A_1 S}(t) = \begin{cases} Rt + b, & t > 0 \\ 0, & \text{otherwise} \end{cases}. \tag{11.46}$$

Then, we have

$$r_0 \ge \left(\frac{b}{\sigma} \right)^{\frac{1}{2D-5}}, \quad r_{0 \min} = \left(\frac{b}{\sigma} \right)^{\frac{1}{2D-5}}, \tag{11.47}$$

$$a_\infty^{-1} \ge \left(\frac{R}{\rho} \right)^{\frac{1}{H}}, \quad a_{\infty \min}^{-1} = \left(\frac{R}{\rho} \right)^{\frac{1}{H}}. \tag{11.48}$$

Proof. Since $Y_{A_1S}(0) = b$, (11.47) holds according to (11.39) and (11.40). In addition, from (11.41) and (11.45), we have (11.48).

11.5 CASE STUDY

We first brief the real traffic data used. Then, we show the computations of $r_{0\min}$ and $a_{\infty\min}^{-1}$ of those real traffic traces for $Y_{A_1S}(t)$ being the affine function (11.46).

11.5.1 Traffic Data

We use two sets of real data of wide-area TCP (transmission control protocol) traffic traces. One was measured by Digital Equipment Corporation (DEC) in March 1995. The other was collected by the Measurement and Analysis on the WIDE Internet (MAWI) Working Group Traffic Archive (Japan) in April 2019. Those traces are used in the academic research, see e.g., [8,10–13,15,19,22,24,26–28,33,75–77]. Tables 11.1 and 11.2 list the data information.

11.5.2 Computations of $r_{0\min}$ and $a_{\infty\min}^{-1}$ of Traffic Traces

In order to find the values of $r_{0\min}$ and $a_{\infty\min}^{-1}$, we have to know the values of σ, ρ, D, and H. We first explain the computations of σ and ρ. Refer to Chapter 8 for the estimates of D and H.

TABLE 11.1   Four Wide-Area TCP Traffic Traces Measured by DEC

Trace Name	Record Date	Duration	Number of Packets
DEC-pkt-1.TCP	08 Mar 95	10 PM–11 PM	3.3 million
DEC-pkt-2.TCP	08 Mar 95	2 AM–3 AM	3.9 million
DEC-pkt-3.TCP	08 Mar 95	10 AM–11 AM	4.3 million
DEC-pkt-4.TCP	08 Mar 95	2 PM–3 PM	5.7 million

TABLE 11.2   Four Wide-Area TCP Traffic Traces Recorded by MAWI

Trace Name	Starting Record Time	Duration	Number of Packets
MAWI-pkt-1.TCP	2:00 PM, 18 Apr 2019	6.77208 minutes	741,404
MAWI-pkt-2.TCP	2:00 PM, 19 Apr 2019	6.65965 minutes	742,638
MAWI-pkt-3.TCP	2:00 PM, 20 Apr 2019	12.55740 minutes	482,564
MAWI-pkt-4.TCP	2:00 PM, 21 Apr 2019	12.66541 minutes	576,495

11.5.2.1 Computations of σ and ρ of Traffic Traces

Given a traffic trace, its burstiness parameter σ in the continuous case is given by (11.5). Practically, a traffic trace is in the discrete case. Let N be the length of a traffic trace. Then, the analogy of the traffic bound $A(t)$ in the discrete case is given by

$$\sum_{i=0}^{n} x(i) = X(n) \leq \sigma + \rho n = A(n), \quad n = 0,1,...,N-1. \qquad (11.49)$$

Since

$$\lim_{n \to 0} A(n) = \sigma, \qquad (11.50)$$

we estimate σ by

$$\sigma = \max[x(i)]. \qquad (11.51)$$

Once the above is satisfied, $\lim_{n \to 0} X(n) \leq \sigma$ can be assured.

When N is large enough, the long-term average rate ρ can be estimated by

$$\rho \approx \frac{1}{N} \sum_{i=0}^{N-1} x(i). \qquad (11.52)$$

The values of σ and ρ of eight traces are listed in Table 11.3.

11.5.2.2 Values of $r_{0\min}$ and $a_{\infty\min}^{-1}$ of Traffic Traces

As previously mentioned in (11.22), $Y_{A_1S}(t) \leq A_1(t) = \sigma_1 + \rho_1 t$. Consider $Y_{A_1S}(t)$ as the affine function (11.46). Then, we have

$$Y_{A_1S}(t) = Rt + b \leq \rho_1 t + \sigma_1. \qquad (11.53)$$

The above implies

$$R \leq \rho_1 \leq \rho, \qquad (11.54)$$

$$b \leq \sigma_1 \leq \sigma. \qquad (11.55)$$

TABLE 11.3   Values of Six Parameters of eight Traffic Traces

Trace Name	σ	ρ	D	H	$r_{0\min}$	$a_{\infty\min}^{-1}$
DEC-pkt-1.TCP	1,460	137.347	1.349	0.989	1.351	0.496
DEC-pkt-2.TCP	1,460	219.401	1.305	0.998	1.336	0.499
DEC-pkt-3.TCP	1,460	151.238	1.474	0.988	1.402	0.496
DEC-pkt-4.TCP	1,460	220.127	1.395	0.999	1.369	0.500
MAWI-pkt-1.TCP	5,778	1,116	1.371	0.629	1.359	0.332
MAWI-pkt-2.TCP	7,354	1,081	1.440	0.560	1.387	0.290
MAWI-pkt-3.TCP	11,650	839.229	1.873	0.782	1.738	0.412
MAWI-pkt-4.TCP	14,920	893.147	1.860	0.810	1.677	0.419

Because σ, ρ, D, and H are known for a traffic trace x, we can obtain $r_{0\min}$ and $a_{\infty\min}^{-1}$ based on (11.40) and (11.45). As a case study, by letting $R = 0.5$ ρ and $b = 0.5$ σ, we have $r_{0\min} = (0.5)^{\frac{1}{2D-5}}$ and $a_{\infty\min}^{-1} = (0.5)^{\frac{1}{H}}$. Therefore, we obtain the values of $r_{0\min}$ and $a_{\infty\min}^{-1}$ for eight traces in the last two columns in Table 11.3.

11.6 APPLICATIONS

11.6.1 Physical Meaning of Asymptotic Scale Factors

Theorems 11.3 and 11.4 reveal interesting scaling properties of traffic. On the one hand, Theorem 11.3 exhibits that $r_0 \sim (D, \sigma, Y_{A_1S}(0))$, where D describes the locally stochastic property, that is, local self-similarity, of traffic; σ characterizes the locally deterministic property, namely, burstiness, of traffic; and $Y_{A_1S}(0)$ is the local value of departure traffic. All three quantities, D, σ, and $Y_{A_1S}(0)$, relate to the local properties of traffic. On the other hand, Theorem 11.4 means $a_{\infty}^{-1} \sim (H, \rho, Y_{A_1S}(\infty))$, where H measures the globally stochastic property (long-range dependence) of traffic, ρ denotes the globally deterministic property (long-term average rate) of traffic, and $Y_{A_1S}(\infty)$ is the long-term value of departure traffic. All three are associated with the global properties of traffic.

11.6.2 Applications

11.6.2.1 Approximations of Traffic Bound

Li's bound (11.15) introduces the scale factors r and a for σ and ρ, respectively. Since ρ may be neglected when $t \to 0$ while σ can be ignored if $t \to \infty$, we can attain an approximation of Li's bound.

Theorem 11.5

The traffic bound $A_1(t)$ can be approximated by

$$A_1(t) \approx r_0^{2D-5}\sigma + a_\infty^{-H}\rho t. \qquad (11.56)$$

Proof. Expression (11.15) can be approximated by

$$X(t) \leq \begin{cases} r^{2D-5}\sigma, & t \to 0, \\ a^{-H}\rho t, & t \to \infty. \end{cases} \qquad (11.57)$$

Since

$$r^{2D-5}\sigma = r_0^{2D-5}\sigma, \quad t \to 0, \qquad (11.58)$$

and

$$a^{-H}\rho t = a_\infty^{-H}\rho t, \quad t \to \infty, \qquad (11.59)$$

(11.56) holds.

Since r_0 and a_∞^{-1} are in inequalities (11.39) and (11.41), $r_{0\min}$ and $a_{\infty\min}^{-1}$ in (11.40) and (11.45) may be used for an approximation of (11.56).

Corollary 11.5

The approximation of Li's bound can be expressed by

$$A_1(t) \approx r_{0\min}^{2D-5}\sigma + a_{\infty\min}^{-H}\rho t. \qquad (11.60)$$

Proof. The proof is straightforward and omitted accordingly.

When $R = 0.5\,\rho$ and $b = 0.5\,\sigma$ in the affine function, we obtain the approximations of $A_1(t)$s of eight traffic traces. We show them and their $A(t)$s for the comparison to demonstrate $A_1(t) \leq A(t)$ in Table 11.4.

11.6.2.2 Applications to Fractal Delay Bounds

Since $Y_{AS}(t) \geq 0$, we have a simplified form of d_{Cruz1} in the form

TABLE 11.4   Approximation of $A_1(t)$ for Eight Traffic Traces and Comparison

Trace Name	$A(t) = \sigma + \rho t$	$A_1(t) \approx r_{0\min}^{2D-5}\sigma + a_{\infty\min}^{-H}\rho t$	$A_1(t) < A(t)$
DEC-pkt-1.TCP	$1{,}460 + 137.347t$	$730 + 68.674t$	Yes
DEC-pkt-2.TCP	$1{,}460 + 219.401t$	$730 + 109.700t$	Yes
DEC-pkt-3.TCP	$1{,}460 + 151.238t$	$730 + 75.619t$	Yes
DEC-pkt-4.TCP	$1{,}460 + 220.127t$	$730 + 110.064t$	Yes
MAWI-pkt-1.TCP	$5{,}778 + 1{,}116t$	$2{,}889 + 557.764t$	Yes
MAWI-pkt-2.TCP	$7{,}354 + 1{,}081t$	$3{,}677 + 540.318t$	Yes
MAWI-pkt-3.TCP	$11{,}650 + 839.229t$	$5{,}825 + 419.614t$	Yes
MAWI-pkt-4.TCP	$14{,}920 + 893.147t$	$7{,}457 + 446.573t$	Yes

$$d_{\text{Cruz}1} = \frac{\sigma + \rho t - Y_{AS}(t)}{\rho} \leq \frac{\sigma + \rho t}{\rho} = d_{\text{Cruz}2}. \qquad (11.61)$$

In the case of $t \to 0$ ([48, Eq. (11.32)]), $d_{\text{Cruz}2}$ becomes

$$\lim_{t \to 0} d_{\text{Cruz}2} = \frac{\sigma}{\rho} = d_{\text{Cruz}3}. \qquad (11.62)$$

On the other side, denoting the right-hand side of (11.28) by $d_{\text{fractal}2}$, we have

$$d_{\text{fractal}2} = \frac{\sigma_1 + \rho t - Y_{A_1S}(t)}{\rho}. \qquad (11.63)$$

Because $Y_{A_1S}(t) \geq 0$, we have a simplification of $d_{\text{fractal}2}$ by

$$d_{\text{fractal}2} = \frac{\sigma_1 + \rho t - Y_{A_1S}(t)}{\rho} \leq \frac{\sigma_1 + \rho t}{\rho} = d_{\text{fractal}3}. \qquad (11.64)$$

When $t \to 0$, we have

$$\lim_{t \to 0} d_{\text{fractal}3} = \frac{\sigma_1}{\rho} = \frac{r^{2D-5}\sigma}{\rho} = d_{\text{fractal}4}. \qquad (11.65)$$

The above is for $t \to 0$. Therefore [48, Eq. (11.33)], we have a fractal delay bound given by

$$d_{\text{fracta 4}} = \frac{r_0^{2D-5}\sigma}{\rho}. \tag{11.66}$$

Note that d_{fractal4} is a number with r_0. The present corollary below gives its maximum.

Corollary 11.6

The maximum of d_{fractal4} is given by

$$d_{\text{fracta 4,max}} = \frac{r_{0\min}^{2D-5}\sigma}{\rho}. \tag{11.67}$$

Proof. Replacing r_0 in (11.66) by $r_{0\min}$ yields $\frac{r_{0\min}^{2D-5}\sigma}{\rho}$. Due to $1 \le D < 2$ and $2D - 5 < 0$, $\frac{r_{0\min}^{2D-5}\sigma}{\rho}$ equals to the maximum of d_{fractal4}.

The values of conventional delay bound d_{Cruz3} and the maximum of fractal delay bound d_{fractal4} are listed in Table 11.5, where we see that $d_{\text{frac-tal4, max}} < d_{\text{Cruz3}}$.

Since the values of r and a can be computed for a given traffic trace as can be seen from the above, the present computation formulas of r and a stand for a significant advance in the aspect of traffic bound and delay bound computations.

TABLE 11.5   Values of Delay Bounds d_{Cruz3}, $d_{\text{fractal4, max}}$ of Eight Traffic Traces

Trace Name	σ	ρ	d_{Cruz3}	D	$r_{0\min}$	$d_{\text{fractal4, max}}$	$d_{\text{fractal4, max}} < d_{\text{Cruz3}}$
DEC-pkt-1.TCP	1,460	137.347	10.630	1.860	1.719	5.315	Yes
DEC-pkt-2.TCP	1,460	219.401	6.654	1.860	1.719	3.327	Yes
DEC-pkt-3.TCP	1,460	151.238	9.654	1.190	1.303	4.827	Yes
DEC-pkt-4.TCP	1,460	220.127	6.633	1.190	1.303	3.316	Yes
MAWI-pkt-1.TCP	5,778	1116	5.180	1.371	1.359	2.590	Yes
MAWI-pkt-2.TCP	7,354	1081	6.805	1.440	1.387	3.403	Yes
MAWI-pkt-3.TCP	11,650	839.229	13.882	1.873	1.738	6.941	Yes
MAWI-pkt-4.TCP	14,920	893.147	16.699	1.860	1.677	8.350	Yes

11.7 CONCLUDING REMARKS

We have presented Theorems 11.1 and 11.2 for the computations of the small-scale factor r and the large-scale one a in the traffic bound $A_1(t)$, giving a solution to the open problem stated in [68]. In addition, we have proposed Theorems 11.3 and 11.4 for the asymptotic computations of r for $t \to 0$ and a when $t \to \infty$, respectively. Moreover, we have put forward the formulas to compute the approximations of r and a in Corollaries 11.1–11.4. Besides, we have brought forward the approximations of $A_1(t)$ in Theorem 11.5 and Corollary 11.5. The maximum of a fractal delay bound has been explained in Corollary 11.6 as an application case of the present computations of scale factors. We have shown that r_0 is solely associated with the local properties of traffic while a_∞ is only dependent on the global properties of traffic. The case study and application of the computations of scale factors show that Li's bound is tighter than the conventional one while Li's bound-based delay bounds are tighter than the conventional ones.

REFERENCES

1. M. Li, W. J. Jia, and W. Zhao, Correlation form of timestamp increment sequences of self-similar traffic on ethernet, *Electron. Lett.*, 36(19) 2000, 1668–1669.
2. W. Stallings, *Data and Computer Communications*, 4th Ed., Macmillan, New York, 1994.
3. H. Inme and T. Saito, Theoretical aspects in the analysis and synthesis of packet communication networks, *IEEE Trans. Commun.*, 66(1) 1978, 1409–1422.
4. J. D. Gibson, editor-in-chief, *The Communications Handbook*, IEEE Press, New York, 1997.
5. L. Kleinrock, Principles and lessons in packet communications, *Proc. the IEEE*, 66(11) 1978, 1320–1329.
6. V. G. Cerf and P. T. Kirstein, Issues in packet-network interconnection, *Proc. the IEEE*, 66(11) 1978, 1386–1408.
7. D. L. Mills, *Computer Network Time Synchronization*, 2nd Ed., CRC Press, New York, 2011.
8. V. Paxson and S. Floyd, Wide area traffic: the failure of Poisson modeling, *IEEE/ACM Trans. Net.*, 3(3) 1995, 226–244.
9. B. Tsybakov and N. D. Georganas, Self-similar processes in communications networks, *IEEE Trans. Inform. Theor.*, 44(5) 1998, 1713–1725.
10. M. Li, Generalized fractional Gaussian noise and its application to traffic modeling, *Physica A*, 579 2021, 1236137 (22 p).
11. M. Li, Multi-fractional generalized Cauchy process and its application to teletraffic, *Physica A*, 550 2020, 123982.

12. M. Li, Long-range dependence and self-similarity of teletraffic with different protocols at the large time scale of day in the duration of 12 years: Autocorrelation modeling, *Physica Scripta*, 96(6) 2020, 065222 (15 p).

13. M. Li, Record length requirement of long-range dependent teletraffic, *Physica A*, 472 2017, 164–187.

14. M. Li, Power spectrum of generalized fractional gaussian noise, *Adv. Math. Phys.*, 2013 2013, Article ID 315979, 3 p.

15. M. Li, Evidence of a two-parameter correlation of Internet traffic, in *Internet Policies and Issues*, Vol. 8, B. G. Kutais, editor, Nova Science Publishers, Inc., New York , 2011, pp. 103–140.

16. M. Li, Generation of teletraffic of generalized Cauchy type, *Physica Scripta*, 81(2) 2010, 025007 (10 p).

17. M. Li, Fractal time series—a tutorial review, *Math. Prob. Eng.*, 2010 2010, Article ID 157264, 26 p.

18. M. Li, Self-similarity and long-range dependence in teletraffic, *Proceedings of the 9th WSEAS International Conference on Multimedia Systems and Signal Processing*, Hangzhou, China, May 2009, pp. 19–24.

19. M. Li, Modeling autocorrelation functions of long-range dependent teletraffic series based on optimal approximation in Hilbert space—a further study, *Appl. Math. Model.*, 31(3) 2007, 625–631.

20. M. Li, Change trend of averaged hurst parameter of traffic under DDOS flood attacks, *Comput. Secur.*, 25(3) 2006, 213–220.

21. M. Li, An approach to reliably identifying signs of DDOS flood attacks based on LRD traffic pattern recognition, *Comput. Secur.*, 23(7) 2004, 549–558.

22. M. Li, *Self-Similar Network Traffic – Its Modeling and Simulation*, PhD Dissertation, City University of Hong Kong, Hong Kong, Mar. 2002.

23. M. Li and P. Borgnat, Foreword to the special issue on traffic modeling, its computations and applications, *Telecommun. Syst.*, 43(3–4) 2010, 145–146.

24. M. Li and S. C. Lim, Modeling network traffic using generalized Cauchy process, *Physica A*, 387(11) 2008, 2584–2594.

25. S. C. Lim and M. Li, Generalized Cauchy process and its application to relaxation phenomena, *J. Phys. A: Math. General*, 39(12) 2006, 2935–2951.

26. R. Fontugne, P. Abry, K. Fukuda, D. Veitch, K. Cho, P. Borgnat, and H. Wendt, Scaling in Internet traffic: A 14 year and 3 day longitudinal study, with multiscale analyses and random projections, *IEEE/ACM Trans. Net.*, 25(4) 2017, 2152–2165.

27. Y. Himura, K. Fukuda, K. Cho, P. Abry, P. Borgnat, and H. Esaki, Synoptic graphlet: Bridging the gap between supervised and unsupervised profiling of host-level network traffic, *IEEE/ACM Trans. Net.*, 21(4) 2013, 1284–1297.

28. P. Loiseau, P. Gonçalves, G. Dewaele, P. Borgnat, P. Abry, and P. Vicat-Blanc Primet, Investigating self-similarity and heavy-tailed distributions on a large-scale experimental facility, *IEEE/ACM Trans. Net.*, 18(4) 2010, 1261–1274.

29. P. Abry, P. Borgnat, F. Ricciato, A. Scherrer, and D. Veitch, Revisiting an old friend: On the observability of the relation between long range dependence and heavy tail, *Telecommun. Syst.*, 43(3–4) 2010, 147–165.

30. M. Pinchas, Cooperative multi PTP slaves for timing improvement in an fGn environment, *IEEE Commun. Lett.*, 22(7) 2018, 1366–1369.

31. M. Pinchas, Symbol error rate for non-blind adaptive equalizers applicable for the SIMO and fGn case, *Math. Prob. Eng.*, 2014 2014, Article ID 606843, 11 p.

32. P. Abry, R. Baraniuk, P. Flandrin, R. Riedi, and D. Veitch, Multiscale nature of network traffic, *IEEE Signal Process. Magaz.*, 19(3) 2002, 28–46.

33. J. Beran, R. Shernan, M. S. Taqqu, and W. Willinger, Long-range dependence in variable bit-rate video traffic, *IEEE Trans. Commun.*, 43(2–4) 1995, 1566–1579.

34. S. Tadaki, Long-term power-law fluctuation in internet traffic, *J. Phys. Soc. Japan*, 76(4) 2007, 044001 (5 pp).

35. O. Markelov, V. N. Duc, and M. Bogachev, Statistical modeling of the Internet traffic dynamics: To which extent do we need long-term correlations, *Physica A*, 485 2017, 48–60.

36. A. Tamazian, V. D. Nguyen, O. A. Markelov, and M. I. Bogachev, Universal model for collective access patterns in the internet traffic dynamics: A superstatistical approach, *Europhys. Lett.*, 115(1) 2016, 10008.

37. V. D. Nguyen, O. A. Markelov, A. D. Serdyuk, A. N. Vasenev, and M. I. Bogachev, Universal model for collective access patterns in the Internet traffic dynamics: A superstatistical approach, *Europhys. Lett.*, 123(5) 2018, 50001.

38. B. B. Mandelbrot, *Gaussian Self-Affinity and Fractals*, Springer, New York, 2001.

39. W. Stallings, *High-Speed Networks and Internets Performance and Quality of Service*, 2nd Ed., Prentice Hall, New York, 2002.

40. F. A. Tobagi, M. Gerla, R. W. Peebles, and E. G. Manning, Modeling and measurement techniques in packet communication networks, *Proc. IEEE*, 66 (11) 1978, 1423–1447.

41. J. W. Wong, Distribution of end-to-end delay in message-switched networks, *Comput. Net.*, 2(1) 1978, 44–49.

42. I. Tejado, S. H. Hosseinnia, B. M. Vinagre, X. Song, and Y.-Q. Chen, Dealing with fractional dynamics of IP network delays, *Int. J. Bifurcation Chaos*, 22(4) 2012, 1250089 (13 p).

43. W. Yue, H. Takagi, and Y. Takahashi, *Advances in Queueing Theory and Network Applications*, Springer, New York, 2009.

44. R. L. Cruz, A calculus for network delay, part I: network elements in isolation, part II: network analysis, *IEEE Trans. Inform. Theor.*, 37(1) 1991, 114–141.

45. J. Y. Le Boudec, Application of network calculus to guaranteed service networks, *IEEE Trans. Inform. Theor.*, 44(3) 1998, 1087–1096.

46. J. Y. Le Boudec and T. Patrick, *Network Calculus, A Theory of Deterministic Queuing Systems for the Internet*, Springer, New York, 2001.

47. Y.-M. Jiang and Y. Liu, *Stochastic Network Calculus*, Springer, New York, 2008.

48. M. Li and A. Wang, Fractal teletraffic delay bounds in computer networks, *Physica A*, 557 2020, 124903.

49. M. Li, W. Zhao, and C. Cattani, Delay bound: fractal traffic passes through servers, *Math. Prob. Eng.*, 2013 2013, Article ID 157636, 15 p.

50. A. Abdelkefi, Y.-M. Jiang, B. E. Helvik, G. Biczók, and A. Calu, Assessing the service quality of an Internet path through end-to-end measurement, *Comput. Net.*, 70 2014, 30–44.

51. Y.-M. Jiang, A basic stochastic network calculus, *ACM SIGCOMM Comput. Commun. Rev.*, 36(4) 2006, 123–134.

52. X. Jia, A distributed algorithm of delay bounded multicast routing for multimedia applications in wide area networks, *IEEE/ACM Trans. Net.*, 6(6) 1998, 828–837.

53. M. Fidler, B. Walker, and Y.-M. Jiang, Non-asymptotic delay bounds for multi-server systems with synchronization constraints, *IEEE Trans. Paral. Distrib. Syst.*, 29(7) 2018, 1545–1559.

54. M. Fidler and A. Rizk, A guide to the stochastic network calculus, *IEEE Commun. Surv. Tutor.*, 17(1) 2015, 92–105.

55. M. Fidler, A survey of deterministic and stochastic service curve models in the network calculus, *IEEE Commun. Surv. Tutor.*, 12(1) 2010, 59–86.

56. S. Mao and S. S. Panwar, A survey of envelope processes and their applications in quality of service provisioning, *IEEE Commun. Surv. Tutor.*, 8(3) 2006, 2–20.

57. R. G. Garroppo, B. Gendron, G. Nencioni, and L. Tavanti, Energy efficiency and traffic offloading in wireless mesh networks with delay bounds, *Int. J. Commun. Syst.*, 30(2) 2017, e2902.

58. V. Gupta, S. Dharmaraja, and V. Arunachalam, Stochastic modeling for delay analysis of a VoIP network, *Ann. Oper. Res.*, 233(1) 2015, 171–180.

59. H. Zhu, M. Li, I. Chlamtac, and B. Prabhakaran, A survey of quality of service in IEEE 802.11 networks, *IEEE Wireless Commun.*, 13(6) 2004, 6–14.

60. Y. T. Woldeyohannes and Y.-M. Jiang, Measures for network structural dependency analysis, *IEEE Commun. Lett.*, 22(10) 2018, 2052–2055.

61. Z. Li, Y.-M. Jiang, Y. Gao, P. Li, L. Sang, Lin, and D. Yang, Delay and delay-constrained throughput performance of a wireless-powered communication system, *IEEE Access*, 5 2017, 21620–21631.

62. S. K. Korotky and T. Pfeiffer, Continuing advances in next-generation communication technologies, services, and networks, *Bell Labs Tech. J.*, 14(1) 2009, 1–5.

63. A. K. Parekh and R. G. Gallager, A generalized processor sharing approach to flow control in integrated services networks: The single-node case, *IEEE/ACM Trans. Net.*, 1(3) 1993, 372–385.

64. D. Starobinski and M. Sidi, Stochastically bounded burstiness for communication networks, *IEEE Trans. Inform. Theor.*, 46(1) 2000, 206–212.

65. J. Liebeherr, A. Burchard, and F. Ciucu, Delay bounds in communication networks with heavy-tailed and self-similar traffic, *IEEE Trans. Infor. Theor.*, 58(2) 2012, 1010–1024.

66. C. Li and E. Knightly, Schedulability criterion and performance analysis of coordinated multihop schedulers, *IEEE/ACM Trans. Net.*, 13(2) 2005, 276–287.

67. C. Li, A. Burchard, and J. Liebeherr, A network calculus with effective bandwidth, *IEEE/ACM Trans. Net.*, 15(6) 2007, 1442–1452.

68. M. Li and W. Zhao, Representation of a stochastic traffic bound, *IEEE Trans. Paral. Distrib. Syst.*, 21(9) 2010, 1368–1372.

69. T. Gneiting and M. Schlather, Stochastic models that separate fractal dimension and the Hurst effect, *SIAM Rev.*, 46(2) 2004, 269–282.

70. M. Li and J.-Y. Li, Generalized Cauchy model of sea level fluctuations with long-range dependence, *Physica A*, 484 2017, 309–335.

71. J. T. Kent and A. T. Wood, Estimating the fractal dimension of a locally self-similar Gaussian process by using increments, *J. Roy. Stat. Soc. B*, 59(3) 1997, 679–699.

72. G. Chan, P. Hall, and D. S. Poskitt, Periodogram-based estimators of fractal properties, *Ann. Statist.*, 23(5) 1995, 1684–1711.

73. P. Hall and A. Wood, On the performance of box-counting estimators of fractal dimension, *Biometrika*, 80(1) 1993, 246–252.

74. M. S. Taqqu, V. Teverovsky, and W. Willinger, Estimators for long-range dependence: an empirical study, *Fractals*, 3(4) 1995, 785–798.

75. P. Borgnat, G. Dewaele, K. Fukuda, P. Abry, K. Cho, Seven years and one day: Sketching the evolution of internet traffic, *Proceedings of the 28th IEEE INFOCOM 2009*, Rio de Janeiro (Brazil), May 2009, 711–719.

76. K. Cho, *Recursive Lattice Search: Hierarchical Heavy Hitters Revisited, ACM IMC 2017*, London, 1–3 Nov. 2017, 283–289.

77. M. Kato, K. Cho, M. Honda, and H. Tokuda, Monitoring the dynamics of network traffic by recursive multi-dimensional aggregation, *OSDI2012 MAD Workshop*, Hollywood, CA, 8–10 Oct. 2012 (7 p).

CHAPTER 12

Postscript

Having explained the main contents of fractal traffic modeling in Chapters 6–9 and its applications to traffic delay bounds in Chapters 10 and 11, I would like to talk about related issues in traffic modeling and delay-bound computations. In Section 12.1, I address the relationships between the measures of local and global properties of a fractal time series. The relationship between the measures of local and global properties of network traffic bounds is explained in Section 12.2. In Section 12.3, I expound a tough problem in delay-bound computations.

12.1 LOCAL VERSUS GLOBAL OF FRACTAL TIME SERIES

Although I did not mention fractal time series and traffic modeling from the point of view of heavy tail distributions, fractal time series, including traffic, has a property of heavy tails (Mandelbrot [1,2]). Due to heavy tails, mean, which characterizes the global property of a time series, and variance, which measures the local property of a time series, may not exist. A typical heavy-tailed probability density function (PDF) is the Cauchy PDF. When a time series follows the Cauchy PDF, its mean and variance do not exist (Korn and Korn [3]).

The Cauchy PDF is an extreme case of heavy-tailed PDFs. There are other kinds of heavy-tailed PDFs, such as the Pareto PDF. The variance of a heavy-tailed time series may not be infinite as that of the Cauchy PDF. However, one thing in common for all heavy-tailed time series is that their variance is large or infinitely large. Therefore, we usually do not mention variance for a fractal time series in general (Li [4,5]). Instead, one uses the Hurst parameter H to measure the global property (long-range dependence) and fractal dimension D to measure the local property (local self-similarity) [1,4,5].

From an early literature by H. E. Hurst [6] to today, understanding of relationships between H and D of a fractal time series is developing. Let D_{fGn} and H_{fGn}, respectively, be the fractal dimension and the Hurst parameter of the fractional Gaussian noise (fGn). Then, following (6.26), we see that both are linearly related by

$$D_{fGn} = 2 - H_{fGn}. \tag{12.1}$$

Therefore, D_{fGn} is completely coupled with H_{fGn}.

Let D_{gfGn} and H_{gfGn}, respectively, be the fractal dimension and the Hurst parameter of the generalized fractional Gaussian noise (gfGn) (Li [7,8]). In (7.35), I expressed the relationship between the two by

$$D_{gfGn} = 2 - aH_{gfGn}. \tag{12.2}$$

The above implies that D_{gfGn} is related to H_{gfGn} with the coupling factor $0 < a \leq 1$. The smaller the value of a, the weaker the coupling between the two.

Denote by D_{GC} and H_{GC}, respectively, the fractal dimension and the Hurst parameter of the generalized Cauchy process. Then, D_{GC} and H_{GC} are uncorrelated, see Chapter 8, Li [9–12], Li and Li [13], Li and Lim [14], Lim and Li [15], Gneiting and Schlather [16], and Gneiting [17].

Recently, I introduced a type of fractional noise, called modified multi-fractional Gaussian noise (mmfGn) (Li [18]). Let $D_{mmfGn}(t)$ and $H_{mmfGn}(t)$, respectively, be the fractal dimension and the Hurst parameter of mmfGn for $0 < t < \infty$ on a point-by-point basis. Then,

$$D_{mmfGn}(t) = 2 - H_{mmfGn}(t). \tag{12.3}$$

Another multi-fractional noise I recently introduced in [10] is termed multi-fractional generalized Cauchy (mGC) process. Denote by $D_{mGC}(t)$ and $H_{mGC}(t)$ the fractal dimension and the Hurst parameter of mGC for $0 < t < \infty$, respectively. Then, $D_{mGC}(t)$ and $H_{mGC}(t)$ are uncorrelated.

The above describes the relationship between D and H for five types of fractal time series I studied, including traffic. Other types of fractal time series, for instance, fractional Levy ones, are not discussed anymore in this book.

12.2 LOCAL VERSUS GLOBAL OF TRAFFIC TIME SERIES

In computer communications, Cruz proposed his deterministic bound of the accumulated traffic in the form

$$\int_0^t x(u)\,du = X(t) \le \sigma + \rho t, \tag{12.3}$$

where σ and ρ are non-negative constants (Cruz [19], Le Boudec [20], Jiang and Liu [21], Jiang [22,23]). The quantity σ is a measure of burstiness, which is a local property of traffic, while ρ measures the long-average rate, which is a global property of traffic. The pair (σ, ρ) is a kind of traffic model called Cruz bound in Chapters 9–11. Two measures are independent of each other. However, that is untrue for Li's bound expressed by

$$\int_0^t x(u)\,du = X(t) \le r^{2D-5}\sigma + a^{-H}\rho t, \tag{12.4}$$

As a matter of fact, r relates to ρ while a is associated with σ, see Chapter 11. Therefore, for Li's bound, the coupling between σ_1 and ρ_1 appears complicated.

12.3 PROBLEM

Traffic bounds are desired in real-time communications. Practically, traffic is considered at the connection level. The simplicity of the Cruz bound attracts the interest of researchers but its use may sacrifice too many resources. Li's bound is tighter than the Cruz one but it needs the computations of D and H of traffic. Satisfactory computations or estimations of D and H need traffic data with enough record length (Li [11]). At the connection level, a traffic trace may not meet the length requirement for a satisfactory estimation of D and H. Desiring traffic traces of all connections have enough length for satisfactory estimations of D and H must be a problem too tough. Once that problem is solved, Li's bound and its delay-bound computations may go a considerable step further in practice.

REFERENCES

1. B. B. Mandelbrot, *Gaussian Self-Affinity and Fractals*, Springer, New York, 2001.
2. B. B. Mandelbrot, *Multifractals and 1/f Noise*, Springer, New York, 1998.
3. G. A. Korn and T. M. Korn, *Mathematical Handbook for Scientists and Engineers*, McGraw-Hill, New York, 1961.
4. M. Li, Fractal time series—A tutorial review, *Math. Prob. Eng.*, 2010 2010, Article ID 157264, 26 p.
5. M. Li, Self-similarity and long-range dependence in teletraffic, *Proc.of the 9th WSEAS Int. Conf. on Multimedia Systems and Signal Processing*, Hangzhou, China, May 2009, 19–24.
6. H. E. Hurst, Long term storage capacity of reservoirs, *Trans. Am. Soc. Civil Eng.*, 116 1951, 770–799.
7. M. Li, Generalized fractional Gaussian noise and its application to traffic modeling, *Phys. A*, 579 2021, 1236137 (22 p).
8. M. Li, Modeling autocorrelation functions of long-range dependent teletraffic series based on optimal approximation in Hilbert space—a further study, *Appl. Math. Model.*, 31(3) 2007, 625–631.
9. M. Li, Long-range dependence and self-similarity of teletraffic with different protocols at the large time scale of day in the duration of 12 years: Autocorrelation modeling, *Phys. Scr.*, 95(4) 2020, 065222 (15 p).
10. M. Li, Multi-fractional generalized Cauchy process and its application to teletraffic, *Phys. A*, 550 2020, 123982 (14 p).
11. M. Li, Record length requirement of long-range dependent teletraffic, *Phys. A*, 472 2017, 164–187.
12. M. Li, Generation of teletraffic of generalized Cauchy type, *Phys. Scr.*, 81(2) 2010, 025007 (10 p).
13. M. Li and J.-Y. Li, Generalized Cauchy model of sea level fluctuations with long-range dependence, *Phys. A*, 484 2017, 309–335.
14. M. Li and S. C. Lim, Modeling network traffic using generalized Cauchy process, *Phys. A*, 387(11) 2008, 2584–2594.
15. S. C. Lim and M. Li, A generalized Cauchy process and its application to relaxation phenomena, *J. Phys. A: Math. General*, 39(12) 2006, 2935–2951.
16. T. Gneiting and M. Schlather, Stochastic models that separate fractal dimension and Hurst effect, *SIAM Rev.*, 46(2) 2004, 269–282.
17. T. Gneiting, Power-law correlations, related models for long-range dependence and their simulation, *J. Appl. Prob.*, 37(4) Dec. 2000, 1104–1109.
18. M. Li, Modified multifractional Gaussian noise and its application, *Phys. Scr.*, 96(12). Doi: 10.1088/1402-4896/ac1cf6.

19. R. L. Cruz, A calculus for network delay, part I: network elements in isolation, part II: Network analysis, *IEEE Trans. Inform. Theor.*, 37(1) 1991, 114–141.
20. J. Y. Le Boudec, Application of network calculus to guaranteed service networks, *IEEE Trans. Inform. Theor.*, 44(3) 1998, 1087–1096.
21. Y.-M. Jiang and Y. Liu, *Stochastic Network Calculus*, Springer, New York, 2008.
22. Y.-M. Jiang, Per-domain packet scale rate guarantee for expedited forwarding, *IEEE/ACM Trans. Net.*, 14(3) 2006, 630–643.
23. Y.-M. Jiang, A basic stochastic network calculus, *ACM SIGCOMM Comput. Commun. Rev.*, 36(4) 2006, 123–134.

Index

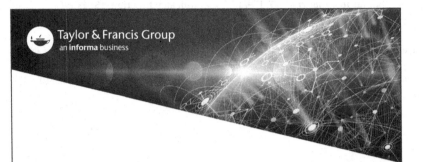

Taylor & Francis Group
an **informa** business

Taylor & Francis eBooks

www.taylorfrancis.com

A single destination for eBooks from Taylor & Francis
with increased functionality and an improved user
experience to meet the needs of our customers.

90,000+ eBooks of award-winning academic content in
Humanities, Social Science, Science, Technology, Engineering,
and Medical written by a global network of editors and authors.

TAYLOR & FRANCIS EBOOKS OFFERS:

A streamlined
experience for
our library
customers

A single point
of discovery
for all of our
eBook content

Improved
search and
discovery of
content at both
book and
chapter level

REQUEST A FREE TRIAL
support@taylorfrancis.com

 Routledge
Taylor & Francis Group

 CRC Press
Taylor & Francis Group

Printed in the United States
by Baker & Taylor Publisher Services

Printed in the United States
by Baker & Taylor Publisher Services